Fraught Decisions in
Plato and Shakespeare

Philosophical Projections

Series Editor: Andrew Benjamin, Distinguished Professor of Philosophy and the Humanities, Kingston University, UK, and Professor of Philosophy and Jewish Thought, Monash University, Australia

Philosophical Projections represents the future of modern European philosophy. The series seeks to innovate by grounding the future in the work of the present, opening up the philosophical and allowing it to renew itself, while interrogating the continuity of the philosophical after the critique of metaphysics.

Titles in the Series
Foundations of the Everyday: Shock, Deferral, Repetition
    Eran Dorfman
The Thought of Matter: Materialism, Conceptuality and the Transcendence of Immanence
    Richard A. Lee
Nancy, Blanchot: A Serious Controversy
    Leslie Hill
The Work of Forgetting: Or, How Can We Make the Future Possible?
    Stephane Symons
Political Loneliness: Modern Liberal Subjects in Hiding
    Jennifer Gaffney
Fraught Decisions in Plato and Shakespeare
    Dianne Rothleder
Refugees: Towards a Politics of Responsibility (forthcoming)
    Nathan Bell

Fraught Decisions in Plato and Shakespeare

Dianne Rothleder

ROWMAN & LITTLEFIELD
Lanham • Boulder • New York • London

Published by Rowman & Littlefield
An imprint of The Rowman & Littlefield Publishing Group, Inc.
4501 Forbes Boulevard, Suite 200, Lanham, Maryland 20706
www.rowman.com

6 Tinworth Street, London SE11 5AL, United Kingdom

Copyright © 2021 by Dianne Rothleder

Citations from Plato are reprinted with permission from *The Republic*, vol. 5 of The Dialogues of Plato (New Haven, CT: Yale University Press, 2006), R. E. Allen, editor and translator.

All rights reserved. No part of this book may be reproduced in any form or by any electronic or mechanical means, including information storage and retrieval systems, without written permission from the publisher, except by a reviewer who may quote passages in a review.

British Library Cataloguing in Publication Information Available

Library of Congress Control Number: 2020944098

ISBN 978-1-78661-627-2 (cloth)
ISBN 978-1-5381-4707-8 (pbk)
ISBN 978-1-78661-628-9 (epub)

For everyone who has wielded duct tape and baling wire with such skill, all my gratitude

Contents

Acknowledgments ix

Introduction xiii

PART I: COMEDY, TRAGEDY, AND NARRATIVE CHOICE

Prologue: The *Republic* and Tragic and Comic Incredulity 3

Section 2: The Comedy of *Othello*, Or, Who Kills Desdemona? 39

Section 3: The Tragedy of *The Comedy of Errors* 61

PART II: POLITY, ECONOMY, AND SOCIO-STRATEGIC CHOICE

Prologue: The *Republic*, Polity, and Economy 85

Section 2: Melancholy and Risk Analysis in *The Merchant of Venice* 109

Section 3: The Economy of the Sea in *Pericles* 127

PART III: BIRTH AND INFINITE DEBT: THE CHOICE OF MEANING

Prologue: The *Republic* and the Philosopher's Birth and Debt 159

Section 2: The Gift of Debt in *Timon of Athens*   181

Section 3: Isabella's Incontinent Incredulity in Her Silence in *Measure for Measure*   213

Conclusion   233

Works Cited   237

Index   243

Acknowledgments

Susan Moller Okin at Brandeis University and R. E. Allen at Northwestern University were my first Plato teachers. With their gift of Plato, a gift they may not have recognized at the time, and which I only had a glimpse of as a gift, this book had its inception. This book was written in their memory.

I want to thank my students over the years who, in good humor, allowed me to spend some seven and two-thirds weeks of a semester going through the *Republic*. A slow reading of the most beautiful text with thirty-five or so students is a professorial paradise, and I have had the joy of this experience regularly for more than two decades. Eventually, Shakespeare joined Plato on the syllabus, and, again, my students read the texts with grace and humor. We worked through tragedy and comedy, debt and death, applications of the texts to the world and to each other and to the lyrics of popular songs. I hope that I have given the gift of Plato in the world as a kind of return for what was given to me.

Numerous people fell "victim" to my "elevator pitches" as I started thinking about this book in more concrete terms. I am grateful to Maria Acosta, Steve Bynum, Mary Caputi, Stefano Giacchetti, David Ingram, James Ingram, Jennifer McCaleb, Jennifer Parks, Trevor Perri, Virginia Strain, Holly Stratton, Jean Tan, and Julie Ward, among others, for coffee, conversation, and thought-provoking questions. John Russon sent me in numerous fruitful directions as I was looking for the community of scholars who read Plato's works through concerns in continental philosophy. His questions and recommendations have strengthened this work immeasurably.

Hanne Jacobs, Peggy Knapp, Jim Knapp, Jacqueline Scott, and Holly Stratton have read portions of the text and given me comments that have strengthened my work. I am especially grateful to Peggy for reading an overly large portion of an early draft and encouraging me to focus my writing. The strengths are theirs, the faults are mine.

Suzanne Gossett generously responded to an e-mail from me, though she does not know me directly, and she helped me try to track down a reference. She went as far as writing a friend of hers in an effort to help track down what I was looking for. A community of scholars like this, willing to reply to relative strangers, makes sustained writing and thinking possible.

Mark Waymack and Jacqueline Scott in the Philosophy Department at Loyola, and Claudio Katz, in the Interdisciplinary Honors Program at Loyola, have had enough confidence in my teaching to let me loose in front of groups of students year after year. I am grateful for this. I would not have been able to think through these issues without the years of teaching these texts.

My colleagues in the Interdisciplinary Honors Program at Loyola have lectured year in and year out, and the lectures on the Homeric texts, Greek tragedy and comedy, the Platonic texts, and Shakespeare have made their way into my thinking. My gratitude to John Danford, Marilyn Dunn, Blake Dutton, Verna Foster, Jonathan Mannering, Virginia Strain, Katherine Swanton, and Chris Whidden, for their insights into the Classical world and the Renaissance. In addition to fundamental insights into the Greek world, Jonathan Mannering has provided insights into Greek translation issues as I have all too frequently requested. Ian Cornelius, Jim Harrington, Tom Kaminski, Claudio Katz, Cristina Lombardi-Diop, David Posner, Father Tom Tobin, and Paula Wisotzki all also lecture in the program and their insights have proved invaluable. My gratitude to the whole group for a wonderful set of lectures spanning the ages and the academic year.

Nancy Ferguson, the director of the MPPA Program at Northwestern University's School for Professional studies, has helped me sustain the policy and world-based side of my brain. Concern for the world and concern for texts, practice and theory, are all one for me, and I am grateful for the many years of teaching public policy at the graduate level. The world calls, the texts call. And the many graduate students who have encouraged my blending of the world and the text are present here, as well.

I am grateful to Andrew Benjamin for his kind reception of my work, for reading the manuscript with care and suggesting ways to improve it, and for helping shepherd it (and me) through the publication process. Frankie Mace, Scarlet Furness, and Rebecca Anastasi at Rowman & Littlefield have been clear, kind, and helpful throughout the process of turning a manuscript into a book.

The editors at Arden Shakespeare have given me permission to quote material and have provided editions of Shakespeare's plays with insightful introductory essays and annotations throughout. Yale University Press has given me permission to use R. E. Allen's translations of the *Republic*. This, too, is in his memory.

I am embedded in a community of neighbors and friends who have, over the years, cheered me on for my (completely non-competitive) half-marathon obsession, who have applied bandages both material (when I "meet" the pavement and cannot bear to look at the results) and abstract (when I "meet" everything else there is, and still cannot quite manage it). Community sustains, we are political animals, and I could not have completed the manuscript and the revisions without all of this support. Jeff Davis, my trainer, has gotten me to appreciate the spirit of always doing ten more, and the many people I run with at the Evanston Running Club have kept my spirits up and my feet moving.

Megan Cutrofello and Quinn Cutrofello have listened with patience to my end-of-writing-day rants and have kept their good humor despite having their own ways to engage with the world. I do not know what kind of world I will leave to them, but I do know what they have given to me. And it is everything.

Finally, but never and always at the end, were Andrew Cutrofello's life laid out next to mine in a myth at the end, I would choose this all over again, comedy and tragedy and philosophy entwined in proper measure with proper understanding, or so I would hope.

Introduction

Through a drunken, sleepy haze at the end of Plato's *Symposium*, Aristodemus, a "real runt of a man, who always went barefoot" (173b) recounting the tale later to Apollodoros, notes that Agathon, Socrates, and Aristophanes were still drinking and Socrates was claiming that "the skillful tragic dramatist should also be a comic poet" (223d). Comedy and tragedy, that is, should coexist in the same creative soul, and if the *Symposium* itself is witness to this coexistence, the two modes should coexist in the same text.[1]

Of the speeches in the *Symposium*, Aristophanes' is perhaps the best example of this coexistence. Nothing is funnier than the hiccups that delay his speech by reminding us of the physicality of the poet; nor can anything top the image of the cartwheeling extra-limbed, joined lovers whose imagined movements make ridiculous the commonplace notion of love that Socrates, in Diotima's voice, will challenge in her speech. And yet, nothing is more tragic than Aristophanes' description of Socrates in the *Clouds* as it is invoked in the *Apology*, where we find that it is these old charges that will lead to the condemnation and execution of Socrates; nor is there anything more tragic than the separation of lovers from their proper wholeness, condemning them to utterly unfulfilled lives of searching for what may not be found.[2] A life lived apart from one's proper love is a tragic life; a life ended prematurely because of the timing of a speech is, as well, a tragic life.[3]

The whole of the *Symposium* is both comic in the drunken antics that lower the exalted figures, and sober, somber, and even tragic in the outcomes of the stories and some of the characters. Alcibiades' inability to hold to philosophy, as he notes in his speech in the *Symposium* (216b) coincides with his turning to his career and to worldly concerns. His career fails and he betrays his own city as Thucydides notes, because he destroys sacred statues and is pulled from the Sicilian Expedition.[4] Aristophanes' comic tendencies in describing Socrates as a buffoon lead to Socrates' death, though not to his betrayal of his city, and even the gentle and loving description of love as soft, treading only on souls, that Agathon, the tragic playwright constructs, has a tragic side to it, in that it is a complete misunderstanding of the nature of love, as Socrates gets Agathon to understand in the cross-examination. Socrates on the porch is comical (175a), Socrates' ability to drink everyone under the table and then have a normal day of philosophizing is equally comical (223d). Alcibiades speaks to the general oddness of Socrates (221c-222b). He is unlike others, but in a kind of amazing way that is either absurd or godlike. Alcibiades presents a version of Socrates that is not miles from what Aristophanes presents, but there is far more respect for Socrates and so the comic outweighs the tragic and the Socrates who emerges from the *Symposium* is worthy whereas the Socrates who emerges from the *Clouds* is the one who is convicted in the *Apology* and is executed in the *Phaedo*. Our knowing as we read, and as the text was written, that Socrates' fate is to die from drinking an altogether different kind of drink is both sobering and a reminder that tragedy underlies the comic in surprising ways.

At the same time, Diotima's account of proper ascent suggests precisely the separations that are tragic in Aristophanes' account and in Socrates' life, but yet are fulfilling when carried through in proper order as a seeking for the gods rather than a punishment from the gods for the kind of seeking that angered Zeus in Aristophanes' tale. Separation is, then, capable of being both tragic and the source of proper delight. Indeed, the last men standing at the party are Aristophanes, the comic poet, Agathon, the tragic poet and host of the party, and Socrates the philosopher (223c-d). Of course, to have them standing next to each other at the end of a long night does not entail their actually recognizing one another as the proper other half. Given that these two fall asleep and Socrates walks away to start a new day, the layering of the comic (last men standing) with the tragic (the failure of recognition) continues to the end of the dialogue.[5]

If Socrates is to live out the comic potential of a seemingly tragic death, Aristophanes and Agathon are there to mark this as each represents one possible interpretation of the nature of the death of Socrates; each may be present to celebrate the meeting and unity of comedy and tragedy (the unfulfilled mention at the end of the text signals this possible reading); and perhaps each may be forgiven for their parts in both Socrates' death and the misunderstanding of the nature of the death, as its nature is indeterminate. If Aristophanes, singled out in the *Apology* as the origin of the old charges, shows how comedy can lead to a tragic end (the death of Socrates), so too does Agathon show how the misunderstanding of the nature of love in his tragic works leads to incorrect thinking. Both Aristophanes and Agathon, then, need correction.

These tragedies are joined to comedy in similar fashion to the whole primal lovers in Aristophanes' speech. Comedy and tragedy belong together as a whole, and when they are separated, they are in a kind of fallen state that is a mark of the human. One could imagine the comic and tragic, fully joined, cartwheeling across a text, as it were, leaving readers dizzy; one could equally see a life, at its end, as a series of events cycling between the comic and the tragic, leaving the soul of the subject dizzy and uncertain.

This joining of comedy and tragedy in a life, in a series of events, in a series of lives, is the focus of the first part of this book. The joining of economic and political structures in the state is the focus of the second part of this book. And the joining of birth and infinite, unpayable debt in a kind of cosmological reading is the focus of the third part of this book. Altogether, then, the text looks at life, the state, and the place of the human soul or its analogues in the cosmos. The decisions we make in the conduct of a life, the decisions we make in the state, and the decisions the state makes for us shape our souls and affect our further decisions. A "soul," in a parsimonious reading, can be thought of as the totality of decisions made across a life and carrying into the future through one or another sort of causation. Given that Socrates says in the *Meno* that he does not insist that everything he says about the immortal soul and the doctrine of recollection is necessarily true, but that we will be "braver and less idle" should we choose to act as if there were immortal souls, it is worth examining the broader suggestions here. The life of a man and the life of a possibly existing human soul, then, are examined in the third part of this text. Keeping in mind, then, the relationships between life, state, and soul, this text will examine closely Plato's *Republic* and six paired plays by William Shakespeare: *Othello* and the *Comedy of Errors*, *The Merchant of Venice* and *Pericles*, and *Timon of Athens* and *Measure for Measure*. In each case, this book will present close readings of the texts and of the decisions the characters make within the texts. The structure of decision-making and the consequences of the decisions will be analyzed. This book will aim to develop an understanding of the fraught nature of interpretative choices and the need to make all choices with great care and with some sense of philosophical understanding.

The starting point for the book is the Myth of Er in Book X of the *Republic*, the choice the first soul there makes for a new life and a new fate, and the effects of that choice of fate.[6] The choice is made with very real comic and tragic possibilities, as these two modes of dramatic presentation are joined. The soul who makes the first choice quickly regrets the choice, and this regret is expressed as a kind of wailing to the heavens, a blaming of everyone save the soul who has chosen. The regret, coupled with the disbelief engendered by this experience, is termed a "moment of incredulity" in this text. This soul's wild and wailing incredulity, refusal to accept responsibility, failure to have studied philosophy in order to mitigate the risk at this moment are central to this book. The book then proceeds to explain the kinds of errors in a life that can lead to such a terrible choice and to the incredulity that follows. The errors are made both by figures in Book I of the *Republic* and by characters in the Shakespeare plays. Errors in decision-making that lead us to the terrible fate of that first soul in Book X of the *Republic* are precisely the errors we most need to understand and we most need to avoid. That first soul is condemned to a fate of eating his own children, and it is a fate he has chosen. This, more than anything else, is the worst.

These characters are all engaged in acts of interpretation that are used to inform actions in the world.[7] Interpretation is fraught both structurally (we never have full information) and in terms of desire (there may well be a preferred interpretation, whether or not it is true). Erroneous interpretations of one's life, one's state, one's cosmic duty, may lead, then, to "incredulity." A moment of incredulity is a moment of shocked disbelief at the consequence of a decision one has made thinking one has made that decision properly. Because of the structure of limited knowledge, we cannot interpret the conditions of our lives with guaranteed accuracy, but we are generally fairly sure we are doing things properly. This structure of assuming one knows, and finding out suddenly and horribly that one does not know, is repeated across Socratic texts and across Shakespeare's plays. Incredulity, then, is the outcome of decision-making. It is at its most intense in the Myth of Er, but is present throughout the *Republic*, and indeed, in the outcomes of numerous Socratic dialogues.

Incredulity, as a psychic phenomenon, is deeply troubling, deeply painful, and tends to lead to externalizing blame. The first soul to choose in the Myth of Er cries out and blames everyone else for his bad decision. His desire has taken hold, he has acted in the name of desire rather than in the name of truth, and his horrible fate is sealed. Equally, in the plays discussed here, there are moments of incredulity that follow from improper decisions and that lead to tragic consequences and final realizations. Othello kills and then rues, Antonio signs a deal and then is shocked when he might have to pay up, Claudio sins and cannot quite believe he may have to die. The consequences are severe: in tragedies they are fatal; in comedies, they still cause suffering. It is incumbent upon these characters, and us, then, to come to terms with comic and tragic structures, the proper balance of political and economic power, and with our obligations at the moment of birth. Failing to do so leads to the most dire consequences and the most painful incredulity.

The book is informed by a close textual and literary reading of the *Republic*, in the spirit of what John Russon describes as "giving the text its due as *text*."[8] The text of the *Republic*, in the reading presented here, becomes both a subject in the discourse of justice—that is, the text is a kind of actor of justice, a participant in the conversation even as the characters whose words we are reading are determiners of what counts as justice—and an object of justice—that is, our interpretations determine how just or unjust the portrayals of justice in the text are. The *Republic* tells us something about what justice might be and it provides its own interrogation of itself. Our duty to the text, then, is akin to the duty that a system of justice has both to those over whom it rules and to itself as a monitor of its own practices. If justice comes about through asking, listening, searching, so too does textual interpretation.[9]

This reading of the text as text plays out in this book as a careful consideration of patterns, repetitions of imagery, circles and cycles, or ring structures, as they appear across the work, taken as a whole.[10] The old man near death in Book I, Cephalus, and his arguments regarding debt and truth, reappear in a number of guises across the text and the reappearances of old men near death, men in death, men after death, men handing legacies to their sons, men dining on their sons, men using up fortunes given them or replenishing them only to have them lost again, men and debt, men and truth—all of these need to be read together as a working through of the ideas of justice presented in the *Republic*. The text presents these images, ties them together, and asks them questions, and judges them. They are, as it were, on trial.

This book presents, as well, careful readings of the Shakespeare plays using a range of techniques inspired by contemporary continental philosophy and psychoanalysis. Jacques Derrida's work on the gift and on debt figure throughout. Some contemporary work in economics, especially discussions of hysteresis (the mark of history, events, or crisis, borne by that which is affected and never returns to its prior state) and the transfer of risk, figure in Part II. Risk-bearing appears in the *Republic* in the ways that philosophers must bear the risk of harm by "going down" and the ways that we all must live out the consequences of all of our decisions, including the most fateful decision in Book X. The study of the transfer of risk, the consequences of transfer, and the need for social organization to manage risk carefully are taken up by public policy analysts, economists, and social scientists more generally. Some of this material has broad implications for this reading of both the *Republic* and the Shakespeare plays. Risks borne by individuals, risks borne by cities, risks borne by souls all have the same basic structures. We are excited by risk, ruined by risk, liberated by risk transfers, and sometimes rendered foolish when we have nothing at risk. Weighing the liberation and the foolishness against each other is a central concern in a number of public policy areas, and it is of clear concern in the texts this book is reading. With this in mind, it is important to ask how much the study of philosophy acts as a kind of insurance policy for souls. If health or automobile insurance is a transfer of risk under circumstances of future uncertainty, so the study of philosophy must be seen as a kind of insurance policy against the risk of having to choose a new life. To what extent does the study of philosophy "pay off," and to what extent does it fail to hedge our risks?[11] Are these the right questions to ask the discipline?

Philosophically what is at stake in this text is a tension of sorts between a desire for something like Cartesian certainty, where judgments and the decisions that stem from judgments are based on clear and distinct perceptions derived by a post-meditation subject who relies primarily on disembodied reason,[12] and keeps a kind of modest skepticism regarding the external world on the one hand and what Derrida notes in the *Politics of Friendship* is a responsibility to extend friendship without advance certainty regarding the result. This tension between a desire for certainty and a responsibility to act in the face of profound and perhaps insoluble uncertainty is at the heart not just of this text but of what we as philosophers must contend with. The world is not now nor ever will be fully unfolded, and yet the world demands that we be in it as agents. To pretend that we are not agents so as to avoid responsibility for action, to stay in this room by this fire with this paper, is to be disingenuous. To act with no philosophical awareness is also to be disingenuous. We must negotiate the spaces between grave uncertainty and false knowing, and it is philosophy that is tasked with this.

Shakespeare, as well, deals with these issues of making decisions with less than full information, and with trying to negotiate responsibility for action under uncertainty. Shakespeare scholars have a long history of working through philosophical, economic, psychological, psychoanalytic, feminist, and historical traces in the plays. I am indebted to many scholars who have contributed to these discourses. Philosophical, psychological, and psychoanalytic readings, and historicist readings predominate.

Part I focuses on the interplay and workings of comedy and tragedy, using both Aristotelian and Shakespearean notions of these terms. That we choose our fate, even as Achilles does in the *Iliad*, and then choose an interpretation of our fate which then guides further choices through the effects of hysteresis (a term borrowed from physics and used in economics) is shown through a reading of the choice that the first soul in Book X makes, and the ways that this unnamed soul might be named by any character in Book I of the *Republic*. Hysteresis describes the change in materials left by exerted forced. Metal bends back most of the way but does not quite return to its original state. Economies are altered by crises and do not quite return to pre-crisis states. And analogously, lives are altered by decisions and though we may return to being something like what we were before the crisis, we are permanently marked by events and by decisions. When we act again, we carry the mark of this experience. The naïf is no longer quite so new, the soul is no longer quite so innocent, even as each still retains its identity.

Othello and the *Comedy of Errors* provide a deeper look at the interplay of comedy and tragedy, the interpretive choices we make in our lives, and the ways that our interpretations of events shape both our reactions and our futures. Desdemona's father, Brabantio, reads his daughter's marriage, and therefore his own life, as a tragedy. This interpretive choice moves the action in the play, gives Iago all the more strength as a manipulator of perception, and leads to the final deaths of the major characters. By way of contrast, early events in *The Comedy of Errors* are read as comic and are meant to be played out as comic, but the choice to interpret life as a comedy leads to a range of events bordering on the tragic.

The characters' interpretive choices provide the narrative scheme that each works through, and using the comic or tragic scheme causes each character to live out a comedy or a tragedy rather than the reverse. If the characters had been able to listen to Socrates' account of the need for both narrative schemes, if the characters had been able to be informed by fully joined narrative modes, their pain may have been reduced.

This choice of narrative form shapes the lives of the characters in ways that leave permanent marks on them. *Othello*, the tragic play, begins in marriage and ends in death for many of the major characters. The focus of the play is the lives of individuals as they intersect and interact, as they interpret their worlds and engage in world-making based on their interpretations. Life, it would seem, is a series of interpretations and actions, each tied together in a kind of feedback loop. *The Comedy of Errors*, as the seemingly opposite comic play, is equally populated by characters who act out assumptions, who start with a tale of loss and end with a partial (comic) reunification.

Part II looks at a different kind of error—that of misusing political and economic structures in ways that misallocate risk or that cause characters to underestimate risk. The terms of analysis are polity and economy. The polity, for the purposes of this book, is the set of structures that underlies the use of force and the appeal to justice, and the human relations that make up a society. *The Merchant of Venice* is, among other things, a courtroom drama, and the court is part of the political system. Appeal is made to the judicial enforcement of a contract and to the ownership of property. Ownership is enforced by the political system. Tied to the polity, and not entirely separable, is the economy. Economics is concerned with the allocation of scarce goods, with the risk of losing goods, with the translation of the value of scarce goods into a medium of exchange. For economic value to be enforced, there needs to be a political system that uses force and that has something like a stable set of meanings to which we can appeal in the face of unfair or unjust exchanges. The economic structure, then, needs the political structure in order to be workable. The political structure, equally, needs some notion of exchange and management of risk. A political system that has no exchange, that cannot manage the risk of human life, will fail. Or rather, perhaps, it does not even exist. If there is no exchange, if risk is borne only by individual actors, there is no mutuality and therefore no social structure that can support a political structure, no polity. The polity, then, is as dependent on the economy as the economy is on the polity. These components of the state must act in some kind of proper balance for either one to exist. If the economic oversteps the political, or if the political oversteps the economic, the entire set of human relations fails. The paired plays in this section reinforce this sense in the *Republic*.

The *Republic* presents economic structures in a number of places including in the relationship between the guardians and gold. There is a clear separation between what the polity or political structures of the city should deal with and what the economic structures should deal with. It is at the moment that these are confused—that private wealth-seeking is again admitted to the city that the fall becomes clearest.

In similar fashion, *The Merchant of Venice* provides us with a way to see the effects of the overvaluation of money on family structures and the undervaluation of money on social structures. That is, just as Shylock overvalues money, so Antonio undervalues it. Antonio invests safely, uses money to buy a marriage, but then finds himself unable to repay what he has borrowed. He fails to see that there is a place for money, even as he uses money and the economy to foster love and to create excitement. Shylock is Antonio's counterpart, in that he confuses money and his daughter, unable to tell them apart in a telling moment of distress. The subplot of the caskets gets at a notion of the proper valuation of the inner and the outer, and it gets at the ways that economic relations can be properly used to manage human affect. Antonio's melancholy comes from too little risk; Shylock's misuse of money comes, perhaps, because being a Jewish figure in a non-Jewish society carries too much risk. The caskets and the decisions that are made around them help manage the risks involved in making fateful choices, and suggest ways to keep economic and social and political issues in their proper places.

Pericles, as well, shows the problems of risk in decision-making and the misuse of political and economic structures to exert control over people. Sexual desire and human love and loyalty are commodified in the play, and this commodification, the economic takeover of the social dimension, has cruel outcomes including famine, a suggestion of cannibalism, and prostitution (as its own kind of devouring). The economic must be properly disciplined and not brought fully into the polity.

Part III looks at the refusal of debt at the moment of birth. That is, it considers what it means to be alive, to take on debt properly or to act in mistaken fashion and assume that birth does not come with some kind of already existing debt that one does not freely ask for, but rather that one is simply burdened with and that one must wrestle with. The sense of the relationship between birth and infinite debt developed in this section carries with it a kind of cosmological concern. The soul, or its various analogues, is the locus of intergenerational debt that must be struggled with, that must be paid, and that cannot entirely be paid. This structure of the necessary but impossible task is present in both the *Republic* and the paired Shakespeare plays. Philosophers, in the *Republic*, are charged with repaying their states, minding their souls, and minding the souls of their fellow citizens. In the face of desire, in the face of the crowd, philosophers fail at this task and the city falls. The duty is still present, but it cannot entirely be fulfilled. Equally, *Timon of Athens* and *Measure for Measure* demonstrate obligations that go unfulfilled, desires that interfere with duty, and uncomfortable restorations of order. The ends of each of these three texts, the fall of the city, the fall of Timon, the Duke's proposal to Isabella, is unsatisfying. The characters are flawed, the duties they are charged with are impossible, and they react in human fashion to the impossibility of answering the call. The philosophers retreat, Timon grows bitter, uses generosity to destroy, and Isabella is shockingly silent.

The central debt of the *Republic* is the obligation of the philosophers to go back down to the cave though they have escaped it and would rather live in the sun, on the earth, above. Their obligation comes simply because they have experienced the truth and the truth itself is a kind of debt. Their fates are fixed, the debt is heavy, failure leads to death, and yet it all must happen inexorably.

That one is fated, as a philosopher, not merely to experience the truth but to tell the truth, is a condition of life. That is, birth is precisely this debt. To misunderstand the nature of this debt is to put oneself in a position of being the first soul to choose in Book X. That is, one risks being a tyrant if one fails to accept this debt and pay it back despite the impossibility of escaping the choice in the afterlife. Even as the first soul chooses the life of a tyrant and ends up incredulous, so other souls may well choose the life of a philosopher. We need to think through whether or not this choice, too, comes with deep regret, incredulity, and a cry to the heavens.

There is, then, a full circle back to the start of the *Republic*. The obligation to pay back, to go back down, to go down to the Piraeus, to engage in philosophical conversation however unwillingly and with however much risk, is a profound and life-ruling obligation. It simply must happen. And though it must happen, it likely will fail as it does with Cephalus and the other figures in Book I. It is either a comic or a tragic repetition, or cycle, or a cartwheeling across life.[13]

The central concern of *Timon of Athens* is the notion of the gift. With Derrida's work on the gift as a background, Timon's generosity as a kind of aggression is presented. He overgives in that he expects return, he seems to invest rather than to give, his gifts are always instrumental rather than free, and yet he resents having any other interpretation of his gift-giving presented. Eventually, Timon's gift giving transforms from a simple kind of aggression to all-out war. He gives death, even as he has given love. His notion of birth as a kind of aggression is tragic in its outcome. He does not merely give because he owes, he gives so that he can be owed. It is investment in the guise of gift giving. It is ruinous.

Measure for Measure provides another reading of obligation that comes from mere existence. Nearly all of the characters have at least one form of incontinence, and the main obligation is to get control over what is not yet controlled. Proper speech, proper rule, proper sexuality, proper reproduction, proper punishment, proper mercy, proper justice—all of these must be imposed on people who feel too much, who want too much, who do too much, who say too much. Birth is a kind of debt that must be paid in proper measure.

We find then, by the end of the book, that we owe the right reading of our lives and the events in our lives, we will struggle to choose the right narrative mode: comedy or tragedy; we will struggle to balance political and economic structures in the right ways so that we do not destroy what we are meant to tend to, and we will struggle as well with the nature of our responsibility at the moment of birth and in the acceptance of life, and we will need to calculate the right ways to repay what we owe. Our lives are fraught with risk, with the risk of making the wrong interpretive choices, getting delicate balances wrong, and refusing to attempt fundamental repayment. Our choices, our balances, our refusals all work to define us even as we define them. The phenomenon of hysteresis gives us no way to hit rewind and try it all over again. The failures mark us.

Most fundamentally, against the need to choose, to choose well, to make proper use of philosophy and the reading of the texts of our lives is the very indeterminacy of this text. We cannot read and interpret at the end of life, for there is always another decision to be made, always some kind of incompletion. Even the souls who choose new lives at the end of the *Republic* are not entirely at the end of their lives. They do not have the completion needed to make an ever-correct choice. The play of the parts of the soul, the play of lives, the play of possibility all seem to work together to limit the soul's ability to choose well. Philosophy is the one discipline arrayed against the temptations to misinterpret or to choose hastily. It does not seem to be powerful enough to guarantee wise choices in all cases and at all times.

To the extent that the *Republic* and these plays offer us some insight, it is the insight that we must find both the tensions and uneasy balances in the relationships between key categories of human existence. It is in our choices of interpretive modes that these balances can be set, and it is in these very same choices that the balances can be thrown off. The choice is ours, the consequences are ours, and these are fraught decisions, indeed.

We turn to philosophy to rescue us from indeterminacy, to clarify our conceptual understanding of our experiences, to help us wrestle with desire. Philosophy, though, brings its own problems as we see from Socrates' confession at the end of Book I of the *Republic*. He has had inappropriate desire and has behaved badly, not from actual overeating but rather from a kind of epistemological overdoing, or desire for more than he should want—a kind of philosophical *pleonexia*. Further, the cyclical nature of the Book X myth suggests that philosophy cannot rescue us in any permanent way, as the inevitable cycles will have us fall and rise in turn. We are left then without heroes and without clarity, perhaps without true tragedy but equally without full comedy. Within this incompletion, with the lack of heroic rescue, we must still make decisions, we must still choose how to live and which social forces to balance against which others, and we must live with the consequences of each decision, from the smallest (what to snack on) to the largest (what philosophical arguments to "eat" and which "children" to "dine" on.) Each of the sections of this text, each of the pairings of Shakespeare plays, each of the concerns about interpretation and choice and duty presents a problem we attempt to solve using philosophy, and perhaps settling on hope rather than on easy resolution.

NOTES

1. See Drew Hyland for a discussion of both the comic aspects of Aristophanes' story and an account of the "pessimism about the human condition." Drew Hyland, "The Animals That We Therefore Were," in *Plato's Animals: Gadflies, Horses, Swans, and Other Philosophical Beasts*. Edited by Jeremy Bell and Michael Nass (Bloomington, IN: Indiana University Press, 2015), 202.

2. Freydberg writes, "There is a symmetry to the treatment of (Aristophanic) comic and (Homeric) tragic themes." Comedy and tragedy, choices regarding interpretation, the responsibilities for reading responsibly all cycle through the *Republic* and the Shakespeare plays I discuss. See Bernard Freydberg, "Retracing Homer and Aristophanes in the Platonic Text," in *Retracing the Platonic Text*. Edited by John Russon and John Sallis (Evanston, IL: Northwestern University Press, 2000), 109.

3. Andrea Wilson Nightingale develops a wonderful reading of comic and tragic moments in Plato and Athenian literature more generally. See Andrea Wilson Nightingale, *Genres in Dialogue: Plato and the Construct of Philosophy* (Cambridge: Cambridge University Press, 1995).

4. See Thucydides, *The History of the Peloponnesian War*. Translated by Rex Warner (New York: Penguin Classics, 1972), Book VI sections 26–28.

5. My gratitude to Andrew Cutrofello for pointing out the relationship between the last men standing in the *Symposium*, and to Jim Harrington for pointing out Socrates' role as the philosophical mediator between them.

6. The choice of fate at the end of Book X of the *Republic* echoes Achilles' choice of a shorter life and *kleos* rather than a longer life of anonymity in the *Iliad*. Achilles says, "Mother tells me / the immortal goddess Thetis with her glistening feet, / that two fates bear me on to the day of death. / If I hold out here and I lay siege to Troy, / my journey home is gone, but my glory never dies. / If I voyage back to the fatherland I love, / my pride, my glory dies . . . / true, but the life that's left me will be long, / the stroke of death will not come on me quickly In the end, of course, Achilles chooses glory or *kleos* over a long life. That he can choose what is fated, that necessity is open to choice, is central to the Myth of Er, and to the notion of choice in general. That glory and time are zero-sum is equally significant. Homer. *Iliad*. Translated by Robert Fagles (New York: Penguin Books, 1990), 9.497–9.505.

G.R.F Ferrari notes that Glaucon, too, has some concern for glory and reward rather than a simple life. G.R.F. Ferrari, "Glaucon's Reward, Philosophy's Debt," in *Plato's myths*. Edited by Catalin Partenie (Cambridge: Cambridge University Press, 2009), 117–119.

7. Jonathan Lear develops a reading of the internal structures of the parts of the soul, the external myths to which they have been exposed, and the dynamics of the interrelations of all of these moving parts. See Jonathan Lear, "Inside and Outside the "Republic"," in *Phronesis* 37(2) (1992): 184–215.

8. John Russon, "Just Reading: The Nature of the Platonic Text," in *Retracing the Platonic Text*. Edited by John Russon and John Sallis (Evanston, IL: Northwestern University Press, 2000), x.

9. Further, as John Sallis notes in *Being and Logos*, "The images of the *Republic* have become so 'self-evident,' . . . that they have long since ceased to provoke us into questioning" (Sallis 312). We need, then, to defamiliarize the text at some level in order to be in a position to do the kind of careful reading that the text deserves. For the purposes of this book, some of that defamiliarization will come from reading the text of the *Republic* with the texts of the Shakespeare plays. An unusual pairing can help with making the familiar a little less so. Sallis cautions us, also, to be careful with the name of Plato as author. See John Sallis, *Being and Logos: Reading the Platonic Dialogues*, third edition (Bloomington and Indianapolis, IN: Indiana University Press, 1996), 312. Drew Hyland raises similar points in the introduction to his book on continental readings of Plato. See Drew A. Hyland, *Questioning Platonism: Continental Interpretations of Plato* (New York: State University of New York Press, 2004).

One issue here is that ascribing authorial intention is always at least mildly problematic. More interestingly though, what is at stake is a kind of short hand or easy way to avoid ambiguity, confusion, incoherence, multiple meanings, difficulties with the texts, and the endless need to read, to circle back to the beginning and re-read, to allow oneself to re-enact the final scene of reincarnation in the *Republic*. If we claim to know what "Plato" says or means or is, we no longer need to revisit, re-read, re-think. In place of "Plato," then is a text that will be read from the end back to the beginning. (Sallis, *Being and Logos*, 1.)

10. Adi Ophir reads the *Republic* through some of these same kinds of structural concerns. Mythos and logos, rings, and the "space of discourse" all appear in the discussion. See *Plato's Invisible Cities: Discourse and Power in the Republic* (Savage, MD: Barnes and Noble, 1991).

11. Satkunanandan points out that there are real questions in the literature about whether or not the turning of the soul is permanent or if a re-turning is required. That is, is the soul changed, does hysteresis mark it, or does it ever fall back to a pre-philosophical state. Is there progress? Shalini Satkunanandan, *Extraordinary Responsibility: Politics Beyond the Moral Calculus* (New York: Cambridge University Press, 2015), 109.

12. See R. Descartes, *Meditations on First Philosophy*. Translated by Donald A. Cress (Indianapolis, IN: Hackett, 1998).

13. David Gallop develops a reading of the cyclicality of the soul, the immortality of the soul, and how we should consider it to be "an opening dialectical move" (Gallop 274). See David Gallop, "Plato's 'Cyclical Argument' Recycled," in *Essays on Plato's Psychology*. Edited by Ellen Wagner (Oxford: Lexington Books, 2001), 263–280.

Part I

COMEDY, TRAGEDY, AND NARRATIVE CHOICE

Prologue
The Republic *and Tragic and Comic Incredulity*

Incredulity, a feeling potent enough to make a character scream out to the heavens despite having been warned by the gods that his situation is entirely of his own making and should not have shocked at all, is the starting point of this book, though this moment appears near the end of the *Republic*. The choices we make to interpret our world according to one particular narrative structure rather than another can lead us to awful suffering and even to horror itself. In what follows, in part I, we will look at characters' choosing to interpret their situation as either tragic or comic such that they foreclose other possibilities. In their choice of interpretive framework, then, there is a kind of fate or destiny under construction. Another choice would make for a different outcome. Somehow the characters presented below do not see that there is some flexibility in interpretation. They spin narratives, they are spun by others, they are ill-prepared and ill-informed. If for Aristotle, the key to moral understanding is the formation of a good character who can make good choices, who can compensate for flaws through the emphasis on their opposites, the characters we will look at in the following sections seem to fail to develop both the right character and the right kind of compensatory mechanisms for managing their worlds.[1]

In *The Politics of Friendship*, Jacques Derrida provides us with a philosophical interpretation of the kind of choice and the stakes of the choice that are at issue here. He writes, "Friendship, the being-friend—what is that, anyway? Well, it is to love *before* being loved. Before even thinking about what *loving, love, lovence* mean, one must know that the only way to find out is by questioning first of all the act and the experience of loving rather than the state or situation of being loved."[2] There is, in Derrida's view, a kind of impossible decision to love, to reach out, to accept, to define oneself, to make a decision, to choose, before knowing anything of the result, the consequences, the worth or pay-off. One must cast out, and one cannot know at the moment of casting what will happen. The subject must choose to enact its subjectivity regardless of any outcome. There is a kind of investment here, but one with such uncertain return that no market could tolerate it.

Friendship, in this reading then, is an act of subjectivity, a choice to invest and trust, a choice to allow an experience of love (a comedy) with no way of knowing the result. Will it end in tragedy or not, will it end in failure or not. The subject cannot know if he or she will be loved in return, smote in return, destroyed some other way, or rescued, requited, returned as one could wish.

Philosophically, then, the gesture of friendship depends on a choice made under complete uncertainty. The Cartesian subject cannot be Cartesian, but rather must trust what cannot be trusted. Friends have betrayed and there is no way to gain a clear and distinct perception of the quality of friendship in advance of the choice to love. This epistemic limit comes before the act, and the act is only possible at this extreme limit.

The characters from both the *Republic* and the Shakespeare plays wrestle with this fundamental epistemic limit. No one can know the outcome of the choice to befriend, to enact, to react, or to respond. Each such act alters the subject and the subject's prospects in unknowable ways, and yet choices must be made and the newly established world must be inhabited.

Tragedy and comedy, seemingly separable modes of dramatic presentation, are not as distinct as it might seem. Though Aristotle provides clear categories that separate the two modes, many dramatists find that mixing the elements of the two provides a heightened dramatic experience. We are often presented with "comic relief" or a sudden moment of drama within a comedy that lends the comedy a certain amount of seriousness and that sets up the next comic moment. We are familiar with the notion of the "straight man" whose job is to provide room for the comic by contrast. A straight man need not be completely tragic but is clearly there as a sober foil to the more manic character. The contrast between the sober and the comic leads us to feel a certain level of pity for the more sober character who either "does not get it" or who is made fun of by the comic's jokes. There is a low-level tragedy in being the butt of much of what passes for comedy.

Further, and more structurally significant than the roller coaster view of drama, is the notion that we cannot determine the boundaries of an experience until the experience is complete. Any comic character or moment can be embedded in a tragedy and any tragic character or moment can, equally, be embedded in a comedy. The result of this dependence on completion for making a determination of mode is that deciding upon the mode in medias res is fraught with error.

To assume one is in a tragedy, or that a character is tragic, or that an event has tragic consequences for a character is to assume that one knows the final moment, the point of judgment, the culmination of events. But as soon as one allows time to become a factor, one must acknowledge that the meanings of events can be recast and the tragic can become comic, or the comic can become tragic.

When we arrive at the final page of a tragedy, and we look back on the deaths or lowered circumstances of the characters, we can, just as well, look forward to the new era to come and that looking forward can alter the way we view the deaths or horrors of the characters we have just held in sympathy. The new era and all the new characters made possible by the end of the old era bring hope for happiness, for marriage, for joy. These hopes are the beginnings of new comic situations and are as likely to grip our imaginations as our looking back has done.

If we were proper readers of drama and dramatic narratives, perhaps we should think about the events that have happened before the drama opens so that we see that the characters have "lives" that predate the comedy we are about to watch, and those "lives" may well have been laced with tragic moments that have led to the current comedy.

The point of this speculation is to highlight the way that time alters our judgments of events so that we become aware that any judgment that makes marriage comic and death tragic is really a judgment contingent on artificially determined ends and statuses of characters and situations. Indeed, the marriage can be the beginning of a nightmare, as it is in *Othello*, and a death sentence can be the beginning of a comedy, as it is in *The Comedy of Errors*. Part I will look at both of these texts to show in more detail the ways that the comic and tragic end up inseparable, and that therefore our judging ourselves to be either comic or tragic is likely to lead us to a moment of incredulity.

Before we get to Shakespearean drama, we will discuss Aristotle's definitions of tragedy and comedy and then look at Plato's expression of the mixing of the tragic and the comic in the *Republic*. For Aristotle, from the *Poetics*, "a tragedy, then, is the imitation of an action that is serious and also, as having magnitude, complete in itself."[3] Further, he writes, "We have laid it down that a tragedy is an imitation of an action, that is complete in itself, as a whole of some magnitude, for a whole may be of no magnitude to speak of. Now a whole is that which has beginning, middle, and end."[4]

Comedy, on the other hand, "is (as has been observed) an imitation of men worse than the average; worse, however, not as regards any and every sort of fault, but only as regards one particular kind, the Ridiculous."[5] From these passages we see that tragedy deals with the serious and has a definite magnitude that makes it complete, brings about pity and fear, and helps with catharsis while comedy deals with the ugly and ridiculous, brings about laughter, and does not bring about pain. Tragedy, with its sense of a certain magnitude, should come to some kind of measurable and markable end, but determining the end of a measure is at some level merely a contingent decision to stop writing after five acts or a few hundred pages or a particular death or event. Reflection on any tragedy, on any limitation, leads immediately to the question of what happens next, and thus the seeming certainty of magnitude falls away into the indeterminate. As indeterminate, any narrative can be recast from one mode to another, and indeed can be recast as a kind of cycle of history or cycle of life. A cycle can have tragic moments, but, according to Aristotle's definition of tragedy, a cycle cannot itself be a tragedy. I will argue that no text, no life, is anything other than a cycle or some other topography of incompletion, and that therefore the judgment of mode must be left in the moment. Further, even momentary judgments fall into paradoxes of time and event and leave us largely unable to decide with certainty if we are experiencing tragedy or comedy. The very question itself becomes problematic.

Each of the characteristics of the tragic and comic modes, then, is subject to modification, play, boundary crossings, and out and out violations. Indeed, the argument in this section is that many texts contain both tragic and comic elements and that distinguishing the comic from the tragic is impossible in any other than a local, temporary, and contingent way. The texts to be dealt with in part I will each violate Aristotelian notions of the separability and distinguishability of tragedy and comedy.

Our inability to distinguish with certainty and finality our position within a tragic–comic nexus, and the idea that the range between tragedy and comedy is less a continuum than it is a major leap in perspective between one mode and the other leads us to a kind of psychic whiplash effect that has significant and lasting implications for our understanding of ourselves, for the stability of our institutions, and for any notion of right living. We do not ever know, at any moment, if we are amidst a tragedy or amidst a comedy because there simply is no absolute standard of judgment, no correct view from nowhere that gives us the correct perspective on our situation. We will find, in the readings of *Othello* and *The Comedy of Errors*, that when characters assume that they are either in a tragic or in a comic moment, they end up causing profound problems for themselves.

Aristotle discusses peripety and discovery—two key notions of dramatic presentation that help negotiate the path that narrative takes. He writes of these two concepts, "A Peripety is the change of the kind described from one state of things within the play to its opposite."[6] And, "A Discovery is, as the very word implies, a change from ignorance to knowledge, and thus to either love or hate, in the personages marked for good or evil fortune."[7] Peripety, as a change in the state of things to their opposite, characterizes the flip in perspective between tragic and comic moments. That events can be suddenly recast as their opposite that we can feel secure in our interpretations and suddenly have to think the very opposite of what we had been so certain about, shows the problems inherent in rendering certain judgment over the meaning of a text, an event, a character, or any other kind of modal claim. We simply do not have the ability to know what is to come, nor do we have a way to guarantee that our sense of the text is the accurate one. A peripety could easily be followed by yet another. The destabilization of emotions and judgments here is significant for the purposes of coming to understand modal play.

The mechanism for a peripety is the discovery. The characters can make a sudden discovery that undermines their sense of the world, and that undermining is then transferred to the audience. Or the audience can discover something a character does not yet know, and the same destabilization occurs, with the added tension of the audience's knowing that the character is in for a rude shock.

The author has a great deal of power over the sense of the audience through the use of peripety and discovery in both the characters and in the conventions the audience is generally known to bring to the text. Marriage can be the start of a tragedy, the end of a comedy, or both. Death, too, can signal either comedy or tragedy, beginning or end. Because we often use rituals associated with marriage, birth, and death to signal tragic and comic narratives, and because we use these rituals both in literary and real narratives, we end up with what this book styles as moments of profound incredulity. In each of these cases, the audience or a character makes some assumption about the worth or location or temporal position of some event or thought, but then discovers that the assumption is mistaken.

Though seemingly characteristic more of drama than of philosophy, the issues of peripety and discovery are freighted with philosophical concern as well. They evince the uncertainty with which we live as subjects in the world, they require us to consolidate our sense of self, to become subjects, as it were, in order to act, and they require us to take responsibility for our actions despite the uncertainty under which we operate. The world, authored or not, can change or disclose or surprise us. Skepticism, seemingly a defense against the surprise, is unhelpful given that we simply must choose and must act. Commitment must be fully engaged in, and yet can only ever be partial. We live out this paradox both in drama and in the institutions of the social and political world.

The incredulity that this book is focusing on is that which comes when we think we are in one kind of narrative structure, say, a comedy, and we turn and find ourselves suddenly in a wholly different structure, say, a tragedy. The whiplash effect here comes from our completely misreading the situation. But this misreading is not one of getting the details about comedy and tragedy wrong; rather, the misreading comes because we do not at all realize that comedy and tragedy are relativistic notions, subject to wild swings, and not ever absolutes that are fixed. The Stephen Sondheim musical *Into the Woods*, which depicts the aftermath of "happily ever after" for a number of fairy tale characters, is a work that shows very nicely how much tension there is between the comic and the tragic, how close to death and horror any marriage is, and how close to comedy any death can turn out to be.

Aristotle suggests that the height of drama comes from the coupling of a peripety and a discovery. There is nothing more awful, full of awe, than the complete reversal of fortune that comes from a new, and suddenly but naturally, found piece of evidence. The discovery we never saw coming, but that we accept as perfectly natural, forces a turning upon our souls or our understandings and we are shocked, surprised, saddened, by the force of the turn.

A moment of incredulity, I would suggest, is a refined version of the coupling of a peripety and a discovery. What makes us completely shocked, and largely unaccepting, of the turn is a sense of the seeming unnaturalness of it because our assumptions had been so deeply incorrect. Our certainty regarding the mode we are operating in, our sense that we know where we are, where we are heading, and how we are getting there all work together to make it nearly impossible for us to manage the kind of whiplash that a peripety coupled with a discovery can lead to.

A further term that is useful here, in laying out the causes of moments of incredulity, is "hysteresis."[8] Hysteresis has a meaning in physics—the tendency of an object to retain some of its history and thus to respond only partially to changed circumstances or to a shock and to return only partially to the original state prior to the application of force. Compression episodes leave a small mark on metal; there is a spring back to nearly its original shape, but not a complete spring back. The shock that bends the metal changes it; the history of the metal forces the return of the shape. But the shock leaves a mark, and the prior history leaves a mark. There is no complete change nor is there a complete return. This notion has been borrowed by economists to deal with the notion of "sticky wages"—the tendency of wages to stay put for the most part, even in deflationary times. The environment changes, but the inhabitants cannot fully adjust as they have something like an identity or a character. The shock, as well, becomes part of the history, and so a shock cannot fully transform nor can a history be fully returned to. The history of wages will tend to slow change, the history of a shock will tend to slow recovery, and the previous interpretations of a situation will tend to mark the response. If you are in a comic mode, the comic will affect your interpretations, and if you are in a tragic mode, the tragic will mark your thinking. Hysteresis suggests, then, a lag in responses to changing situations, and that lag causes problems for adjustments to peripeties and discoveries. Hysteresis, to the extent that it is a force, limits flexibility and limits the return to the normal. Further, it plays a role in the repetitions we will see in some of the plays in later sections. Repetition, in contrast, is an endless return to a prior state regardless of changes, shocks, incredulity, or cries to the heavens. We can think of hysteresis as working in ways similar to trauma (a trauma leaves a permanent mark on a psyche) or to character (a character's character, as well, is a permanent state that bends and mostly re-forms.)

The signal moment of tragic incredulity is the Myth of Er from Book X of Plato's *Republic*.[9] The tale starts with a tragicomedy, the battlefield death of Er. That Er dies is a tragedy of the moment, but in time ends up being less a tragedy as the death is temporary and Er returns to report on what he sees in the afterlife.[10] This cycle of death's being returned to life is repeated within the myth itself, though without the addition of reportage.[11]

Er journeys to a "marvelous place" (614c) where souls are judged and sent either up to the right or down to the left based on their previous life (614c). The tale continues:

> He [Er] said he saw souls depart by each of the two openings of heaven and earth after judgment, while from the other openings, some souls came up travel-stained and dusty from out of the earth, while from the other opening others came down from heaven clean and pure. Those who kept arriving appeared to come as from a long journey, and departed rejoicing into the meadow and camped as if at a festival. (614d-e)

There are comic and tragic elements throughout the description Er gives us. The almost mechanical arrivals and departures of souls have a comic edge to them, but the mechanistic treatment of the human can seem at the same time dehumanizing. Further, the greetings of the dead are mixed between happy joy and horror. The thousand-year reward is delightful, the thousand-year punishment horrific. Suffering for some, unsurpassed beauty for others. There is a notion of helping friends of justice and harming enemies of justice. Except that just as the helping and harming confounds Polemarchus's notion of justice, so too will this most ultimate version cause problems for our souls.

Socrates tells Glaucon,

> the sum of it is this: for every injustice they had ever done to anyone, for every person they had wronged, they paid a penalty for each in turn tenfold—that is, once every hundred years, because this is the span of human life—in order that the punishment imposed might be ten times the crime . . . ; and again, if they had worked any benefit and become just and holy, they reaped their due in the same measure. (615a-b)

The penalty is both natural, tied to human lives, and contrived as ten times the crime, and the reward as well is both natural and contrived. Helping and harming are proportionate to the help and harm that individuals do during their lives.

The next step, after the punishment and reward phase of the afterlife, is the return into the cycle of life. An Interpreter of Lachesis speaks thus,

> So begins another period of membership in the race of mortals, whose birth brings death. No fate shall fall to you by lot; you shall choose a fate. Let him to whom the lot first falls first choose a life which shall of necessity be his. Virtue is without master: each shall have more and less of her according as he honors or dishonors her. The responsibility is his who chooses. God is not responsible. (617d-e)

The significance of the choice stems from the profound responsibility for the choice, the lack of blame of any deity for the choice and the consequences, and the concomitant lack of fate as a structure. These souls choose, based on whatever wisdom they have accrued, and there is nothing but choice here.[12] That "virtue is without master" means that virtue itself is the highest good, as it comes up in the *Euthyphro*, and virtue is to be the guide, not chance or fate, not gods or God, not random luck. The choice is absolute. It must be cared for. We owe the choice by its nature as the highest thing. And it is necessity itself in its most profound reading. This choice, of all choices there are, is the structure of infinite debt as it is laid out in part III.

Socrates describes the scene in this manner:

> [T]he Interpreter laid the patterns of lives on the ground in front of them, more numerous by far than those who were present, and very various, for there were lives of all kinds of animals, and especially all kinds of human lives. There were tyrannies among them, some permanent, others destroyed in midcourse and ending at last in poverty and exile and beggary. There were also lives of men distinguished for beauty in respect to their form, others for bodily strength and athletic prowess, or for birth and the virtues of their parents; and there were lives undistinguished in these same respects, and so similarly for women. (618a-b)

There is, here, an economy of plenty—enough lives and more for every soul to choose well. The lives are themselves varied from simple to complex, from beautiful to ugly, from animal to human, from comic to tragic.

Such a plenitude, such choice should, it seems, be a comic moment when a happy character, having lived well, continues in the same way, or when a sad character finally discovers riches and becomes a happy character and lives on in plenty, comfort and joy. And yet, despite the warnings, we find that

> [T]he first to choose at once came forward and chose the greatest tyranny; due to folly and greed, he chose without sufficiently examining it all, and it escaped his notice that he was destined to eat his own children, along with other evils; when he examined it at leisure, he beat his breast and bewailed his choice. But he disregarded the admonitions of the Interpreter: for he did not blame himself for these evils, but blamed fortune and fate and everything except himself. He had come down from heaven, having lived his previous life under a settled constitution, and had gotten a share of virtue by habit without philosophy. (619b-d)

The moment of incredulity that this first soul faces when he reads of his life at leisure is marked by both peripety and discovery. The peripety is the going from a happy heavenly well-ordered life which this soul thinks is a comedy to the tragic life of tyrannical dieting. The discovery comes from the reading of that life, and so in Aristotle's sense, this moment is the highest moment of tragedy, when peripety and discovery meet. There is, further, a moment of hysteresis as the passage below illustrates, for the souls all use their previous lives as a historical guide to choosing a new life. Many do not entirely understand the role of their own history in their own choosing, they remain unphilosophical, they seem to carry with them the desires and fears they have built up over the course of the previous life and the last thousand years of reward and punishment, and those who choose badly will suffer from their bad choices because they do not, at some fundamental level, understand their situations. Hysteresis makes them unable to react carefully and openly to the scene in front of them, and their prior beliefs and prior states of mind carry great weight.

Because our children are imitations of us, to use the worrisome language of the text, we both care too much for our children and too improperly.[13] We assume we are well and good and so our children, as copies of us, will also be well and good, and so we do not worry. We assume, equally, that our children will take on our best qualities rather than losing "information" over the generations, and so we care more about them than we do about what is actually better than our children, what Socrates might call the Forms. That something could be higher than the lives of the children who replicate us is not a thing we see well.

With this lack of vision, what stands out to us is the fact of our children and our concern for a kind of mirror image of them, which really is a mirror image of ourselves. Book X's discussion of mirrors, imitations, copies of things made so easily, must be applied to children as well. Imitations are less good because they are made with less care and less skill than they need. And yet, we are taken with imitation in our narratives, our making and doing, our studies, and of course, in our children.

The improper regard is outsized, misplaced, and leads the first soul to his greatest mistake. Presumably he chooses this easy life both because he does not know how to make non-imitative decisions (after all, he has lived in a well-ordered city under a constitution he could merely imitate, but could not actually create), and he wishes for great power and great wealth that he can inherit and pass down. He thus chooses for himself, for whom he has too much regard, and for his children, for whom he also has too much regard. His imitative action, which is at the core of inheritance, leads him to an incorporation rather than a copying of his children. Such an incorporation is precisely the opposite of what he had wanted, and it is the height of horror at the moment of the discovery.

We can also hear an echo of Derrida's discussion of Aristotle on friendship, the numbers of friends one can have, and the extent or reach of friendship. Derrida writes, "It is possible to love more than one person, Aristotle seems to concede; to love in number, but not too much so—not too many. It is not the number that is forbidden, nor the more than one, but the numerous, if not the crowd."[14] If this soul loves too many of his own, he chooses them as they reflect on him. The crowd, which cannot be loved fully, perhaps occasions this bad choice for it has muddied the soul's ability to see himself in his proper place, to be judged properly. Derrida continues, "A finite being could not possible be present *in act* to too great a number. There is no belonging or friendly community that is *present*, and first present *to itself, in act*, without election and without selection."[15] If the soul in his previous life thought himself an easy friend to many, he was no friend to any. The nature of prior social relations, the possibilities for friendship, the development of proper regard, philosophical contemplation, and decision making under profound uncertainty all play a role in how this first soul to choose makes his choice.

Socrates continues, repeating Er's language,

> For indeed, Er said, it was a sight to see how the souls each chose their lives; it was pitiful to see, and ridiculous, and surprising. They for the most part chose according to the character of their preceding life. Er said he saw the souls which had once been Orpheus choose the life of a swan; he hated womankind because of his death at their hands, and refused to be conceived and born of woman.... By chance, the soul of Odysseus drew the very last lot of all and came to make its choice. (619e-620d)

With no time to recover from the shock of someone's cannibalizing (metaphorically or literally) his own children, we are presented with a comic tableau of reactive choices. Socrates denotes the comic with "pitiful," "ridiculous," and "surprising" as the chief descriptors. People become animals, animals become people, complex people want simple lives, prejudices from the previous life continue unschooled and overcorrected for.[16] Humans, having hated humans, give up on humanity. None of these choices speaks well for how the soul lived his or her previous life. The underlying suggestion is that no one has really gotten it right, and that getting it right is far more complicated than one might hope for. The complexity can play out either comically, as when one chooses to be an animal, or tragically, as when one chooses unwittingly to eat one's children.[17] That there is a cyclical repetition pushes the whole choice-making away from Aristotle's notion that tragedy has a certain magnitude, though, and so it becomes impossible to distinguish the comic from the tragic here.[18]

The underlying concern in this myth, perhaps the greatest discovery in Aristotle's sense is that the people who choose most badly are the ones who have been most rewarded and have been the least suffering among men in their previous lives.[19] That reward and unsuffering lives would lead us to the greatest tyranny is a peripety and discovery moment that is profoundly disturbing.

From the beginning of the *Republic,* the motivating questions have been just what is justice and whether the just life profitable. Justice is clearly, at this point, whatever allows you to make this ultimate choice well, but the profit, the reward for justice, may well be a thousand years in heaven during which a soul loses sight of justice and picks the wrong life, or it may be a well-ordered constitution that prevents the proper training of one's soul in the ways of justice. We have to reconsider then the idea that justice is more about harming one's friends in a particular sense—helping them suffer enough that they retain modesty and study philosophy. The right kind of harm of friends is a help, and the wrong kind of help is a harm.[20]

The possibility of friendship, then, is a central part of working out what Socrates leaves us with. Can we ever be positioned to make this particular decision well, can we be philosophical enough, skeptical enough, committed enough, comfortable enough with paradox, to do the work of choosing our lives? Again, we should think about what Derrida notes regarding friendship—that we must love without knowing the return on investment. We must cast out, and we cannot know where we, our souls, our lives, will land. We do not have Cartesian certainty, nor can we in an act of faith. To cast our lots with others, or even to cast our lots with ourselves, is to choose with no guarantee.

That concepts flip over into each other, merge at the edges, and become indistinguishable from their opposites, or are relativistic, fall within what Socrates calls summoning, and is where the lack of delineation between the comic and the tragic becomes ever clearer.[21] Because this first soul has lived well and been rewarded, he feels certain that his reward is deserved, that he already knows what he needs to know, and that he is in a comedy rather than in a tragedy. He is pleased with rewards, and feels immune to punishment. He is unprepared for the reality of the reward system, and is shocked beyond shock at the peripety and discovery that await. He does not want to come to dinner, but his fate, chosen only by him, is to do just that. Just desserts?

The realization that rewards are not perhaps what we should want, that justice is not at all about profit, that nothing is as it seems, will be explored in this section. The exploration will consider just who this soul is, given that it comes at the end of a lengthy dialogue, and what this soul should have done in its previous life. We will tease out the comic and tragic elements of the journey to the fateful conscious choice, from comic overdetermination of who the soul was in his previous life (assuming we have met the man in our reading of the *Republic*) to the various comic elements in the characters as they move through the dialogue. We will, then, tie together the elements of narrative, character, action, and place, in order to see the murky nature of the boundaries between the tragic and the comic, and the ways our assumptions of certainty regarding these uncertain boundaries cause us a number of moments of incredulity.

More than this, we will try to understand why the soul rejects the consequences of his own choice. That is, he seems willing to accept the choice in the moment of making it, as it seems an easy, rewarding, worthy thing to do. The soul, as a consolidated identity when all seems good, falls into fragments as soon as the stakes are clear. This move illustrates Derrida's note that we must extend friendship even before we know if we are to be loved in return. This soul who is first to choose attempts to extend friendship (to himself though the choice of his next life) but is not genuine in the attempt. Once the consequences are revealed, once the seeming certainty is unmasked, the soul rejects his own choice. We can appreciate Descartes' anxious quest for greater certainty here, and then we need to undertake a philosophical project that allows us to approach Cartesian certainty while accepting Derridean responsibility.

The first thing to wonder about, though, with this terrible choice is who the soul is who managed to do so badly when given so much freedom and reward for living well. We know from Book I that Cephalus is old, ready to die, pious, is self-certain in his definition of justice, is tired of sex and the body and wants to concentrate on philosophy long enough to blurt out his Polonius-like philosophy of life. He then retreats to his pious sacrifice and leaves the conversation to his son, Polemarchus, as an inheritance. This part is all easy. Cephalus ends the discussion by stating, "Indeed, I bequeath the argument to you . . . for I must at this point attend to the ceremonies" (331d). Time intervenes for Cephalus, showing that he is aware he has limited time, aware that the conversation could continue past his time, and that he is really unable to answer Socrates' charge that "tell[ing] the truth" and "return[ing] what is received" "is not a defining mark of justice" (331d).

But what really is Cephalus's notion of justice? Telling the truth and paying debts seems to be a simple formulation that suggests more profoundly that things should be put to rights, that place and person should be respected, that one ought to leave the world without leaving a trace of oneself either in terms of marking another by betrayal or by leaving an unpaid debt (which in itself is a kind of lie-telling, as debt is an unreturned promise to pay.) The Cephalean promise, then, is to return all that must be returned to its proper place such that an exit is a full release with no further obligation. It is, in many respects, a kind of minding of one's own business.[22]

The many subtle issues with Cephalus's notion of justice are touched on (what is debt, what is proper payment, what are the temporal issues, to whom does one actually owe, how does one pay, and so on), but not fully engaged because Cephalus does not have the philosophical comfort to engage nor the sufficiency of remaining life span to make amends for any mistakes he has made. That is, he cannot repay a new kind of debt should there be one, so he must return to a more traditional notion of debt, the sacrifice, and pay that instead. Cephalus, then, simply contradicts his own definition of justice. He cannot face the truth, and therefore of course cannot tell the truth. He cannot pay his debts because he has a false notion of the truth. But he has so totally run out of time that he is simply not ever able to pay anyway. Happily, Cephalus has a son, Polemarchus, to whom he can hand the argument, the legacy, and thus defer the debt repayment. Whether or not this kind of debt can be deferred endlessly is certainly a question worth asking, but for now, it will be deferred as we look at Cephalus as a possible answer to the question of who would have made the terrible choice in Book X.

We know, from Book X, that the soul who chooses the first life has lived in a well-ordered society, has been just out of habit and custom and social expectation and not at all out of understanding or philosophical care. Certainly, Cephalus would seem to be thoroughly socialized into behaving as he does. He falls in the midpoint between grandfather and father regarding wealth, he has many friends, he has had a lot of desires over the years, and as the desires have faded, he has found a new love of philosophy that he pursues with very little energy but he does seem to think it is important and that he is pursuing it with the right amount of energy.

Of course, giving up sex because you are impotent is not quite the same as giving up sex for philosophic conversation. And talking about how great it is that Socrates has made it down to the Piraeus to talk is not quite the same as engaging in real transformative philosophical discussion. And building up your father's wealth is not quite the same as understanding the point of wealth. Indeed, Cephalus seems to be missing out on the content of philosophy, and it is not even clear that he has the form down. It is not clear that

Cephalus has even the slightest idea of what he should be doing to prepare his soul for death.

An unprepared as he is, Cephalus could certainly be one to devour his child (Polemarchus) in a new and more tyrannical life. He has certainly outdone his own father, if not his own grandfather, suggesting some kind of thematic tie to Thrasymachean thinking. In the current life, then, he has fallen from any kind of ideal but has some half-remembered sense that his son should learn something from his inheritance. He may have some elements of a private tyrant who is overly concerned with money and the unnecessary pleasures it buys, though he expresses some relief at being done with desire as he has aged. He has some sense that money buys the necessity of justice, and thus he still sees justice as something worthy of pursuit; but he finds himself unable to pursue justice properly. His society has kept him from doing worse, but he has not converted his soul to that of a philosopher such that he would ever be able to make an independent decision about anything. His total lack of independence of thought is precisely what chases him out of the conversation. He does not really engage, and then he passes the buck, as it were, to his son, the son he will devour in a few hundred pages, or in a thousand years after his rewards are granted him, rewards that are the repayment for his being just.[23]

Book I has other possible culprits, however. Polemarchus, as the heir to the conversation, easily fits the role. He has grown up in a well-ordered state, will inherit wealth, is only mildly concerned with what is right, and may be less concerned than his father even if more willing to talk and change his mind. Even his very willingness to change his mind adds an interesting tension. One should of course wish to be willing to change what is imperfect and improve one's beliefs, but that Polemarchus so quickly jettisons his views means that his level of commitment and certainty were always already inappropriate. He simply never should have held views that he could so easily alter or that have been so totally mistaken. So much for the courage of one's convictions.

Polemarchus suggests that justice entails helping friends and harming enemies. The first round of discussion gets Polemarchus to the point that he is willing to say that justice is useful only when things are useless, that the just man is good at keeping things, that justice is more for wartime than for peacetime, that the just man is a thief, and that really, when we want an expert, the last thing we want is a just man. We want a horse breeder to take care of our horses, not a just man. To the extent that, so far, we have encountered commonly held views of justice, we are now getting a set of the opposite. Justice is for the moment completely absurd, worthless, pointless, and not at all what we think it is. That Polemarchus can hold these views under the notion of justice suggests the logic of summoning and thus is a call for philosophy.

From the issues regarding expertise and the status of the just man, Socrates moves on to point out that we can easily confuse friends and enemies and thus can unwittingly harm our friends. Further, when we do harm, we worsen others, and worsening others does not seem particularly just. Polemarchus quickly assents to the thrust of Socrates' arguments and concludes by agreeing that he will join in the fray to fight anyone who would argue that the poet Simonides suggests that it is a good idea ever to harm anyone. Polemarchus completely misses the irony.

Could Polemarchus be the one to choose badly in Book X? He is more open to argument and more willing to engage than is his father, but he still lacks the ability to construct independent arguments and he is still wedded to some notion of a fight for justice rather than a quiet attitude of being oneself just. Father and son, then, may well both be implicated in the terrible choice and the terrible realization. And yet neither one is prepared to understand how wrong are the views he holds. The moment of incredulity comes because neither father nor son has the slightest idea of what the nature of justice is, despite each one's certainty of the nature of justice.

Still, we have to consider the more open tyrant, Thrasymachus. Sallis describes him as a "flesh-eating hellhound of Hades."[24] He does not at all hide his desires or preferences behind gentle language.[25] He certainly argues forcefully for his position and he seems to respond to Socrates' arguments with counter arguments. Further, Thrasymachus eventually professes to agreeing with Socrates, but he may well not be telling the truth, and he may well not be gentle. His blush suggests something has happened to him, but it is unclear if the blush is a mark of the realization that he has been wrong all these years, or if it is a mark of his inability to convince Socrates.[26] If justice is the will of the stronger, and Thrasymachus proves weaker, he must capitulate. But his very capitulation is actually an affirmation of the power of his own argument. Socrates, in being the stronger, is actually the tyrannical determiner of the nature of the just.[27]

That Socrates and Thrasymachus are so closely tied here is significant for trying to figure out who the soul is in Book X who chooses so tragically. If Thrasymachus is right that the stronger proves to be the tyrant, and the just, simultaneously, then suddenly not only is he implicated in Book X but so also is Socrates. Thrasymachus' use of physical strength and his emphasis on his own desires as the source of the just together suggest that he is tyrannical. Socrates is implicated in a somewhat different way. Given the cyclical nature of the movement of souls, even philosophers may fall into tyranny. Further, given Socrates' failure to persuade his interlocutors, he may be a fallen figure at some level. Any fall off from philosophy suggests the further, and inevitable, cycling down. No one seems to escape from the fall described in Books VIII–X.

Claudia Baracchi suggests yet another way to implicate Socrates which is that as Cephalus hands off the argument to his son, he also hands off his son to Socrates and Socrates becomes a father, as it were.[28] That Socrates and Cephalus both are inadequate parents and that they both might fail in very different ways, Cephalus for not engaging in thought, and Socrates for not engaging in successful conversation, adds to the Polemarchean tragedy. He might very well be devoured, even as he devours. And indeed, a tyrant is one who would commit any deed and eat any food, parricide and cannibalism included (574e).

Would Socrates choose badly? Would he choose a life in which he is the stronger such that he could determine what justice is? Further, given Socrates' mission in Book I, to go down to the Piraeus, or down to the cave, to meet and greet, to converse and turn souls, and given Socrates' own self-confessed bad behavior at the banquet, perhaps Socrates is as much a failure as are the others, and perhaps Socrates, too, would end up behaving badly at the choosing ground. He has entered the conversation under duress, somewhat unwillingly and so has not quite properly chosen the life of a philosopher, he has given in to his desire for more, *pleonexia*, and has been a bad guest and bad host. He has dined, as it were, badly. Given the Book V stipulation that our troubles will not cease unless philosophers become kings and kings become philosophers, we can see that the very specific structures of Socrates' choices are implicated. Socrates must choose to become a king, the interlocutors from Book I who might become kings must choose philosophy. Even then, though, the cyclical nature of the soul suggests that this choosing will not happen. There will be reluctance, spirit and appetite will intrude. Not only, then, is Socrates unwilling to enter the conversation at first, he is also self-confessedly greedy once he does enter. And further, he fails to fulfill his appointed duties in Book I. He does not rescue or retrieve the interlocutors because they are not fully retrievable at this point. He has chosen, but has chosen incompletely. He has labored, but labored unsuccessfully, has ruled but ruled unsuccessfully and has been momentarily ruled by his fear of Thrasymachus. Though Socrates is the philosophical hero of the text, he is, perhaps, an imperfect hero, and may well be implicated in the Book X choice. Too much philosophy, *pleonexia,* is condemned equally with too little philosophy. Getting the balance right, then, is the central task for the philosopher-king or king-philosopher.

The terrible tragedy of a life misspent such that at a crucial decision point one chooses so badly that one destroys precisely the underpinnings of one's life is at the heart of tragic incredulity. Philosophically, what is at stake is the nature of subjectivity and the operations of certainty. Can we be consolidated Cartesian subjects ever certain that what we are doing is the proper thing to do, error-free and firm and lasting, or must we maintain a kind of skeptical readiness to disavow our actions, apologize as Pyrrho does for deciding to flinch at an attack by a dog.[29] To agree to a consolidated notion of subjectivity and to the resulting responsibility for action could be so paralyzing that we stand frozen not in skepticism but in fear of responsibility. Philosophical thought about the nature of the subject, the accepting of decisions and consequences, the effects of these decisions on our souls seems to be a central concern in these texts.

The contemporary analogues to the soul in Book X include Bernard Madoff, a corrupt financier who managed a wealth fund that turned out to be a pyramid scheme, and whose son Mark committed suicide despite his father's vast ill-gotten fortune, and Jeffrey Skilling, another corrupt financier whose work included stripping the pension fund from Enron and running the company into the ground, and whose son, John Taylor Skilling also committed suicide. Neither father would likely have chosen this fate had he known, but then, when we are choosing our fates, we do not really know what they will bring. It takes philosophy to teach us better, but then, who is more philosophical than Socrates? And yet, it is possible that even Socrates would choose badly, especially after having been rewarded for a just life.[30]

The greatest incredulity of them all is that we should not wish for just desserts, rewards for a good life well lived. The economic and political rewards themselves can overpower our ability to choose well and can provide incentives that lead us away from proper decisions and from proper valuations. And if Socrates suffers from a kind of philosophical *pleonexia*, even philosophical desire itself is implicated. We should, perhaps, wish for less. No fortune to hand our children, no appetites of our own, no social conventions that protect us from knowledge, no banquets, no gold in our souls.[31]

The structure of tragic incredulity is that the loss we experience is a terrible one we cannot really recover from. Whoever is fated to eat his children in Book X has failed to live well, has failed to learn how to make decisions, has been hasty, has felt too comfortable and self-satisfied. Such a person has not suffered sufficiently. That we should be "punished" for a good life that is not good enough is terrible indeed.

At the same time that this tragedy is slowly unfolding, there is a comic dimension to the *Republic* that makes it far harder to figure out how to draw a bright line between the tragic and the comic.[32] Cephalus, like Shakespeare's Polonius, can be played as a bumbling fool who has everything comically wrong. He dodders, he seems thrilled to have Socrates visit for a conversation, and yet he completely fails to engage in the very conversation he has seemed so excited about. He even gets in a line about being grateful to have no more desire for sex. He gives a seemingly straightforward definition for what justice is—doing basically what he has done his whole life. But then he is plunged into this foreign world of Socratic discourse in which he is the naïf, and comically he cannot engage. He exits stage right and lets his son take over.

If we occupy the dialogue only at the moment we are reading, there is clearly a comic element to the old but not wise, self-obscure but claiming transparency, and fatherly but foolish figure that Cephalus enacts. Talking with Cephalus is closer to visiting an aging relative in a nursing home than it is to sitting at the feet of a wise man on top of a mountain, and yet the journey to reach Cephalus's advanced wisdom should be more of a mountain climbing expedition than a trip to the nursing home in the next suburb over. The surprise Cephalus provides here, of being far less wise than he should be, is comic as long as the consequences are simply that he is foolish and his son, too, is foolish. We do not mind fools, we enjoy them.

Enter Polemarchus whose confusions, willingness to do harm in a bumbling sort of way, and easy position changes are still more on the benign side, though indeed the willingness to fight could be of concern. Polemarchus is still comical but with more of an underlying tone of potential nastiness. He is, after all, willing to harm his enemies, and quite able to mistake friends and enemies and thus to harm friends.

After engaging with Socrates, Polemarchus, still in comic mode, manages to contradict pretty much everything he has argued throughout his time on stage. There is, then, in Polemarchus, the figure of one who cannot keep arguments straight, who confuses terms, who falls back on convention even as his father does. The convention Polemarchus falls back on is not sacrifice or piety, but rather belligerence. Polemarchus will fight. But we can be sure that his fight will be no more effective than his argumentation, and therefore we are spared tragedy in this moment.

Thrasymachus, the next ninja in line to do comic battle with Socrates, comes in as a lion and goes out as a sheep (to mix metaphors in comic fashion).[33] The lion side is scarier and carries more belligerence and more threat, but then its fall is in some ways funnier, if still disturbing. As long as we identify with Socrates, we worry about the threat Thrasymachus presents, but we see that the battle-ready figure really has a hard time with issues like how to tune instruments or whether or not mistake-making makes you the thing you are or makes you an exception to yourself, so that you are most precisely not the thing you are. If mistake-making negates us, or makes us be what we are not, then any practitioner's error is a source of comic transformation. One only is what one is when one is that thing, and one stops being what one is when one errs. That you could be an exception to yourself is sufficiently paradoxical that Thrasymachus falls right into a comic argument without trying too hard. That Thrasymachus has to note that in fact there is a non-competitive way to tune instruments and a non-competitive way to be a thief and indeed a number of non-competitive ways of being suggests that Thrasymachus's whole notion of the need for competitive justice and belligerence is fruitless and foolish.[34] If Thrasymachus is erring in his reading of the nature of a thing and the nature of identity, then Thrasymachus himself is not what he is, but rather is a negation of himself. An erring Thrasymachus is not strong, but is, rather, a failed tyrant, a failure in the practice of justice, and a failed interlocutor. He has negated himself or outdone himself.

Because much of the underlying threat in Book I has been based on the acceleration of competition, having Thrasymachus lose an argument about how competitive arguments should be turns the entire first threat well away from the potential tragedy of a war into the comic moment of a bunch of fools arguing foolish points and contradicting themselves throughout. The comedy of Book I remains as long as there is no further perspective from which to view the events. It is not until the Myth of Er and the choosing of a new life that we can see the tragic element in the problems that our naïve interlocutors all share. Thrasymachus' argument that a mistake undoes your identity and thus your culpability suggests an interesting reading of the first choice of a new life, one that is not upheld by the divine caution.

The final scene in Book I, Socrates' apologizing for his greediness, is high comedy (345a-c). An old man at a banquet shoving food in his face, sticking his fingers in every dish, grabbing what can be grabbed while completely disregarding any social conventions about the handling of food and desire in a public forum is a scene one could use in film. Oversized desire, huge and rapacious appetites, gross behavior—these are things we laugh at routinely, and they are scenes we play out to show both how foolish and gross some individuals are and how foolish and silly some social conventions are. Again, it is worth seeing this scene through the text's concerns regarding *pleonexia*. Every desire for "more" has its boundaries, and exceeding these boundaries is problematic on every level.[35] That there could be "more" desire for philosophy than is seemly, proper, even properly philosophical is a significant problem for philosophy to wrestle with. Can a philosopher want too much philosophy, even as Thrasymachus wants too much power?

Socrates says of himself, "I haven't dined well, however, though it's my own fault, not yours. Gluttons keep grabbing at each new dish that's passed, and tasted it before they've properly enjoyed the previous course" (345b). This line prefigures the choice of a new life and the caution of the divine voice. Socrates is, perhaps, implicating himself here.

If we look further into the *Republic*, there are a few more moments of high comedy worth looking at as they hit on the points of tension that make comedy and tragedy bump up against one another. Briefly, even the very first violent encounter, when Socrates is "invited" into the conversation by the servant, there is a comic element. Socrates, the philosopher, is stopped, held and threatened by first one servant and then by a group. He is not told to "dance" with a gun pointed to his feet, but rather to "talk" while a group of men circle and threaten. And at the same time as he is being force to talk, his audience is refusing to listen. One can imagine a comic element in which the thing being commanded is always rejected even in the command or one could imagine a tragedy from the same material. The line is unclear in this scene, as comic and tragic moments are in tension with one another. An old man threatened by a crowd, a philosopher told to speak, an impossible necessity, these moments play off of each other and make it impossible to settle on a particular reading of the opening moments of the dialogue.

Book I is an ordeal. From the declarative certainty of Cephalus through the oscillations of Polemarchus and right to the belligerent certainty of Thrasymachus, Socrates has managed to survive through some version of binge eating. Just as he emerges from the piggish feast, he is thrown right back into the fray as Glaucon and Adeimantus demand a more muscular defense of the just life.[36]

The two brothers contribute two crucial comic devices, one a preference for couches and pastries over justice and the other a portrayal of the best, justice, as the worst possible way to live.[37] The just life, they suggest in someone else's voice, is a miserable life, and one we would all reject if there were no monitoring of our conduct. And further, the just life is uncomfortable and should be rejected on that count alone.

We know, going into the *Republic*, that justice is "worth" some number of pages, some amount of thought, some effort on Socrates' part to talk with others about it. We generally feel that justice is worthy, and yet we find ourselves frequently rooting for the bad guys in film, feeling that a lovable gang of thieves really ought to win out over the general run of society. We also seem to prefer some amount of comfort, and so Glaucon and Adeimantus present us with images of justice as difficult, uncomfortable, and not really what we would actually choose if we could choose otherwise. This issue of choice will come back to haunt them in Book X, but for now it seems to make sense to prefer couches and pastries over a pile of straw or boiled roots. And it makes sense that Gyges would start as a grave robber and become king. Rags to riches stories are compelling. And rags to riches stories that bypass hard work are even more compelling. Because there is something of a longing for ease and comfort, we do not merely dismiss Glaucon and Adeimantus's pressing Socrates on these issues. Yes, justice seems worthy, but comfort is the more immediate preference, and the more immediate is more concrete, more present, more what we are willing to fight for.

Because justice will turn out to be a highly abstract notion that cannot be put into words, there is yet another comic strain running through the opening books of the *Republic*. Glaucon and Adeimantus, and the servant and Polemarchus in Book I, all demand that Socrates speak. They claim to want to hear what justice is, that the just life is worthy, and that Socrates explain it all. And yet they refuse to listen. And yet they get stymied by holding to the concrete world, unable to grasp the abstractions to which Socrates gestures. And yet they cannot really understand what Socrates needs to speak, as the speaking itself is the wrong medium for coming to know what justice itself is. The Form of the Good is gestured at through metaphor and image but is itself beyond metaphor and beyond image. The sense of the "beyond-ness" of justice is such that language fails to show it, and it must be known directly (as the line image suggests in Book VI).

The figure of the impossible necessity, of the inaccessible thing that must be accessed, is at the heart of what we mean by "Kafkaesque" and is what provides the comic-tragic tension in the *Republic*. We both need to hear what justice is and cannot hear. We both need Socrates to explain and must laugh at his explanation. We both demand justice as a concrete figure and must come to grasp it as an idea. Doing what cannot be done is heroic, comic, and tragic all at the same time.

Book V presents us with another comic moment. The discussion of the nature of justice and the education that children require in order to be just is interrupted by Polemarchus's adolescence, in the same manner that growth in general is interrupted by hormones. Polemarchus whispers to Glaucon and Adeimantus, and they all agree that the most interesting part of the discussion thus far is the bit about how all things should be in common, especially women. Adolescent men agog at women, both naked women who are wrestling and the related group sex, is nothing if not comic. Except of course when it is tragic.

Seth Benardete characterizes this moment as follows, "A whisper initiates the second phase of the *Republic*. It is meant to be noticed. The revolt which it sparks is as much a sham as Polemarchus' earlier threat to force Socrates to stay . . . . Just before he whispered, Polemarchus brought Adimantus over toward himself."[38] The whisper Benardete notes marks a point where private desire intrudes, much the same way as does the preference for couches and pastries, the shock at the life made for pigs, and other reminders that Socrates' interlocutors have very much their own lives and preference schemes that are really their starting points. Socrates has to work with the material he has, and the material he has is a group of men whose habits, customs, and desires are constitutive of the world they would create. The meeting of the low purposes of sexual congress and the higher purposes of Socratic dialogue are rife with comic and tragic potential.

The turning upside down of standard family life and education in the *Republic* is comic the way that portrayals of how other people live can be hilarious, or the way that futuristic narratives can be hilarious. It is precisely because there is no imaginable way to imagine, no possible route from here to there, no chance at all of the changes' actually coming into being that it is safe to discuss them in great detail. The safety of distance and impossibility makes the contemplation of these changes possible. But contemplation here is fraught with the same kind of impossibility that runs through much of the rest of the dialogue. We are not about to do any of the things Socrates recommends, we are not about to alter our lives, stop performing sacrifices, move away from habit, do away with honor or belligerence, or really listen to philosophers. Because these things will never happen, we can laugh about the idea of their happening. They are truly comic.

The three waves that provoke incredulity are ordered in both a ranking of increasing hilarity and in a ranking of libidinal investment and deferral, both of which are significant for the structure of the *Republic*.[39] The first wave is naked co-ed wrestling in the palestra, the second wave is the collectivization of women and children, and the third and most absurd of all is the rule of philosopher kings or king philosophers. There is a libidinal logic to the order here that I will trace through as it signals an important sub-theme in the *Republic*, and in the nature of incredulity.

Naked co-ed wrestling stands in for the desexualization of both sexual contact and war. That women can bear justice, bare bodies, and be taken seriously in both modes without comic results or tragic results shows that Socrates is calling for a revolution in male desire. No longer are men to invest in either the satisfaction of their own desire or the satisfaction of a woman. Indeed psycho-sexual investment must be deferred, denied, desexualized if the wrestling is to be proper preparation for a just life and a warrior life.

While Cephalus is ready to give up sex because he is old and impotent, the wrestlers will not have it quite so easy. There will be consequences to their giving up their libidinal investments, and the payoff will be uncertain. It seems clear from this "wave" that the wrestling, and justice itself, depend on the disruption of a fundamental human desire that simply is not going to go away. And this point is only the first wave.

The second wave is a further disruption of the reward system and the libidinal economy. Not only will men and women wrestle together naked in full view of others, but they will not then be allowed to pair off for sex as a reward for their efforts. Further, when there is reproductive sex, it will not be rewarded with the gratification of children who look just like you, are just like you, and who thus fulfill the narcissism of self-reproduction. Children will not be imitations of their parents, and their parents will not be narcissistically involved with love relations that reflect on their own desires. The complete disruption of the cycle of lust and love, and of attachment and reproduction, means that these feelings have to be displaced onto the city or suppressed completely.

The final, and most difficult wave of all, is the philosopher king/king philosopher wave. The key to the absurdity here shows up in the disruptions of the first two waves. The first wave does away with desire for the opposite sex during physical contact and with the social norm of disrespect for women's ability to be very much the same as men when it comes to justice or any other universal. The second wave does away with the next part of the reward system for desire and attempts to defer it indefinitely.

In this third wave we see that the reward for desire cannot be deferred to the political system as the most powerful and sexiest of the interlocutors, Thrasymachus, cannot rule. What we get instead is a "wall-eyed, snub-nosed" man with a "peculiar rolling walk" as our fearless leader.[40] We cannot, then, displace our libidinal energy to the political ruler who would enact our desires in the absence of our being able to do so on our own.

This issue of the libidinal economy, a ruler's attempts to manage it, and a ruler's succumbing to libidinal demands will come up in a number of the Shakespeare plays throughout the text.[41] The Duke in *Measure for Measure* has extra-rule preferences and his substitute Angelo has deep desires unbeknownst to himself; Antiochus's bizarre desires in *Pericles* make him completely unfit for rule; and Portia's absent father sets up a fascinating system for managing desire and channeling it properly in order to ensure that his daughter marries well despite his posthumous absence from the scene. Desire and rule are forces to be reckoned with more thoughtfully than any of these characters starts out doing.

If we were simply to disrupt via the first or the first and second waves, there might be a chance of something akin to success. If the libidinal energy has a place to go, it can be channeled. Since Socrates is most assuredly not trying to found a city of old, impotent men, he cannot simply assume that we will all be Cephalean about our desires. They will not simply melt into aged air and leave us ready to talk. Indeed, we are founding a city of youth whose whole innate desiring system must be regulated and channeled toward the good. We must be confronted with what we most desire in its most unclothed, and we must learn not to desire that. We must learn not to desire to copy ourselves, and we must learn not to need to move these desires into another realm.

To disrupt the entire structure of sexual desire, then, is what these middle books of the *Republic* are after. And since the biggest part of desire is the fulfillment or reward side, we must learn to stop desiring rewards. Of course, the need to move away from reward is precisely what the Myth of Er is working toward and what the whole *Republic* is pushing us toward.

What gets us into trouble is making the leap from the value of justice to a demand for a reward for the effort of justice. That we are hoping for an afterlife above and to the right, that we want someone to notice that we are good, that we likely will abuse the Ring of Gyges because it takes away the risk of punishment and gives us only rewards, suggests that it is the disruption of desire that we most need in order to bring about justice. The lack of reward for doing something good, the idea that our enemies might not be punished for doing something bad, the idea that the rules of comedy and tragedy might not be followed are indeed a central cause of incredulity.

Once the society is constructed, and the general hilarity is fully stated, there are several realizations to be dealt with before we come to the tragico-comical fall of the system. First, if indeed justice can only be realized in a system of repression of desire and obedience to Socratic-style rule, we are simply not going to have a just system. Chasing the impossible certainly has its comic element. The absurdity of the tasks before us, exiling all people over the age of ten, destroying family and gender relations, teaching people, contrary to all experience, that they emerged from the belly of the planet, never speaking a range of ideas and fantasies that are far more autochthonous than anything Socrates dreams up, none of these tasks is likely ever to be completed, or even ventured.

Justice, seen from this vantage point, then, is a purely comic and false state we will ever chase and never reach. Further, it may be that reaching a state of justice is closer to the tragic than we realize. That is, the bulk of what we think of as human qualities, passion and creativity, imagination and the body, flights of fancy and pure physicality all would be limited by a regime that sorts us, limits us, and forces us to replicate the same from generation to generation with no variation and no mistakes.

We know from Books VIII and IX that indeed whatever is invariant and whatever constitutes the replication system are destined to break down. Either from the mathematical structures of Socratic numerology (whatever comes into being must pass) or from the very fact of human desire, the system will not be handed down to the next generation in pure form. The passing of the torch on horseback that begins the *Republic* also puts an end to the city. Any time a thing is copied, it loses information, and the torch bearer passes along a different fire to the next bearer. Doing all this passing at horseback speed simply speeds up the decline of the city. And the skills that might allow a successful pass on horseback are the same skills that will interfere with slow contemplation.

The torch race is, of course, another comic element.[42] One can no more imagine a deep philosophical conversation during a horseback relay race (using torches as the batons handed off) than one can imagine Polemarchus's ever understanding the irony of his own position. Relay races are competitive, torch-batons burn, concentration is on horsemanship, and there is not much in the way of careful speech. Whatever truths could be passed on in such a race are unclear. The intergenerational collapse we see in VIII and IX is simply the detailed account of what happens during the race, when immediacy, intensity, and victory matter more than abstract cares. The race pulls us to earth, the fire burns us. Philosophical wisdom pulls us up and away, and though there may be pain, it is not physical pain that afflicts the philosopher.

Humans replicate physically through sex, and culturally through conversation. Each of these kinds of replication is flawed and fraught with the risk of falling away from the ideal. Improper sex, improper conversation, poorly designed torch races all lead to poor copies and poor transmissions of information. We cannot copy what is good and hand it down to the next round of people. We cannot give light, we cannot give words, we cannot give justice. Try as we might to build this edifice, we fail in comically absurd fashion.

At every moment in the *Republic* that Socrates attempts a positive project of building and enacting justice, something quite human intervenes in the process. False insights and traditions and habits, foolishness and lack of self-awareness, temperament and competitiveness, and desire all wreck the best plans. Further, there are structures in place that cause a whole other level of problems. Copying must need result in loss of information, so any generational transfer of knowledge is doomed. Speaking the ineffable is clearly impossible, so any attempt to communicate the truth is doomed. And because the gulf between philosophical wisdom and any other kind of wisdom is so vast, the issue of absurdity will always arise and philosophical wisdom will always be rejected by those who most need it.

We are doomed by all of these structures. But even more, we are doomed by the desire for reward for living justly. It is the reward of justice that motivates us to be just, that sends the souls up and to the right, that makes them not study hard, that makes them forget that they are still capable of the greatest harms, that leads the soul in Book X to choose the worst life possible. That is, living in a just state dooms us to a new life of injustice. If we choose a just life to avoid punishment and horror that very choice will doom us to a new life of punishment and horror. It is only by choosing suffering that we will have the insight at our next choice to choose the simple life of an animal. Every comfort we pick sends us the wrong way and lets us forget how important it is to live philosophically.

If Glaucon and Adeimantus's major claim against Socrates initially is that the just life is one for animals, then we should keep in mind that indeed, a life as an animal is yet another choice made in Book X, and it is a far better one than the life of a tyrant. The animal will not eat its children, the tyrant will. Depending on where you stand as you look back over the course of the *Republic*, you will find either a tragedy or a comedy, with no clear reference frame for determining which is the true narrative type. The eating of one's children is tragic, the choice of a life as an animal is comic. Cephalus and Polemarchus are either a sit-com father/son team or a tragic tale of family failure. Either they will laugh at how absurd life is or they will devour and/or be devoured in turn.

We should take to heart the cycles that the *Republic* emphasizes repeatedly. One lives a life, goes to the afterlife, is rewarded or punished in turn, and starts all over again. Good people make bad decisions, bad people get tired and make humble decisions that protect them from evil. There is simply no way to privilege one reference frame, as it were, over another and know with certainty the proper mode of narrative one is embedded in. From the point of view of the moment the soul in Book X chooses the life of a tyrant, the tale is tragic. But we know that life will be lived out, in a specificity of horror that could be written up by any tragedian, and then that soul will be punished and will return as an animal. What is called most into question here is whether or not education can be considered a turning of the soul, after all. It seems to require more than a revolution to permeate an entire soul with the knowledge of the weight of this choice. Because the body leads the soul astray, and yet it is only the soul that is present at the moment of choice, the chances of any kind of real permanent knowledge are slight at best. Is it a comedy, then, or a tragedy?

The moment of incredulity comes when we adopt a particular and rigid stance in the tragico-comedic continuum and assume that we have an absolute rather than a relative stance for our analysis. If we think we are in a comedy, and a tragedy unfolds, we, the audience or the participants, feel betrayed. And if we think we are in a tragedy but a comedy unfolds, we may feel relief but nonetheless we feel uncomfortable as our expectations are unmet. The two directions, comedy to tragedy and tragedy to comedy are not quite equivalent, but they do have enough structural similarities in terms of surprise, incredulity, and irritation that it is worth thinking them through together.

When we first encounter Cephalus, we may well feel something akin to respect for the old man who has taken care of his family and who will leave behind a legacy for his offspring. He quickly becomes a foolish figure though, and then at the end of the *Republic* becomes a tragic figure. Sallis notes that his notion of justice is concerned with the benefits he will receive after death and that he does not entirely conceive of justice as related to the treatment of others. Indeed, paying debts is more about clearing one's own soul's obligations than it is concerned about the good of the recipient's soul.[43] Baracchi notes the transactional nature of Cephalus's view, as well.[44] That Cephalus could be tripped up by the idea of paying back debts out of season or out of reason suggests that Sallis and Baracchi are right to emphasize this point. The improper payback is fraught with potential comedy or tragedy in indecipherable measure. We cannot say that he is either a comic or tragic figure definitively. He is both of these, depending on the moment of evaluation, the position of the evaluator, and the concerns that the evaluator brings to the evaluation. Indeed, all of the interlocutors share this basic characteristic. We, the readers, cannot really read them definitively but only relatively. Should we overly identify with one or another interpretation, we set ourselves up for a moment of incredulity.

Seth Benardete argues that "The myth of Er is wholly nontragic, for the equivalent to the removal of pity is the discounting of remorse."[45] The tragedy, though, comes from the sense of identification we feel with the characters we have come to know, from the sense that even Socrates could get the decision wrong, and of course from the personal knowledge that we, the readers, may just as easily be operating under false premises and incomplete or incorrect notions of justice as do the souls in the *Republic*. That we, too, desire, and that we, too, desire reward, and that the very desire for reward could be the thing that causes us to make the worst decisions seems to traverse the distance from irony to tragedy. Further, that the consequence of the decision is that one devours one's preserver and continuation, one's motivation and production, is all the more horrific. Horrific, for it is the destruction of one's cause, and tragic because it is caused by the most basic of desires, the desire for reward for one's labor. While Benardete does not see the fundamental tragedy of the consequence of being what one is and suggests instead that there is no pity available for this soul, indeed it seems that the tragic moment is present in the inevitable destruction of one's cause, and therefore the self-destructive moment that is part of the structure of being. And while the comic is surely just as embedded in the moment of choice as is the tragic, the tragic is not to be made light of.

Tragedy makes use of comedy, and comedy makes use of tragedy, in order to tell a tale. Settling on either category requires fixing a moment of interpretation rather than interpreting within the flow of the narrative. While it might be something of an acceptable strategy to wait to interpret a fixed written text until the last page, it is a more problematic strategy to wait until the last page of a life to figure out its tragic or comic status.

Aristotle brings up this issue in the *Nicomachean Ethics* when he discusses how one knows if one's life is happy or not.[46] Must we wait until the end of a life, must we see how the descendants do? Can we freeze a moment during a life to figure out if it is a happy life or not? How do we interpret a life that has both joy and sorrow? If we are to contend with moments of shock and incredulity, we need a framework for answering these questions implied in the *Republic*, made explicit by Aristotle, and taken up subtly by Shakespeare.

We can see, looking over the issue of decision-making at this point, that philosophical inquiry will push us to a space where Cartesian certainty cannot operate. We have to act in the world, we have to act with incomplete information, we cannot retreat and await a kind of absolute clarity. If the last line of the *Meditations* encourages an acceptance of the possibility of error, that line stands against the previous meditations and the crisis they present. The desire for certainty runs smack into the acceptance of error, and one side must be left behind when decisions are made.

Derrida points to this issue in the *Politics of Friendship* as he discusses quoting the line about friendship, "O my friends there are no friends."[47] Quoting, or even more, quoting a quotation, or ever further, removing oneself many times from the words one speaks or writes, acts as a kind of distancing method, a way of avoiding responsibility for the words and their effects, and for avoiding the need to respond to the words. Thrasymachus refuses to be a ruler at the moment he is ruling badly, Socrates "eats" from every dish, Polemarchus accepts his father's bequest, Cephalus does what is socially expected. In each case, each figure is "quoting," as it were, some other figure. This quoting, the distancing it represents, runs against a more direct philosophical engagement with words, with meanings, and indeed with others. This engagement is something we will see in an occasional moment in the Shakespeare plays this book looks at, but it is something often missing from Shakespeare's characters as well.

Philosophical engagement, done properly, refuses the deferral of responsibility and yet absolutely enters into engagement with others before it knows the results. Thus, Cartesian anxiety and Pyrrhonian distancing and the method of quoting to avoid the weight of words are all to be pushed aside as philosophy engages, errs, attempts.

NOTES

1. See Aristotle for a full discussion. Aristotle, *Nicomachean Ethics*. Translated by David Ross, J.L. Ackrill, and J.O. Urmson, revised (Oxford: Oxford University Press, 1980), Books II and III, "Moral Virtue."
2. Jacques Derrida, *Politics of Friendship*. Translated by George Collins (London: Verso, 1997), 8.
3. Aristotle, *Poetics*. Translated by Ingraham Bywater (New York: Modern Library, Random House, 1984), 239.
4. Aristotle, *Poetics*, 233.
5. Aristotle, *Poetics*, 229.
6. Aristotle, *Poetics*, 237.
7. Aristotle, *Poetics*, 237.
8. See Olivier Blanchard and Lawrence Summers, "Hysteresis in Unemployment in Europe," *NBER Working Paper 2035* (Cambridge, MA: National Bureau of Economic Research, 1986).
9. Stephen Halliwell reads the Myth of Er within Socrates' discussion of narrative form, so that we can see the ways the story is structured, the ways that poetry and truth, recounting and dramatizing, are played against each other. See Stephen Halliwell, "The Life-and-Death Journey of the Soul: Myth of Er," in *The Cambridge Companion to Plato's Republic* (Cambridge: Cambridge University Press, 2007), 445–473.

10. Baracchi notes interesting parallels between Er's role as a messenger when he goes down to the underworld and Socrates' role as messenger when he goes down to the Piraeus. Baracchi also notes the nice continuum along which we can locate Cephalus as a failed messenger and Er as a more successful messenger. Baracchi's insight is complicated by Socrates' own role as messenger and his failure to communicate. See Claudia Baracchi, "Animals and Angels," in *Plato's Animals: Gadflies, Horses, Swans, and Other Philosophical Beasts*. Edited by Jeremy Bell and Michael Nass (Bloomington, IN: Indiana University Press, 2015), 211 for the Cephalus and Socrates comparison.

See Claudia Baracchi, *Of Myth, Life, and War in Plato's Republic* (Bloomington, IN: Indiana University Press, 2002), 211 for the Socrates and Er comparison.

Sallis, as well, notes the relationship between Er and Socrates and the *katabesis*, with the Piraeus standing in as the figure of Hades, and that Bendis is a figure associated with the underworld, as well. John Sallis, *Being and Logos: Reading the Platonic Dialagues*, third edition (Bloomington and Indianapolis, IN: Indiana University Press, 200), 314–315.

11. Andrea Wilson Nightingale links Er's journey and Socrates' journey to the *theoria*, a journey to an oracle or a religious festival in order to gain some kind of significant insight or to have some kind of vision. Nightingale emphasizes the visual metaphor. See Andrea Wilson Nightingale, *Spectacles of Truth in Classical Greek Philosophy: Theoria in Its Cultural Context* (Cambridge: Cambridge University Press, 2004), 3.

12. H.S. Thayer enlarges upon the nature of the choice in "The Myth of Er." That the choice must be made and made well, that there are real choices presented in a kind of ideal fashion, and that "justice is an intrinsic good to be valued for its own sake" (p. 370) all run through this piece. See H.S. Thayer, "The Myth of Er," in *History of Philosophy Quarterly* 5(4) (October 1988): 369–384.

13. Note that in the *Apology*, Socrates asks the jury, "When my sons grow up, avenge yourselves by causing them the same kind of grief that I caused you, if you think they care for money or anything more than they care for virtue." Here we see Socrates' concern for his sons, his understanding of what justice and intergenerational inheritance are concerned with. We also see what the nature of revenge is, for Socrates. The "harm" that makes a soul good is of profound concern. Plato, *Apology*, in *Five Dialogues*, second edition. Translated by G.M.A. Grube and revised by John M. Cooper (Indianapolis, IN: Hackett Press, 2002), 41e–42a.

14. Derrida, *Politics of Friendship*, 21.

15. Derrida, *Politics of Friendship*, 21.

16. See Gonzalez for a full discussion of the economy of choice as human and animal forms are exchanged. Whether or not the animals retain some kind of rational soul so they can choose a new life is considered. It is also interesting to think through whether or not a human's choice to become an animal is really a kind of giving up on any hope for the rational soul. A soul that struggles among the rational, the spirited, and the animal is a soul that is not at ease. To the extent that a choice could do away with both the spirited and rational parts, such a life would likely be more peaceful, though it would also lack any of the greatness that either spirit or reason grants a

life. Francisco J. Gonzalez, "Of Beasts and Heroes: The Promiscuity of Humans and Animals in The Myth of Er," in *Plato's Animals: Gadflies, Horses, Swans, and Other Philosophical Beasts*. Edited by Jeremy Bell and Michael Nass (Bloomington, IN: Indiana University Press, 2015), 225–245.

17. Baracchi discusses the "oscillation" between kinds of lives, noting that souls oscillate between making "wise choices and deleterious ones." See Baracchi, "Animals and Angels," 219.

18. There is an interesting offshoot here from a social science perspective regarding the way choices are made by people who are not governed by rules. Daniel Kahneman, a winner of a Nobel Memorial Prize in Economics for his work in psychology, discusses the ways that choosing well or badly can be ascribed to either "noise," or "bias," or both. Seeing the souls making their choices without a clear pre-determined algorithm or rule frees the soul to make choices that either have some kind of random quality to them or that are pre-set by bias or the workings of hysteresis. Philosophy, if it works, then, must push back on the randomness of decisions and on strongly held priors. Daniel Kahneman, et al., "Noise: How to Overcome the High, Hidden Cost of Inconsistent Decision Making," *Harvard Business Review*, October 2016.

19. Zdravko Planinc reminds us to consider not merely the first soul to choose, but also the last soul, Odysseus. That Odysseus chooses the life of a man who minds his own business after having lived a life of wandering, suffering, and seeking for *kleos*, shows the extent to which Homeric themes underlie the *Republic* and the extent to which Socrates is patterned on heroic elements in both the *Iliad* (Achilles' choice, and the need to fight for truth) and Odysseus (cleverness, and eventual concern for a smaller life.) Whether or not minding one's own business, in Socratic fashion, requires a smaller life or requires a heroic life, is certainly an issue in the text. And whether or not a just life requires some kind of suffering or discomfort, as Glaucon has wondered, is also an issue here. See Zdravko Planinc, *Plato Through Homer: Poetry and Philosophy in the Cosmological Dialogues* (Columbia, MO: University of Columbia Press, 2003), 18.

In a similar vein, it is worth thinking through the links between Odysseus' choice of a modest life, Achilles' choice of a lowly life above rather than a kingly one below, and the choice of Socrates to do away with the Homeric texts in Book III only to bring poetry back in through the inclusion of Odysseus, imagery, and myth. The reincarnation of Odysseus, the reincarnation preference of Achilles, and a general wonderment regarding the position of Homer or the Homeric in the *Republic* gives us just enough room to stretch and consider whether or not there is any suggestion in the text that poetry itself is reincarnated as philosophy—this more perhaps than the possibility that "Homer" becomes "Socrates," or that "Socrates" becomes "Homer." Note that Benardete concludes his book with, "Socrates himself seems never to have been Odysseus. His daimonion, he said, was probably unique (496c4-5). Perhaps, then, philosophy is a rare strand in the bond of the cosmos, and when babies who die at birth choose a life at random, they sometimes get lucky." Seth Benardete, *Socrates' Second Sailing: On Plato's Republic* (Chicago, IL: The University of Chicago Press, 1989), 229.

Freydberg notes, "Contrary to the received wisdom on Plato and Homer (a wisdom which, happily is receding more and more), the Platonic dialogues do not advocate censorship, nor are they 'against' poetry." See Freydberg, "Retracing Homer and Aristophanes," 99. Bernard Freydberg, "Retracing Homer and Aristophanes in the Platonic Text." In *Retracing the Platonic Text*. Edited by John Russon and John Sallis, (Evanston, IL: Northwestern University Press, 2000), 99–112.

And Fagan, too, notes, "What *Republic* 3 reveals to us, though, is that the traditional material has a meaningful life of its own that reminds us repeatedly that Socrates's claims about these untraditional myths and their effects cannot be true." Traditional material is preserved at some level, transformed as needed, and most certainly is not absent from the Republic as a city. See Patricia Fagan, *Plato and Tradition: The Poetic and Cultural Context of Philosophy* (Evanston, IL: Northwestern University Press, 2013), 48.

20. In his chapter, "Plato's Pharmacy," from *Dissemination*, Derrida discusses the nature of the *pharmakon* in Platonic writing. The *pharmakon* is both a therapeutic drug and a harmful poison, but because the two meanings are always present together, they are hard to separate. The *pharmakon* Socrates drinks in the *Phaedo*, the very *pharmakon* that threatens Socrates throughout the *Apology* and the *Crito* turns out to be liberatory or curative rather than harmful for it releases Socrates' soul to knowledge. When Socrates concludes that "Which of us goes to the better lot is known to no one, except the god," at the end of the *Apology*, it is an expression of this doubling. (42a) The jury of Athens thinks it has the cure and Socrates has the poison, but they have their friends and enemies confused. A similar kind of dynamic runs through Cephalus' thinking. Socratic *elenchus* is a kind of *pharmakon*—it cures and harms. What it harms is that which goes by the name "Cephalus" insofar as Cephalus is comfortable with being "Cephalus." The harm to that which is "Cephalus" is something he detects in the course of the gentle conversation and questioning, and he makes escape before he drinks. But, in saving "Cephalus" from Socrates, Cephalus actually ends up drinking that which he had meant to avoid, or, perhaps, eating that which would horrify. The double nature, then, of substances, knowledge, and encounters with Socrates is worth keeping in mind throughout the reading of the text. And, again, Polemarchus' arguments regarding friends and enemies and the ease of telling them apart such that one can hurt enemies and not friends fall under this same logic. The confusion is real because the line between friends and enemies is unclear, as is the line between harming and helping. See Jacques Derrida, *Dissemination*. Translated by Barbara Johnson (Chicago, IL: The University of Chicago Press, 1981), especially 126–127, but throughout, as well.

21. At 524b in the *Republic* Socrates introduces the notion of that which summons calculation. If an object, a finger or the like, can be seen as both what it is and as its opposite, long and short, hard and soft, big and small, then it "summons" calculation as a way to determine precisely what it is. It cannot be both what it is and the opposite, in the end, so some kind of middle status must be figured out, or calculated. If, then, the comic and the tragic are indistinguishable on this reading, then there needs be a kind of calculus to help us determine which it is. Relative thinking, relations of concepts, degrees, measurement, and rational thought are all brought to bear on behalf of summoners. They "summon" reason because the *prima facie* thought is incoherent. Plato, *Republic*, 522e–524d.

22. Russon points out a nice paradox of sorts with Cephalus' definition of justice and his quick exit. Russon writes that Cephalus, "offers a definition of justice (ironically, he defines it as "paying back," that is, as *nemesis*) and considers the issue closed. Socrates, however, does not accept this closure, but shows, by his challenge, that there is more to the question, that the question of *dike* has not been given its proper due Cephalus, then, fails to live up to his own definition by failing to pay justice its due, its proper share of discourse." That language or conceptual understanding or *logos*, too, deserves to be paid back is significant. See Russon, "Introduction" in *Retracing the Platonic Text*, x. John Russon, "Just Reading: The Nature of the Platonic Text." In *Retracing the Platonic Text*. Edited by John Russon and John Sallis (Evanston, IL: Northwestern University Press, 2000), ix–xix.

23. Gregory Kirk discusses an interesting offshoot of what we have seen so far with regard to Cephalus and his son. Kirk sums up his basic point by saying, "Overall, my argument is that true self-knowledge is a state of inherent insecurity that puts upon us the need to engage with others in the life-long pursuit of self-understanding that is, on the one hand, in principle non-completable, but on the other hand, essential for progression towards the good life." This is in keeping with my sense that Cephalus wants a kind of certainty that Socrates' philosophizing disrupts, and that though Cephalus seemingly invites Socrates in for conversation, in fact, Cephalus has nothing but anxiety at the thought of engaging with Socrates. Further, that self-understanding is noncompletable, in Kirk's terms, fits nicely with my sense that one can never settle on a narrative, given the incompletion of life at any decision point. See Gregory Kirk, "Self-Knowledge and Ignorance in Plato's *Charmides*," in *Ancient Philosophy* 36 (2016): 305–306.

24. Sallis, *Being and Logos*, 334.

25. Schmid draws a contrasting picture of what a successful Socratic encounter looks like. Where Thrasymachus is not modest and not self-aware, Schmid suggests that a proper encounter with Socrates requires moderation, self-knowledge, and being examined in an elenchic process and being able to examine oneself. Further, Schmid suggests that *elenchus* is therapeutic. Psychoanalytic literature has numerous accounts of resistance, transference, and counter-transference. Likely the same could be found in Socratic "therapy." See Walter T. Schmid, "Socratic Moderation and Self-Knowledge," in *Journal of the History of Philosophy* 21 (3) (July 1983): 342.

26. There is a stretch one could make here regarding Thrasymachus' blush—that he is enacting a philosophical version of a Homeric battlefield death. In Homeric texts, such deaths are bloody, but in philosophical argumentation, the loss is experienced differently. For Sallis, the blush comes most directly because Thrasymachus has "been robbed of his art," but we can see that it is a kind of defeat and any kind of defeat may well be akin to a battlefield injury. Sallis, *Being and Logos*, 343.

27. Thrasymachus, and all he stands for, and perhaps even the father/son pairing of Cephalus and Polemarchus may well be captured by Derrida's discussion of haunting and negativity in *The Politics of Friendship*. Derrida, discussing Schmitt, notes the ever present ghostlike figure of opposition, the one lurking and ready to leap out and attempt a coup. Against that figure, others consolidate, and the social is marked by oppositional politics, always ready to fight a ghost. See Chapter 6 of Derrida, *The Politics*

of Friendship. Jacques Derrida, *Politics of Friendship*. Translated by George Collins (New York: Verso, 1977).

28. Claudia Baracchi, "Beyond the Comedy and Tragedy of Authority: The Invisible Father in Plato's *Republic*," in *Philosophy and Rhetoric* 34 (2) (2001): 151–176.

29. See Philip P. Hallie's "Polemical Introduction" to Sextus Empiricus *Selections from the Major Writings on Scepticsm, Man, & God*, p. 11–12 for the anecdote of Pyrrho's being attacked by a dog.

30. Brooke Holmes discusses a range of notions that may play into all of this in her book *The Symptom and the Subject*. Holmes' concern in the book is the development in ancient thinking of concerns regarding health and disease, the body and the psyche. There is room to think through the decision making of a soul along the health/disease/desire axis. See Brooke Holmes, *The Symptom and the Subject: The Emergence of the Physical Body in Ancient Greece* (Princeton, NJ: Princeton University Press, 2010).

31. The desire for a reward is a desire for a kind of repayment of a debt, as if doing justice requires getting something in return. Satkunanandan discusses this notion of debt-justice, relying on G.R.F. Ferrari's term. She writes, "Debt justice, in my gloss, understands justice (whether as the attribute of an individual's disposition or of a polis) as the settling of debts between humans and between humans and gods." The question, then, is whether or not justice is the kind of obligation that deserves repayment. Satkunanandan points to Heidegger and others to suggest that justice is "beyond calculable," which is in keeping with my sense of the infinite and unpayable nature of obligation in the *Republic*. Satkunanandan, *Extraordinary Responsibility*, 95–96. Shalini Satkunanandan, *Extraordinary Responsibility: Politics Beyond the Moral Calculus* (New York: Cambridge University Press, 2015).

32. Sallis, too, finds comic moments in the *Republic*. Sallis, *Being and Logos*, 371–378.

33. Roslyn Weiss reads Thrasymachus as a kind of "wise guy" and Glaucon and Adeimantus as "smart alecks." The ways these characters are drawn help us evaluate the nature of their arguments, and the extent to which we should accept or reject or refine what they say. See Roslyn Weiss, "Wise Guys and Smart Alecks in *Republic* 1 and 2," in *The Cambridge Companion to Plato's Republic* (Cambridge: Cambridge University Press, 2007), 90–115. See also Ruby Blondell, *The Play of Character in Plato's Dialogues* (Cambridge: Cambridge University Press, 2002). Blondell discusses the philosophical and literary responses to Plato's work, situating character and argument with respect to one another. Gordon also discusses the literary side of Plato's works in Jill Gordon, *Turning Toward Philosophy: Literary Device and Dramatic Structure in Plato's Dialogues* (University Park, PA: The Pennsylvania State University Press, 1999).

34. Thrasymachus accuses Socrates of a kind of insincerity during their interchange. Gregory Kirk defends Socrates on this charge, one leveled by numerous critics, not simply by Socrates's own interlocutors in the dialogues. Kirk notes that Socrates initiates his interlocutors into a life of questioning, and shows that we must "build a life around engagement in Socratic questioning, and to do so is to build a life whose relationships and vocations are, to the best possible extent, built around the persistent possibility of transformation." To accept this idea of transformation as a real possibility

is to accept that one is not yet, or that one is incomplete, or that one is wrong. Note that Thrasymachus precisely says that being wrong means that one is not what one is, and so to accept the possibility of always being wrong means, for Thrasymachus, that one never is, in some fundamental way. It means, therefore, that the decisiveness and justice-determining qualities of the ruler are misplaced, and it means, further, that the help friends/harm enemies definition given earlier by Polemarchus is equally self-negating. Indeed, there is broad indeterminateness that makes the definitive impossible. See Gregory Kirk, "Initiation, Extraction, and Transformation: What It Takes to Answer Socrates's Question," in *Idealistic Studies* 45 (1) (2015): 117.

35. The issue of philosophical *pleonexia*, that is, whether or not one can want too much "more" philosophy, whether or not one heads toward *hybris* with this desire, whether or not Socrates wants more than his proper share, is worth thinking through in depth. If Socrates can be seen as wanting more than he should, we can then see why he might be implicated in the soul choosing scene in Book X, and we can see why there is no real escape from the cycle of reincarnation. Not even philosophy can save a soul from a bad decision in the underworld, not even philosophy can rescue us from the profound incredulity of choosing the wrong fate. Thomas Smith discusses *pleonexia* in the context of the spirited part of the soul, and notes that *pleonexia* is "a clinging possessiveness" implicated in "projects of power and self-protection." (Smith, 34) And further that "*Pleonexia* [is] an evasion of the Good. *Pleonexia* means 'having more' and connotes overreaching or possessive grasping for external goods" (Smith, 34). Socrates is under some threat because of Thrasymachus and because of the way he is accosted in the street by the servant at the very beginning of the text, and so a kind of physical self-preservation may well be in order here. He does not quite "evade" the good, so much as he avoids a kind of discursive patience. That there are some distinctions here would suggest that philosophical *pleonexia* shares some characteristics with spirited and material *pleonexia*, but has its own peculiarities as well. (Smith, "Love of the Good as the Cure for Spiritedness") Charles Kahn develops a reading of the *Republic* based on the textual notion that each of the three parts of the soul has its own pleasure. (Kahn, 81 and *Republic* 9.580d7). If each part of the soul has a proper pleasure, it is not, in my extension of this argument, hard to think that there may well be an improper pleasure for each as well. Too much of a good thing, then, perhaps, is a problem. (See Charles H. Kahn, "Plato's Theory of Desire," in *The Review of Metaphysics* 41(1) (September 1987), 77–103. In another way into the issue of appetite and reason in the *Republic*, James Wilberding wonders whether or not reason can educate appetite so that appetite, like spirit, becomes more sophisticated, or becomes better at choosing what to desire and how to desire. Wilberding notes that the appetitive soul is ruled rather than educated, and yet, nonetheless, "the just soul that corresponds to Kallipolis is surely moderate in the narrower sense, and this seems to imply that the education has created a belief in the appetitive part and in this way made it friendly to the other part" (Wilberding, 130). Putting this material together should get us thinking all the more about the role of desire within the rational part of the soul, whether or not reason itself needs some amount of education to limit its own desire, and what this education might look like. The text of the *Republic* gives us some clear space to wonder, especially given Socrates' own confession in Book

I. He confesses to a kind of philosophical appetite improperly practiced, and he has to learn how to comport himself at this particular banquet of words. He seems more successful in subsequent books of the text, but then, he is limited to talking mostly to the like-minded by this point. We should wonder if he learns to be "friendly" to the other parts of the soul as they are represented by the interlocutors. And we should think through the possibility of Socrates being implicated in the choice in Book X. The relationship between justice and *pleonexia* also comes up in Gregory Vlastos, "Justice and Psychic Harmony in the Republic," in *The Journal of Philosophy* 66(16) (August 1969): 505–521. Having one's own and no more is clearly central to what Socrates suggests comprises justice. Again, that he confesses to grabbing at dishes inappropriately suggests that there is a Book I violation. *Pleonexia* comes up as well in Sarah Brill's work on Plato. She writes about ruling, living, and psychic excess. "While Plato explores the relationship between ruling and living, he is also careful to document the emergence of anarchic psychological tendencies that make constant the threat of instability. In the absence of an account that would unify ruling and living into a single act, soul defies the economy of labor that will prove to be so crucial for the coming organization of the city (Brill, 86)." The breakaway need for more, possibly in each part of the soul, makes the rational soul's task of ruling fraught and requires decision-making and strategy throughout. We can apply this dynamic to the way Book I plays out. Socrates must readjust for each interlocutor, for each train of argument, for each part of his own soul. Instability rules, decisions are fraught, failure abounds. See Sarah Brill, *Plato on the Limits of Human Life* (Bloomington, IN: Indiana University Press, 2013).

36. Here it is worth noting, again, the parallels to the Homeric texts. Odysseus journeys, battles, struggles, and eventually returns. Odysseus' struggles are partly structural—he is fated to return late, alone, and unrecognized—and partly his own responsibility—his desire for *kleos* and his desire for guest gifts motivate him at the cave of the Cyclops, and it is Poseidon's response that provides the material cause for Odysseus' delayed return. There is, as well, a kind of Iliadic parallel with the battlefield *aristeia*. Socrates takes on a number of arguments, defeats them, and then takes them up again in their new incarnation, as it were. The text cycles on itself, and seems to rest on the Homeric texts, even as it raises explicit concerns with portions of the Homeric texts.

37. David K. O'Connor, in "Rewriting the Poets in Plato's Characters," dives in to what Glaucon and Adeimantus represent in the text, and in to the ways Homer and Hesiod are appropriated within the *Republic*. He includes a nice discussion of the image of descent in the text. See "Rewriting the Poets in Plato's Characters," in *The Cambridge Companion to Plato's Republic*. Edited by G.R.F. Ferrari (Cambridge: Cambridge University Press, 2007), 55–89.

38. Benardete, *Socrates' Second Sailing*, 110–111.

39. Benardete gives a reading of the Book II discussion of using justice in the city to help us see justice in the soul. I want to extend that discussion, and perhaps clarify some of what the text is doing, by relating that image to the discussion of the three waves, the spinning top, Leontius, and the parts of the soul. The issue underlying all of these is the proper separation of what is thought to be joined, and the proper joining of what is thought to be separate. The city image needs to be brought to bear on the soul because

the soul is thought to be unitary, but Socrates is arguing for there being parts or aspects of the soul. We can easily see parts of a city, even a city that needs to be one, and so making the city/soul argument clarifies the parts that really are too small to be seen, if by "small" we mean that we have never seen them. The discussion of the parts of the soul is continued later in the dialogue with the images of the spinning top (in motion and still at the same time, seemingly paradoxically), Leontius (both wanting to see and not wanting to see at the same time.) The resolution is that the whole is made up of parts or aspects, and it takes some kind of calculation to understand what the parts are, how opposites can occupy near space, how things are separate though they seem to belong together.. The three waves, on the other hand, bring together that which has been thought to be disparate, and they each do so in a way that seems at first completely absurd. Women and men share the same kind of justice, and so justice is unitary, not multiple, and it needs to be rejoined through the contention of a wrestling practice at the gymnasium. The family structure needs to be unified because reproduction is a kind of oneness, not something separate and private. Desire, too, is unitary and for a single purpose. And finally, political rule and philosophy most absurdly are one. Each of these waves, then, disrupts multiplicity and creates unity—as if bringing back together that which is split in Aristophanes' story in the *Symposium*. See Benardete, *Socrates' Second Sailing*, 45, for the discussion of justice in the soul and justice in the city. See also Ronna Burger, "The Thumotic Soul," in *Epoche: A Journal for the History of Philosophy* 7(2) (Spring 2003): 151–167, for a careful consideration of Benardete on Leontius and the spirited part of the soul.

40. R.E. Allen, "Introduction" to *The Dialogues of Plato*, Volume I. Translated by R.E. Allen (New Haven, CT: Yale University Press, 1984).

41. The phrase "libidinal economy" is Lyotard's, but my use of it is not Lyotardian. Lyotard is trying to bring together the Dyonisian impulse with the impulses of the moves of economics and bodies, so that desire, exchange, and physicality all dance, as it were, in ecstatic fashion, and so, too, does the language used to describe this ecstasy. My use of the phrase is more prosaic. Characters I discuss in this book have desires, the desires are either managed or not managed by the political and economic systems in which they occur, and the management or lack thereof creates something like a system that one could call a "libidinal economy," but without the Dionysian impulse, either in writing or in enacting it. See Jean-Francois Lyotard, *Libidinal Economy*. Translated by Iain Hamilton Grant (Bloomington, IN: Indiana University Press, 1993).

42. Benardete notes that "a series of frustrations initiates the *Republic* and marks its course throughout." They never actually go to the torch race, and a number of other events fail to take place. This can be a comic structure, as thwarting is a comic device. See Benardete, *Socrates' Second Sailing*, 11.

43. Sallis *Being and Logos*.

44. Baracchi, "Beyond the Comedy and Tragedy of Authority."

45. Benardete, *Socrates' Second Sailing*.

46. Aristotle discusses whether or not we can know a life is happy before it is complete, or only after it is complete, or only after our descendants have lived their lives. See the *Nicomachean Ethics*, Book I, Ch. 7.

47. Derrida has a wonderful discussion of responsibility and quotation. See the *Politics of Friendship*, 228.

Section 2

The Comedy of *Othello*, Or, Who Kills Desdemona?

Othello opens with a set of overlapping comic and romantic layers that surprisingly devolve into tragedy in the span of a few acts. Roderigo's complaints, Iago's and Roderigo's juvenile behavior below Brabantio's window, the fact of the romantic elopement, the befuddled father figure all would suggest a comedy of intergenerational tensions, unrequited and foolish love, and a fool to be used comically.

Further adding to the potential comedy is Iago's feeling that he has been passed over for a promotion that he rightly deserves.[1] The slide into tragedy comes because Iago does not accept his status in a comic way, but instead gives it a vengeful and ultimately tragic reading.[2] That is, Iago rejects the comedy underlying the situation and through his agency turns each of the comic motifs into a tragic one. It is, then, his choice that settles the matter of the mode of presentation.

The underlying comic sensibility is preserved all the way through, as mistaken identities build up, absurd deceptions suddenly seem true, events are spun most ridiculously, foolish hopes are believed to be real, and the kind of corrections the characters need are never actually made. The structure, then, is one of comedy, with its attendant fools and fakes, but the comic structure plays out in genuine horror because the characters fail to recognize the links of comedy and tragedy. It is not until the end of the play, when death is spreading that the major realizations pile up, that the comic moments of marriage and foolery are found to be tragic instead.

By way of placing *Othello* into the history of comedy, Stephen Rogers sums up briefly some of the critical takes on the comic elements of the play. He discusses the comic traditions from which Brabantio, Roderigo, Emila, Cassio, and even Iago have been drawn.[3]

Othello, then, clearly has these moments of comic-like characterization and action, but it transforms these moments into a kind of tragedy that depends on the tension between the two modes for its success. It is precisely the success-gone-wrong side of the play that draws us in. Each of the characters, in his or her place at the beginning of the play, is doing well enough. Roderigo's unrequited love of Desdemona, Iago's unrequited love of promotion, Othello, possibly of Desdemona, Brabantio's unrequited love of or, or at least deep fascination for, Othello, and perhaps even Othello's own unrequited love of himself would all be manageable were the characters not overtaken by the power of Iago's world-spinning narration to spread discontent. Iago, though, would be unsuccessful were the other characters not responsive to his narrativity. The comic beginning then makes a tragic turn through the mechanism of storytelling, and indeed the comic and tragic are fully intertwined such that each event could be taken to be of either mode depending on the position of the interpreter. I will trace through the comic and tragic overlays in order to show the indistinguishability of these two narrative modes, and further will show that it is the structure of the indistinguishability that causes the move from the comic mode to the tragic.

In the text cited above, Rogers writes, "I shall try to show that *Othello* achieves much of its tragic power through the adaptation, often the rearrangement or inversion, of techniques, devices, and other materials traditionally belonging to comedy."[4] Rogers uses Roman comedy as a source to help identify the comic elements that underlie the fundamental tragedy of *Othello*. Beyond merely pointing out the underlying comedy, this section will show that the comic and tragic are inextricably linked and misunderstood by the characters involved. Their very misunderstanding of their own situation, the very mistakes they make in not recognizing the comic elements of their situation pushes them toward a tragic finale that could have been avoided had they reinterpreted their own situation as one of unstable meanings rather than committed truths.

WHO KILLS DESDEMONA?

Just as the question of the identity of the soul who chooses first in Book X of the *Republic* is an issue that is central to the structure of the whole text, so the same kind of question is at issue in *Othello*. We know that Othello himself holds the pillow over Desdemona's head and so is the efficient cause (in Aristotle's language) of her death, but Shakespeare gives us a number of other more distant causes of Desdemona's death, each of which adds to a comically overdetermined fate.[5] These causes may all refuse their responsibility, yet they are indeed causes and they do indeed need to be thought through as forces that bring about the tragic end of Desdemona. As such, these characters need to be thought through in terms of the nature of what they offer, what they accept, and what they say to justify their actions. This philosophical investigation into the nature of the justification of decisions these characters make is central both to understanding the play and to seeing how it is that philosophical engagement can shed light on decisions made in the face of uncertainty.

Soon after Act I opens, there is a balcony scene not of love and eternal promises of gloves and hands and cheeks, but rather of the absurd, seemingly drunken and ribald Iago and Roderigo calling up to Desdemona's father that his daughter, a "white ewe," is being tupped by "an old black ram" (*Othello*, 1.1.87-88). That Desdemona is not properly within her home, and that instead the "old black ram" is within Desdemona is both a shocking displacement for Brabantio, and a source of ribald humor. His daughter, he soon discovers, has eloped in direct defiance of his preferences. This wedding should, of course, be joyful and romantic, and should signal a comedy, as weddings do for Shakespeare. But this wedding is a little different because Iago sets a frame for it of unacknowledged sexuality and defiance of the father. Brabantio adds on his own a notion of kidnapping and the use of magic against a child.

As the scene plays out, Brabantio begins to realize that indeed the marriage is voluntary, and he unhappily gives his daughter to Othello, but not without noting, "Look to her, Moor, if thou hast eyes to see: / She has deceived her father, and may thee" (1.3.293–294). This caution plants a seed in Othello's thinking, gives Iago some material to work with, and within the bounds of speech act theory may create the very fate it is describing. It is both a curse and a prediction, a caution based on knowledge of the past and worry that the future is all too likely to be similar to the past. It is, however, completely wrong as Desdemona deceives no one at all. She is more a mark of changing father/daughter relations than she is a mark of deception, and she does not at all deceive Othello. But because Brabantio suggests the possibility of deception, he actually creates the interpretation that Iago and Othello will make use of. This example is one of many throughout the play in which narratives will alter beliefs in the comic world such that the moments become tragic. Here we can see that Brabantio is part of the causal mechanism that will eventually lead to the death of his own daughter. Had he simply accepted the marriage with joy, as marriages are supposed to be greeted, then he would never have given Iago this little bit of ammunition, nor would he give Othello the first real moment of doubt. Had he seen himself as a causal agent, had he engaged with his beliefs, extended his friendship with Othello to include his daughter, had he done a number of different things, he would have avoided being an agent in his own daughter's horrific death.

In yet another way, Brabantio is again a notable cause of the death of his own daughter. In this part of the story, Brabantio is the one who introduces the couple, who himself courts Othello at some level, and who makes possible the marriage that he then cannot believe has happened. Brabantio has mistaken the romantic comedy he helped set up for some kind of tragic and thus doomed love. It is this very mistake, of course, that leads to the beginning of the end for all the characters. Of course, "mistake" may not be the operative term here as there may be room for choice of narrative mode. If Brabantio's tragic interpretation is a choice, he is creating his fate, just as the first soul to choose in the *Republic* creates his own fate through choice. The choice of interpretive mode, then, is fraught with peril and ought to be made with careful consideration.

Adding an extra layer of tension to Brabantio's tragic narrative is the possibility that he has something of a homoerotic attraction for Othello and has himself been "courting" Othello at some distant level. The text is ambiguous enough on this point to allow some jealousy on Brabantio's part to enter the mix of causes of his outrage at the marriage and his tragic, rather than comic, narrative. Othello describes the quasi-courting,

Her father loved me, oft invited me
still questioned me the story of my life
From year to year—the battle, sieges, fortunes
That I have passed.
I ran it through, even from my boyish days
To th' very moment that he bade me tell it,
Wherein I spake of most disastrous chances,
Of moving accidents by flood and field
Of hair-breadth scaps i' th' imminent deadly breach,
Of being taken by the insolent foe
And sold to slavery. (1.1.129–139)

We can see from this very dramatic account that Othello's words attracted Brabantio, "Her father loved me," Othello says above, even as they attracted Desdemona. The text does not explicitly indicate a homoerotic attraction, but there is just enough of a suggestion in this passage that it is worth considering as an additional layer. Brabantio clearly has some kind of fascination with Othello, and he clearly does not want his daughter with Othello. There may be a range of reasons for Brabantio's reaction to Othello, but it is worth keeping in mind some kind of attraction that goes beyond acquaintanceship or friendship. The fact that Othello was "oft invited" to recount his tale, from beginning to the moment he is talking to Brabantio, suggests that there may well be something to this reading. Of course, we are getting only Othello's account here, but Brabantio certainly does not challenge this version of the tale and so it maintains reasonable legitimacy. That the father and the daughter could perhaps be equally taken, or overtaken, by the same man suggests the sexual tension at the heart of the emerging tragedy. It is less that the Moor is hated, perhaps, than it is that he is loved too well by too many that causes so many problems.

This entangled love polygon (for it is far larger than a triangle) would seem to be at the heart of the conflict among the characters.[6] Clearly, unrequited love, love triangles, intense fascinations, the absurdities of love, the way that, in the case of this play, every character is taken by images of "men with their heads beneath their chests" and the "anthropophogi" cross into absurd territory. Or, to give the oddly headed and oddly dieting people some narrative significance, we could wonder both where everyone's head is, below or in place of the heart, and what everyone eats. The odd placement of the heads may suggest the kind of blindness Othello suffers from, or the lack of heart that Iago suffers from. A head that cannot see or a head in place of a heart, then, would be both exotic and characteristic of the people in the play. And, further, if each character is, as is the fashion in the *Republic*, at least cannibal-curious, there is a whole other dimension to Othello's stories, and to the fascination everyone seems to hold them, and him, in. Tales of wrong headedness and tales of wrong eating are fascinating. They are also perhaps familiar, and they play into the linked senses of fascination and horror as we, and the characters, watch the drama unfold.

The entangled love of the characters in the play and the willful blindness to some of the more absurd tales suggests a potency of attraction that can spin out of control if the narrative it is embedded in pushes that direction. Iago, of course, is a master spinner of tales and his framing is of great consequence. But it is, indeed, Brabantio who strikes the first blow against Desdemona.

Roderigo must, as well, be called to account as his "love" of Desdemona gives Iago both money and incentive to make public the elopement of Desdemona and Othello, and their insults directed to Brabantio as the play opens make it all the more likely that Brabantio will feel deep shame at his ignorance of his daughter's marital status, sexuality, and absence from his home. It is, in a way, this balcony scene that moves the play along and starts the inexorable march toward Desdemona's eventual death.

Underlying both Roderigo's and Brabantio's culpability in Desdemona's death is a conflation of love and ignorance that is part of a kind of self-focused blindness that runs throughout the play. Roderigo loves but does not see that he is unloved. He gives money to Iago but does not see that Iago takes him for a bank. Iago's repeated "Put money in thy purse" does not even convince him that Iago is using him (1.3.335–362). Iago's speech is laced with attempts to get Roderigo to think that Desdemona's love is changeable, that the Moor's love is akin to that for a particular food, and that change in his purse for Iago to draw on is the one catalyst needed. Iago's speech is as follows,

> Put money in thy purse, follow thou the wars, defeat thy favour with an usurped beard; I say, put money in thy purse. It cannot be that Desdemona should long continue her love to the Moor—put money in thy purse—nor he his to her. It was a violent commencement in her, and thou shalt see an answerable sequestration—put but money in thy purse. These Moors are changeable in their wills—fill thy purse with money. The food that to him now is as luscious as locusts shall be to him shortly as acerb as coloquintida. She must change for youth; when she is sated with his body she will find the error of her choice: she must have change, she must. Therefore, put money in thy purse. (1.3.335–353)

The speech incites Roderigo to the most literal reading of the request, and Roderigo agrees to sell his property to get the money to put in the purse to hand to Iago so that Iago can live while Desdemona dies. He says, "I am changed. I'll sell all my land" (1.3.380). Roderigo, unwitting and blind, in "love" or infatuated, and thoroughly self-regarding, empowers Iago. Indeed, it is Roderigo's change ("money" and "change" [alteration in mood]) that allows Iago to continue his work of changing the changeable Desdemona and the changeable Moor from lovers to the opposite. Change for change, and the request changes Roderigo.

The background events of the play also have a role to play in Desdemona's demise. The war, the ships, and the need for Othello's soldiership all legitimate Othello's importance beyond the boundaries of the household, and they force Brabantio to regard Othello outside the scope of the domestic. As a soldier, Othello carries the weight that has made each character fall for him, and though this soldiership framing is shifted momentarily to the domestic, where Othello is weak, the war brings back the proper focus from which to see Othello. The war, then, delays the reckoning momentarily, but by doing so, allows the marriage to continue and thus dooms Desdemona. She, like the drowned Turks, will be a casualty of nature's fury coupled with political intrigue.

Desdemona, herself, is implicated as well in her own death. She has listened to his romantic tales. Othello recounts the courting thus:

> ... antres vast and deserts idle,
> Rough quarries, rocks and hills whose heads touch heaven
> It was my hint to speak—such was my process—
> And of the cannibals that each other eat,
> The Anthropophagi, and men whose heads
> Do grow beneath their shoulders. This to hear

Would Desdemona seriously incline,
But still the house affairs would draw her thence,
Which ever as she could with haste dispatch
She'd come again, and with a greedy ear
Devour up my discourse

. . . .

She loved me for the dangers I had passed
And I loved her that she did pity them. (1.3.141-169)

Othello's tales of exotic creatures attracted Desdemona, caused her to cry, to sigh, to come again and again to hear more. The pity and the wonder, the attraction of the repulsive and strange, and the fact that what Othello really falls for is her pity of his tale all suggest that this marriage is not one of mutual regard so much as one of her desire for the strange and his desire to be pitied for his suffering.

There is something of the second order in their love. She loves not him but his tales, and he loves not her but her pity of his tales. The center of the love, then, is the tale, and as we have seen from the beginning of the play, the meta theme is that of narration and narrative control. That each of the characters sees and is seen within a narrative frame, that each character thinks of him or herself in a comedy or tragedy, but then gets the narrative mode wrong or fails to see a shift in the mode, leads to the tragedy of Desdemona's death.

Michael Cassio, too, is implicated, and his being implicated becomes more and more obvious as he presses for Desdemona to press his case with Othello. Every time Desdemona begs for attention for Michael Cassio, she reinforces the narrative Iago has constructed. Every time she quotes him, it is as if she is enacting what Derrida cautions should not be a refusal of responsibility. Quotation may seem to distance, but it should not distance. And though it is comic, her repetitions of hope in this scene:

But shall't be shortly?
Shall't be tonight at supper?
Tomorrow dinner then?
Why then, tomorrow night, or Tuesday morn;
On Tuesday, noon or night; on Wednesday morn!
I prithee name the time, but let it not
Exceed three days: I'faith, he's penitent (3.3.56–63)

show how overeager she both is and seems. Time feels unbearable to Desdemona in this scene. Though she was patient in listening to Othello's tales, she was impatient in marrying him, and that impatience shows up as a character trait here. She can wait no more than three days for the tale of Cassio to be resolved within a plotline of her preference. Her pity for Othello, it turns out, is equally a pity for Michael Cassio, and is thus not a special pity reserved only for her husband. Pity is what their marriage is based on, and in this scene her "infidelity" is on full display. The infidelity is one of pitying someone other than Othello.

Just as Brabantio misunderstands the new rules of courtship, still locked in a patriarchal sense that he, as the father, should determine his daughter's marriage partner, so too does Desdemona misunderstand this same change in the way things are done. That she marries out of pity means that giving her pity to another is as much an infidelity as would be sexual impropriety. The rules of her marriage are made, not by tradition, but by the new world Emilia suggests in the unpinning scene later in the play. This idea that one can sin and then make a new world in which the sin is undone is an idea that undoes each character who attempts to spin a new world.

At once comic and tragic, seeing Michael Cassio's good side and blind to his drunken violence, and equally blind to Othello's violence, Desdemona is perhaps comic in her repeated pleas for Michael Cassio, and certainly doomed. As a new denizen of a new world tied together by a new kind of marriage, Desdemona is separated from the kinds of protections tradition grants. Tradition gives us rules of behavior; new worlds create rules as we go along. It can be funny to be a naïf in a new world, and indeed the comic is often taken with how ridiculous a naïf seems, but it can also be profoundly alienating, frightening, and even fatal to be new or to be in a new world, unmoored.

Iago reports to Othello a dream scene that is replete with homoerotic content that may bolster the sense of homoeroticism elsewhere in the play, including perhaps between Brabantio and Othello,

I lay with Cassio lately
And being troubled with a raging tooth
I could not sleep. There are a kind of men
So loose of soul that in their sleeps will mutter
Their affairs—on of this kind is Cassio.
In sleep I heard him say 'Sweet Desdemona,
Let us be wary, let us hide our loves,'
And then, sir, would he gripe and wring my hand,
Cry 'O sweet creature!; and then kiss me hard
As if he plucked up kisses by the roots
That grew upon my lips, lay his leg o'er my thigh,
And sigh, and kiss, and then cry 'Cursed fate
That gave thee to the Moor!'. (3.3.416–428)

With this report of the dream, we clearly have a conundrum. Is Iago telling the whole truth, a partial truth, or spinning a world out of nothing. The scene as described is comic. One can easily imagine Iago's pained expression as his tooth throbs while Cassio is lost in his dream world, calling out his love for Desdemona and getting more and more physical with Iago. Because we know that Cassio already has a second self when he is drunk, it is not impossible that he has a third self when he is asleep. This third self could be less demonstrative than Iago makes him seem, but it is not unthinkable that a dreaming Cassio could behave thus.

At the same time, we know that Iago can spin worlds, frame scenes to seem what they are not, and we know that he wants to stoke Othello's rage. Thus, it is possible that Cassio had some quiet dream with some movement and Iago added some details to increase Othello's concerns about Cassio's designs. On this interpretation, the drunken Cassio's behavior still reinforces Othello's credulity, and Othello's own jealousy adds credence to the story that Iago spins. It is also possible that the dream is Iago's own, as he says "In sleep I heard him say" The references are unclear enough here that we cannot know precisely what Iago means.[7]

Comic misunderstandings can allow for either version of the story, one resting on Iago's truth telling and the other resting on outright lies or mere exaggeration. That Othello takes the dream to be indicative of Cassio's true intent, and further that he assumes that Cassio's dream speaks to more than Cassio's intent, that it actually represents Desdemona's preferences and perhaps even her actions, is the more important part of this scene for this reading. Othello will grasp at anything at this point, real or not, to reinforce the sense he now depends on that his wife is profoundly unfaithful.

Just below the comedy of the scene with the toothache, the over-exaggerated declarations of love, and the throwing over of the leg is the tragedy that Othello takes the ridiculousness of the dreamworld, or of Iago's spun world, as proof of the reality of his own inflamed daylight dream/nightmare. Othello is living in a spun narrative, and fails again and again to grasp the comedy of the spin. His failure to laugh at this scene is one more part of Desdemona's doom.

Emilia declares to Iago "I have a thing for you" (3.3.305), and of course the "thing" has both a sexual connotation and so could be humorous, and an object denotation. The "thing" in this case is the handkerchief Othello gave to Desdemona and which is dropped by the two of them as Desdemona attempts to ease Othello's head with it. That Desdemona offers the thing to Othello, and that Othello rejects that very thing, and that the thing is picked up by Emilia and handed over to Iago links these four characters in a chain of underlying sexual desire and overt object desire. They all want this magical thing that

> Did an Egyptian to my mother give,
> She was a charmer and could almost read
> The thoughts of people. She told her, while she kept it
> 'Twould make her amiable and subdue my father
> Entirely to her love; but if she lost it
> Or made a give of it, my father's eye
> Should hold her loathed and his spirits should hunt
> After new fancies. She, dying, gave it me
> And bid me, when my fate would have me wive,
> To give it her. I did so, and—take heed on't!
> Make it a darling, like your precious eye!—
> To lose't or give't away where such perdition
> As nothing else could match. (3.4.56–70)

The thing, then, is part of a narrative tradition that either Othello is fabricating or telling the truth about, just as Iago has either fabricated or told the truth of another sexual adventure, the dream scene with Cassio. In this narrative, we find that a thing given by one woman to another woman could help control a man's desires and keep him subdued. Without the thing, he would then loathe her and horrors beyond horrors would result.

As with the other stories the characters tell to shape one another's world views, this story can be comic in intent. The threat that a thing, a napkin or handkerchief, could be so potent a symbol of romantic attachment that to lose it is to risk all is clearly overly magical in thinking and fits more with the anthropophogi than with rational thinking about the ways that marriages remain stable.

At the same time though, this thing is freighted with intergenerational assumptions, the difficulties that accompany romantic marriages as opposed to father-determined mating, and indeed this "thing" is linguistically and emotionally tied to female fidelity in marriage. The thing is virginity, the loss of it and its showing up in Michael Cassio's room, transported by a combination of Othello and Desdemona, Iago and Emilia (and later actually given by Cassio to Bianca!), suggests all the more that there is significant underlying sexual desire among these characters.

The loss of this thing, a symbolically white cloth with embroidered symbolically red strawberries, has, of course, a tragic and terrible effect. The handkerchief is one of the final bits of "proof" of Desdemona's infidelity, it is the mechanism through which Emilia realizes her betrayal of her friend and her husband's horrific behavior, and it is the object that leads most directly to Desdemona's death.

Iago's guilt, without a doubt, is supreme for it is his stage managing, world spinning, insincerity, misuse of honesty and reputation that occasion the worst in the other characters rather than the best. Indeed it is this playing to the worst that makes Iago the worst.[8]

Social assumptions themselves are called into question in the play, from Brabantio's loss of control of his daughter through the breaking of class and race barriers to the casual betrayal of friendship that underscores the handing over of the handkerchief. The chief motivation of this undermining of the social is summed up in Emilia's declaration that the world can be remade to undo sin, and is supported all the way through by the various spinners of world narratives. In her emphasis on redefining justice through spin and making it mean what the spinner, and winner of the world, wants, Emilia is recapitulating not just Iago's views, but also those of Thrasymachus. It is the tyrant who most wants to redefine terms to fit the moment, it is Desdemona who suffers most from the redefinition of the world, and it is Othello who is most blind to having the "real" world replaced by spin.

Because narrative substitutes for world, because story replaces grounded reality, Iago has both a huge responsibility to use story for the good and a strong temptation to use story for his own pleasure, power, and status. Iago chooses the bad over the good, and this choice marks him as wicked, despite all the comic conventions his character satisfies. He is fiendish to a ridiculous level and his fiendishness seems to have little cause, and what cause there is seems to vary some.[9] Is it really that he has been passed over for promotion and so has class status rage? Is it really that he thinks Othello either has had an encounter with Emilia or that Othello might at least have designs on Emilia? Is it his "sport and profit"? (1.3.385). He soliloquizes,

And what's he then that says I play the villain?
When this advice is free I give and honest . . . (2.3.332–333)

Further complicating Iago's motivation is this speech,

That Cassio loves her, I do well believe it,
That she loves him, 'tis apt and of great credit.
The Moor, howbeit that I endure him not,
Is of a constant, loving, noble nature,
And I dare think he'll prove to Desdemona
A most dear husband. Now I do love her too,
Not out of absolute lust—though peradventure
I stand accountant for as great a sin—
But partly led to diet my revenge,
For that I do suspect the lusty Moor
Hath leaped into my seat, the thought whereof
Doth like a poisonous mineral gnaw my inwards . . .

And nothing can or shall content my soul
Till I am evened with him, wife for wife . . .
Or, failing so, yet that I put the Moor
At least into a jealousy so strong
That judgement cannot cure. (2.1.284–300)

What we see with every justification Iago comes up with for his behavior is a kind of thinness of evidence. He thinks himself honest, and yet declares he is not what he is. He thinks Othello has slept with Emilia, but he has feelings of some sort for Desdemona. He thinks maybe Cassio loves Desdemona and that Desdemona's love of Cassio is a proper kind of love and not a perverted or unacceptable love. He thinks Othello loves Desdemona well. He hates Othello and yet can describe him as "constant, loving, noble" (2.1.287).

In order for Iago to continue in his plot to destroy these people, he has to spin tales that justify the transition from a moral order in which his actions are repugnant to a world that calls for his actions. He has to give himself narrative permission to destroy what is good. A comic character needs precisely this kind of ambition or insanity to justify the wicked deeds he is about to do. A purely tragic or evil character would not worry about justification but would merely act according to desire or rage.[10]

In brief, then, Desdemona's death is caused by nearly every character in the play, just as nearly every character in Book I of the *Republic* is implicated in Book X's drama. With the overdetermined nature of Desdemona's death comes a kind of comedy of overdoneness. It becomes absurd to have a death with so many murderers, each of whom is more properly a lover or a beloved.

Several times throughout *Othello* there is an issue of framing of sight, sound, and story such that a character makes either a false discovery (as when Othello thinks Michael Cassio is referring to Desdemona in 4.1), or a false peripety (Othello's becoming convinced multiple times that Iago's framing of events is the true one, and Roderigo's frequent switches from doubting Iago to reaffirming faith in Iago), or a moment of hysteresis (as when Othello reaffirms his jealous nature with Iago's prompting). These false moments come because the power of narrative framing is the deitific power to make the whole world. Though Emilia talks about having the whole world, or acting to receive or have it, indeed what narrative does is to create the whole world. Emilia says,

The world is a huge thing: it is a great price
For a small vice (4.3.68-69)

and right after this line, she says,

By my troth, I think I should, and undo't when I had done. Marry, I would not do such a thing for a joint-ring, nor for measures of lawn, nor for gowns, petticoats, nor caps, nor any petty exhibition. But for all the whole world? ud's pity, who would not make her husband a cuckold to make him a monarch? I should venture purgatory for't. (4.3.70-76)

Emilia's suggestion here is that to gain not a trivial material good, but the whole world, to make one's husband a monarch, to seize power in an unnuanced Machiavellian reading of the world, the ends justify the means because the world can be redefined to wash away the sins of the power grab. The end, gaining the world, is worth the means, cuckolding one's husband.

Given Iago's possible concern that indeed Othello has taken his place in bed with Emilia, these lines can make us wonder if Iago is right in his suspicion or not. And further, we can wonder if Emilia's willingness to betray her husband in the sure knowledge of absolution in a future new world, is she also happy to betray her friend by handing over the handkerchief, the thing, to her husband.

If narrative can undo what has been done (an issue that comes up in *Macbeth*, as well when Lady Macbeth says that "what is done cannot be undone" (*Macbeth*, 5.2.71)) then we have come to another twist in the plot, as it were. The issue of time becomes central to the notion of event.[11] If an event in the present, say, betrayal, can take on a new meaning in a future to be determined by the actor, then the temptation to turn to tragic action merely to reduce it to the comic in the future becomes overwhelming. Emilia is a character whose complexity on this issue is striking. She hands over the handkerchief, presumably with the sense that whatever ill might come of it, the good that can come and the redoing of the ill will compensate. She does, though, care about the good, and she does in the end sacrifice her life to speak truth to power. That one can recreate the world, then, through narrative and over time, gives us the idea that the world is less real, that consequences can be avoided, that finality is not the judge, that tragedy can be changed into comedy, that comedy can be established regardless.[12] She neglects to see the opposite, though, that comic cuckolding can be transformed into the tragic. Emilia's interpretation of the movement of events, then, is incomplete. The incompletion is balanced, though, by Iago's reversals, for Iago moves the comic to the tragic.

Iago constructs worlds for each character from the material each provides him. Roderigo receives a world in which his money can buy his fantasy Desdemona despite the fact that the real Desdemona hardly knows he exists. Roderigo slowly spends down his fortune on Iago's false promises of true love. Roderigo's moments of true discovery are quickly met by Iago's false discoveries and are recast as proofs of Roderigo's wishes rather than proofs of the falsity of Roderigo's hopes. Roderigo is a foolish lover, a foolish spender, a comic mess for being worse than us, and yet a tragic figure for loving what cannot be attained. Iago's work on Roderigo's worldview transforms him from a comic incompetent and ridiculous and unrequited lover to a tragic, impoverished, and finally murdered unrequited lover.

With Roderigo's help, Iago creates a world for Brabantio in which his beloved daughter has been badly used by Othello. While Othello, in his own defense, notes that Brabantio invited him in, listened to and loved his stories, and it was precisely these stories that charmed Desdemona, Iago has colored the scene as one of crude "tupping," racial impropriety, and loss of control over the daughter. Brabantio, in the middle of the night has handed to him a narrative world he cannot manage. It is only when other versions of the tale emerge that he can even begin to come to terms with the choice his daughter has made. His love of Othello and his being charmed by Othello's tales form one layer of narrative world-creation. On top of that layer comes Iago's tale of impropriety. And then on top of that comes Desdemona's own testimony about her love for Othello, for his narratives, and her willingness to marry him. Brabantio has to acknowledge, though he cannot accept, the world he has been handed. A very different introduction to this world, not in the middle of the night, and not through Iago's language, may well have gone differently. And had Brabantio been introduced to his daughter's marriage under different terms, perhaps he might not have introduced the notion of her ability to betray her husband as she has done her father. After all, the duties of wife to husband are not symmetrical with the duties of daughter to father. Fathers are to be left behind, are to be betrayed, are to die first. Husbands deserve very different treatment. Betrayal, then, has to be constructed narratively in order to transfer from the father to the husband.

Clearly, Othello's stories of war bravery fit under the construction of reality through the use of narrative. It is these stories that make Brabantio, Desdemona, and potentially the Duke's daughter fall in love with Othello. It is the stories of the anthropophogi and the men with heads beneath their shoulders and the deprivations of war that call on Desdemona's pity of Othello and on Othello's pity of himself. What people fall in love with are his exoticism and his ability to construct a world out of tales. Iago, ever attracted to Othello and yet jealous of Othello, is able to see where Othello cannot, goes further in world construction than even Othello can imagine. The servant outdoes the master, in true comic fashion, but has certainly learned the craft of worldspinning from his master.

Michael Cassio, to the extent that he might actually be merely an arithmetician, with mere book learning and "mere prattle without practice," (1.1.25) may also be one who has succumbed to narrative. He is promoted based on his ability to use war tales to shape how he is seen, and he perhaps tells tales to himself regarding his love of Desdemona. If the wine and the dream are taken as significant events, we see a very different version of Michael Cassio from the one he shows more publicly. This other Cassio is angry, out of control, lusty, unkind, and not really prepared for the lieutenancy. Of course, we have to choose which narrative to believe here, that told by Iago, by a story of a dream, by a glass or two of wine, or by Cassio himself, and by Othello's regard for Cassio.

As the play progresses, Iago spins more and more of the world we and the characters all see. As he spins more, we lose any sense of what has really transpired and what he has made up for a purpose that is most unclear. If he destroys everyone, he has no world to claim. If jealousy really is its own thing that takes no account of the world at all then he has no goal regarding the world save to let his jealousy run rampant and destroy everything. To the extent that he does destroy everything, he does so with the help of everything, for he does not conjure feelings that are not already present at some level. It is wit, not witchcraft, after all. Thus, it is narrative creation, not world creation, that Iago engages in.

From the spin room, then, Iago sets up the meanings of the missing handkerchief, the conversation he has with Michael Cassio, with the meaning of "lie," with the proper death of Desdemona. Each of these narrative spins is taken up by Othello as more real than anything Othello experiences more directly, and as more real than any other source of meaning. When Emilia declares Desdemona's complete innocence, Othello decides that Desdemona is a subtle whore. When Desdemona declares her own innocence, this declaration, as well, is proof of her guilt. Anything that contradicts the dominant narrative Othello operates under becomes more proof of the truth of the dominant narrative.

Iago has created both a world and a belief system for Othello that confirms Othello's own sense of being outside the language, outside the customs, outside the meanings of the society he has to negotiate. It is precisely this outsider status that allows him to ignore contradicting sources of information. Were Othello familiar with, and trusting of, such a source, he would be more insider than outsider. It is only Iago, the bridge between Othello's war-self and domestic-self, that is given the power to script the narratives. If Othello has charmed by telling wild tales of the oddities of humankind, he has now been charmed by tales of the complexities of human desire. The oddities of humankind are thrilling, the battles full of risk, and so there is a kind of sexual excitement to it all. The complexities of desire have a very different kind of risk—the risk of humiliating sexual loss in an alien world, and so are intolerable.

There is a standard tale of attraction to an appropriate mate, love, marriage, and the unfolding of a life. Brabantio assumes that his daughter is very much in this standard narrative, and so her refusals to marry any of the proper suitors he has presented her are taken as proof that she is opposed to marriage. Brabantio has the wrong notion of love and marriage in his thinking.

But then, every relationship in *Othello* is orthogonal to this very conventional narrative. The lack of conventional relationships both motivates Iago and makes his job much easier. The subtle attractions between Iago and Othello, Brabantio and Othello, Iago and Desdemona, Michael Cassio and Desdemona, and even Desdemona and Emila are all full of jealousy, impropriety, and falsity. They are based on narrative and a strong tie between love and hate rather than on a kind of selfless concern for the other. Further, these relationships defy convention in ways that make it hard to keep them under control. Michael Cassio's freedom with Desdemona, Desdemona's exposure to Othello, the elopement, Othello's outsider status, Iago's sense of power over and attraction to Othello, Emilia's split loyalties—each of these causes divisions and divided duties, room for doubt and intense longing even through the doubt.

THE WAR BETWEEN THE NARRATIVES

In the background of *Othello,* there is one war between Cyprus and the Turks and another between varying narratives the characters use to describe events, themselves, and others. As we have seen, both Othello and Iago are storytellers, spinners of tales that both frame and shape events and meanings for other characters. As Iago takes on more of Othello's storytelling ability, and as Othello loses his own ability and eventually falls into a wordless epileptic seizure, the two characters switch places. Eventually, the peripety, a kind of false peripety, is overturned and Othello regains his gracious, if exaggerated storytelling, for a moment before his death, and Iago falls silent for the rest of his likely brief and tortured existence.

The battle for narrative dominance is played out on the field of the meaning of "Desdemona" for the various characters, and the instability of the meaning of her existence is central to the meaning of her death. For Brabantio, "Desdemona" is a dutiful daughter, one reluctant to marry and therefore both devoted to her father and to her chastity. For Othello, she is clearly devoted to his stories, charmed by them, full of pity for him and his experiences, and therefore at some level, Desdemona is Othello. She pities him as much as he pities himself. She gazes at him as much as he gazes at himself. She places his narrative of himself at the center of her being. The narrative construction of "Desdemona" as Othello's other self is a major cause of her death, for no one can ever really be entirely wrapped up in another person.

Every now and then, during the play, there is a clear separation between Othello and Desdemona, and these moments of separation, when her desire is not his desire, when her pity falls on Michael Cassio, when she drops the napkin unawares, when she wonders about Lodovico's suitability, when she fails to see herself as Othello sees her, that is, when she is Desdemona, and not "Desdemona," are the fundamental cause of her death.

Another narrative construction of "Desdemona" is Michael Cassio's attraction to her and his use of her to regain his reputation. Of course, the attraction is inappropriate and his use of her to press his case empowers Iago's narrative work. Each time Michael Cassio presses his case, Desdemona's pity for him increases and she makes pity for Michael Cassio supplant the pity she feels for Othello's suffering over his jealous rage. That he no longer comes first in her pity, that she does not see the world through his eyes, but now through Michael Cassio's completely undoes the relationship. It is this change in her subject position that Othello cannot bear. But he only sees the change in her position as such because Iago has spun a narrative of the battles for Desdemona's loyalty as a wife.

Emilia's handing over of the napkin to Iago is one of a few efficient causes of Desdemona's death. But underlying the mere efficiency of the action is an entire narrative framework that has made possible Emilia's act of betrayal. For Emilia, "Desdemona" is fully loved, fully chaste, but still fully other such that there is room for Emilia to use the napkin to improve her own marriage. It is as if there seemed such excess in Desdemona's marital status that Emilia could borrow or steal from it with impunity, with clear conscience, and use that "stuff of marriage" for her own foundering relationship. And if it were a small sin that allowed her to gain the world, she could simply re-spin the world to make amends, to cleanse the sin.

Because, once again, "Desdemona" exists for others and in the narratives of others and is herself something of a cipher, she is not really herself, she is not what she is. The result of the lack of clear subjectivity in or of Desdemona is her own death. That Emilia could think of her friend, her better, her companion, her employer as containing such excess that a little borrowing around the edges is fine, that she could so miss the growing tensions in the marriage and be willing to hand over the napkin shows that pity for oneself is no better a bond than that between Othello and Desdemona which is based on his pleasure at the pity she has for him. Pity is an insufficient glue for a marriage.

COMEDY AND TRAGEDY IN THE NARRATIVE STRUCTURES

Roderigo's foolish love is, of course, comically ridiculous. Desdemona has made clear her lack of regard, Iago has demonstrated multiple times that Roderigo is merely a purse (perhaps a feminine image), and Roderigo willingly endures this treatment for an infatuation that has no ground whatsoever.

He allows Iago to tell a story of hope, but it is a ridiculous story of ridiculous hope. With each new selling of possessions and each renewal of foolish hope, Roderigo sinks further in our regard. His character is comic until Iago's knife sticks him. At that moment he has a peripety and a discovery, and this coming together of these moments in what he thought was a comic love story is a moment of incredulity and realization that he has had the narrative wrong all the way through. His instincts had told him as much, but his desires led him astray.

Emilia starts with a kind of comic sensibility. She is playful with Desdemona, seems to champion women, is hopeful that her husband can be purchased with the price of a napkin, and seems to think that gaining the world will allow her to change all the darker meanings to bright. The eternal hope of rewriting the narrative gives her a comic attitude until she realizes the enormity of her sin and the impossibility of rewriting. Her peripety and discovery come together as well, her moment of incredulity leads her to her death at Desdemona's side.

Desdemona, too, has comic mis-timing and comic misunderstandings. There is much that is akin to mistaken identities in her read of Othello. Her starstruck sensibility, her wonderment at the exaggerations, her headlong fall into ridiculous love all suggest that she is comic. And yet her death at the hands of her husband has a tragic sense to it. Her peripety and discovery, too, come together as she realizes that love and death are, for her, one.

Othello's comedy lies in his tales, his blindness as a soldier, his outsider status, the epileptic seizures that remove him from himself, his ridiculous jealousy based on something as flimsy as words and a napkin. He utters the words "I have no wife," and perhaps he realizes that at some level he has never actually had a wife, for a wife is a person in her own right, with an existence of her own, self-pity of her own, and preferences of her own. The comic marriage that begins the play ends in tragic death at the end of the play.

Brabantio's comic love for Othello's tales leads to a tragic marriage between his daughter and Othello, and his tragic death off stage leads to comic relief that he never finds out that his words of caution are the guiding cause of Desdemona's death. A father's concern for his daughter becomes the stuff of her death. The reversal is shocking as is the admixture of comedy and tragedy.

If, at each point in the plot where a character decides on an interpretive strategy, there were a moment's pause to reconsider, to make a different choice, the tragic story could be interrupted and the action could be shifted to a romantic comedy. Triumph in war, triumph in love, promotions and handkerchiefs for all, a little drunken revelry, reunions of lovers, marriages all around, this is the stuff of comedy. But because the characters all tend to fall for tragic interpretations, because Iago is not what he is but is rather a narrative construct endlessly at odds with the world that is what it is but is cloaked in narrative, everyone ends up stuck in a slowly unfolding tragedy, and everyone has a hand in Desdemona's "suicide" and the "murder" of Othello. We can hearken back to the warning to the souls in Book X of the *Republic* that we must choose our next life carefully, and we can see clearly here that this warning goes unheeded, with the direst of effects.

Emilia's choosing to speak, her realization that worlds cannot be made and remade, is the central philosophical gesture in the play and is at the heart of the resolution. It is speaking rather than quoting or echoing or being spun by Iago that has significance. It is the philosophical understanding that the world is and must be shared, that Cartesian isolation cannot work. Emilia realizes this too late, but she does realize it, and she dies for her speaking, for her not having spoken, and for her having accepted Iago's desires as her own. The offer of friendship is indeed fraught, and though it may be proper to accept Iago as a friend, he is a friend who comes with destructive force. Where philosophy can help with a figure like Iago is perhaps where Emilia's belated realizations occur.

NOTES

1. Berger notes that our sense of what is going on at the beginning of the play is distorted at first and only becomes clearer later. That is, "At first, Iago's rhetorical attack on Othello the Moor and Cassio the Florentiene has the effect of coupling them together as comical outsiders, while he represents himself as the quintessential insider. But there must be something wrong with this representation, since he failed in his suit to get promoted." The lack of clarity is significant for the play. We of course do not quite know what to make of "things," but so, it turns out, many characters also have confusions. This confusion is part of what I call world-spinning. Eventually, the play brings us back to "the world." But we spend a fair amount of time in a kind of confused space and time scape. See Harry Berger, Jr., "Acts of Silence, Acts of Speech: How to Do Things with Othello and Desdemona," in *Renaissance Drama*, New Series, 33 (2004): 4.

2. Jennifer Ann Bates turns to Hegel on tragedy to read Othello and emphasizes "collision" as a significant characteristic of tragedy. The plot resolutions come from "inevitable disaster or peaceful union" as Bates quotes Hegel (Bates 25). See Jennifer Ann Bates, *Hegel and Shakespeare on Moral Imagination* (New York: State University of New York Press, 2010). Bates also notes the importance for Hegel of something more than mere luck to drive the plot. Mere luck, or contingency, weakens the effect of the drama, and as Bates writes, "We have seen that Hegel requires that drama have comprehensive and universal import" (Bates 28).

3. Stephen Rogers, "*Othello*: Comedy in Reverse," in *Shakespeare Quarterly* 24 (2) (Spring 1973): 210.

4. Rogers, "*Othello*: "Comedy in Reverse," 210.

5. Berger writes of Iago as Vice character, "The wickedness of his figure represents is not his own but everyone else's. Shakespeare inserts the villain into this position in such a way as to set up an ironic structure of agency." This notion that Iago is acting out the vices of the other characters, that he is at some level the locus of the displaced wickedness of others, lends credence to my sense that nearly every character in the play has some hand in Desdemona's murder. See Berger Jr., "Acts of Silence," 32.

6. Berger sees triangles with Othello, Iago, and Cassio as based on envy, and Othello, Cassio, and Desdemona as based on jealousy. He discusses the significance of Cassio's having been a go-between in Othello's and Desdemona's courtship, and he notes Othello's discomfort with the intensity of Desdemona's desires. See Berger Jr., "Acts of Silence," 11–14.

7. See D. Rothleder, "The Evil Deceiver and the Evil Truth Teller: Descartes, Iago, and Scepticism," in *The Routledge Companion to Shakespeare and Philosophy*. Edited by Craig Bourne and Emily Caddick Bourne (New York: Routledge, 2019), 323–335.

8. Draper presents a reading of Iago as a cuckold who must, according to Elizabethan social convention, take revenge. He notes the thin line between tragedy and comedy in Iago, that the character of Iago could have been written as a comic figure, but in the end, the play "is a double tragedy of supposed adultery, worked out with unflinching logic according to the social and ethical concepts inherent in the profession of the characters in the age." This reading suggests that Iago is not a Machiavel, a purely evil character, but rather is conventional and is responding in conventional fashion to the probable cuckolding. There is a fair amount of scholarly debate about the nature of Iago, his status as "honest," and his wickedness. See John W. Draper, "Honest Iago," in *PMLA* 46 (3) (September 1931): 727.

9. Coleridge famously describes Iago's actions as the "motive-hunting of a motiveless malignity." Much literature on the character of Iago struggles with whether Iago's stated motives can be trusted. He does gives motives, but he couches them in language that suggests that perhaps he has no motive other than malignancy. Readers have to decide how much to trust what he says about his inner thoughts. See R.A. Foakes, edited and selected, *Coleridge's Criticism of Shakespeare* (Detroit, MI: Wayne State University Press, 1989), 113. For an opposing view, see Frank Prentice Rand, "The Overgarrulous Iago," in *Shakespeare Quarterly* 1 (3) (July 1950): 154–161. Rand suggests that in Iago's soliloquies there are explicit motives stated. See Rand, 154. See also Rothleder, "The Evil Deceiver and the Evil Truth-Teller" for a reading that suggests that Iago uses virtue to destroy virtue as a method and that he is motivated by a belief in Emilia's infidelity as attested to when he cries out at the end, "Thou liest."

10. Berger notes that Iago's "power of soliloquy" shifts in Act 5. Once Iago no longer has that power, the power of world-spinning, in my terms, Iago has lost. See Berger, "Acts of Silence," 31.

11. There is a standard set of interpretations of *Othello* that argue that the play takes place in "double time." That is, events cannot unfold quite in the time that the stage presence would allow. Some things happen too quickly, some props are moved

impossibly (the handkerchief shows up in a kind of untimely fashion.) The critical response to these temporal issues is to suggest that the play takes place in two different timescapes. What is especially intriguing about reading the play this way is that Othello's sense of time and Iago's sense of time and Desdemona's sense of time all must differ given the kind of emotional intensity or craftiness or involvement in issues each has. For one reading of the double time, and what the author calls, a solution to the problem, see Steven Sohmer, "The 'Double Time' Crux in *Othello* Solved," in *English Literary Renaissance* 32 (2) (Spring 2002): 214–238. See also Berger, "Acts of Silence," 15, for a read of "inverted time" rather than double time. The inversions come because we find the justifications working *post hoc ergo propter hoc*. See 15–16.

12. Cavell addresses the temporal issue here from a somewhat different angle. He suggests that the overly quick change from Othello's love to his hatred, and presumably other such changes in the play are the result of "the rhythm of skepticism." That is, doubt works in sudden fashion, as much for Othello as for Descartes in the *Meditations*, as Cavell notes. If what is at stake in *Othello* is skepticism and certainty, certainty can take time and be slow, skepticism is sudden, and the step back into certainty takes an event such as a death to precipitate. Certainty could perhaps be thought of as the comic moment, and skepticism could be thought of as the impulse to tragedy. To the extent that Iago impels doubt where there has been certainty, he is the figure of tragedy. Cavell writes further that "Othello's mind continuously outstrips reality, dissolves it in trance or dream or in the beauty or ugliness of his incantatory imagination; in which he visualizes possibilities that reason, unaided, cannot rule out." Here we see the effects of Iago's world-spinning on Othello's thinking. The world-spinning affects both time and perception. See Stanley Cavell, "Epistemology and Tragedy: A Reading of Othello," in *Daedalus* 108 (3) (Summer 1979): 34–35.

Section 3

The Tragedy of *The Comedy of Errors*

From the title on, *The Comedy of Errors* conveys a central tension between the comic and the tragic. Though the end of the play is comic, getting to that comedy requires going through a range of tragic misunderstandings, errors, separations, and losses. To err is to have a failure of knowledge that leads to wrong action. *Othello* can be read as a tragedy comprised of comic elements, and so, conversely, *The Comedy of Errors* can be read as a comedy comprised of a series of tragedies. If, overall, the structure tends toward the comic, at any moment in the play one can identify a tragic sensibility, a sense of deep loss of meaning and connection, a deep misunderstanding about the world the characters inhabit. Othello could be in a comic situation but chooses to misidentify it as a tragedy, and so enacts tragedy and suffers. In contrast, the characters in *The Comedy of Errors* confuse the tragic and comic impulses by turns, and though they end up in the comic, they intensify their suffering through their errors and interpretive choices. A proper understanding of their worlds, were it possible, would save them all from the suffering and losses they endure. Lacking that proper understanding, either for structural reasons or for reasons of willful refusal to entertain possible other narrative interpretations, means that each character has an epic, Odyssean journey through tragedy to comedy. When the world is put to rights again, the tragic moment passes, and the comedy takes over for most of the characters.

Clearly as well, the title should point to the Cartesian anxiety over error and the need to be certain in order to avoid error, and to Derrida's discussion of the need to extend friendship even in the face of uncertainty. Both of these philosophical concerns shed light on the action in the play. Overly blithe actions, overly comedic interpretations, have bad consequences, and yet it would be improper for many of the actions were skepticism to take over and trust not be extended. The play shows clearly how fraught decisions can be and yet how unavoidable they often are.

Mistaken pride, mistaken identity, mistaken notions of marriage, and the incursion of the commercial sector into the lives of families are among the errors that the play recounts. In each case, there is missing knowledge or a lack of recognition of proper boundaries. Tying all of these errors together is the confusion of comic and tragic moments such that the characters enact the wrong strategies for dealing with their situations. From Emilia's initial overweening maternal pride to Egeon's overwhelming melancholy, from the assumptions that the confused twins make about their situation to the misunderstandings about the nature of marriage, from the initial selling of people to the selling of the chain, the assumptions that guide the characters are erroneous. The main result of these errors is the loss of family life, the loss of marriage, and the major disruption of commerce. The Law itself must come to a better self-understanding such that all of these domains can be put to right, all of the relations can be set properly against one another, and the whole framework of human sociality can be restored with a proper sense of the comic and the tragic.

Northrop Frye distinguishes between two kinds of comedy he sees in the Greek tradition, "Old Comedy" and "New Comedy."[1] He writes of New Comedy that "there is a social as well as an individual theme which must be sought in the general atmosphere of reconciliation that makes the final marriage possible."[2] Frye goes on to note that the characters involved in comedy are driven by some kind of "mental bondage" that directs their behavior.[3] Thus we have, at the outset, a guide for looking at the comic elements in the play. There are separated characters, with inner drives, social integrations that have to develop in opposition to the social breakdown that pervades the play from the start, and there are, of course, marriages and re-marriages; family reconciliation and law and mercy come together as well.

The Comedy of Errors, then, is clearly, in Frye's terms, a New Comedy. It has as well, some elements of Aristotelian comedy in that there are some lower characters who provide comedy, but there is less of the foolishness that makes the audience feel superior. Rather than have foolish characters whose lowness elevates us, Shakespeare uses the irony of our being able to tell the twins apart, even as the characters have to wait until the end of Act V to find out what we, the audience, already know.

Frye notes, further, that, "At once—for the process is beginning in *The Comedy of Errors*—he started groping toward that profounder pattern, the ritual of death and revival that also underlies Aristophanes, of which an exact equivalent lay ready to hand in the drama of the green world."[4] What Frye is pointing to here, in the notion of the "ritual of death and revival" is precisely the tragic tone underlying the comic, or accompanying the comic.

Mere buffoonery, or mere laughing at the low born in anxious restatement of one's own higher status is not particularly profound, but a death before a life, an accounting for one's errors before one is permitted to marry or remarry, a trial before a triumph is, as Frye notes above, a "profounder pattern."

In an essay entitled "The Comic Structures of Tragic Endings" Martha Tuck Rozett notes the intertwining of comic and tragic elements in *Romeo and Juliet* and *Antony and Cleopatra*: "[B]oth sets of lovers must overcome social and political obstacles to be united; both are surrounded by variations on comic character types who contribute to the complications in the love plot; and both entangle themselves in tragic renditions of the pattern of misunderstandings and confusion leading to clarification and reunion."[5] Rozett notes, then, that there are entangled comic and tragic elements in Shakespeare's works, and it is these patterns we will disentangle in *The Comedy of Errors* as we have done for *Othello*.

Because these texts are reversals of each other and because their reverse structures come together in moments of incredulity, reading them against each other will reinforce the difficulties in distinguishing between tragedy and comedy, and will demonstrate all the more that our interpretive choices or misreadings of our situations cause us enormous difficulty. The peripeties, discoveries, and moments of hysteresis in each of these texts all reinforce the strategic errors and failures of knowledge that lead us to enact the wrong courses of action, and finally push us toward terrible mistakes.

The *Comedy of Errors* opens with a death sentence and a tale of woe. Egeon, a merchant from Syracuse, now in Ephesus, declares to Solinus the Dukes of Ephesus, "Proceed, Solinus, to procure my fall, / And by the doom of death end woes and all" (1.1.1-2). There is no comedy at all in Egeon's words; rather, there is a heaviness and a readiness to die as both his woes and the non-woeful remainder overwhelm any preference he might have to continue life. Right from the outset, then, is Frye's "ritual of death." The tension here between ending woe with the "doom of death" and ending "all" with the same "doom" is important because the notion of the remainder, the part of Egeon that is not woeful, really ought not be subject to a death wish. There is, then, an error in Egeon's wish for death, but because the error is embedded in a comedy, the wish cannot be fulfilled. Rather, the remainder will trump the major part, and Egeon's past woes will be overtaken by present joys. Before this crossing from woe to joy can happen, though, Egeon has a long and troubled trail. And indeed, the trail will be one that goes from near death to a return to life rather than from near death to complete death.

It is notable that it is precisely the subversion of Egeon's desire to die that allows him the chance to live happily ever after. Happiness, then, at least in a comedy of tragic proportions, is still tragic in its refusal to fulfill desire. Admittedly, Egeon may not really want to die when he says he wants to die, or perhaps he simply changes his mind or has only a surface desire to die, but a deep preference for life. But it is notable that he has his life-preference granted only by losing his death wish. Not all wishes can be granted, and there is a kind of tension in the choice of which wishes are the proper ones, and which kind of happiness is the accepted outcome. One could imagine Egeon's looking back at this series of unfortunate events and not really being able to understand how he had come to want to die, or to want to live.

Solinus, the Duke, and the personification of the law and of justice, replies to Egeon by saying that the laws condemning Egeon stem from the way that the Duke of Syracuse has treated the merchants of Ephesus. Solinus says of the law,

Nay more, if any born at Ephesus
Be seen at Syracusians marts and fairs;
Again, if any Syracusian born
Come to the bay of Ephesus, he dies,
His goods confiscate to the Duke's dispose,
Unless a thousand marks be levied
To quit the penalty and to ransom him. (1.1.16-22)

There is, in Solinus's characterization, a reciprocal treatment of misplaced people. If you are born in Ephesus and go to Syracuse, you die. If you are born in Syracuse and you go to Ephesus, you die. The evenhandedness of this agreement suggests a kind of justice because it is mutual and evenly agreed to and enforced. Of course, the title word "errors" should instantly call to mind the problems Polemarchus has with declaring that justice is in keeping with doing harm, for error can intervene and the result is the harm of the undeserving, even if at some level there is equal opportunity harm-doing.

Further, in Solinus's speech is the workaround based on the notion of the equivalence of money and life. To retain your life, should you in error be in the wrong place, or have been born in the wrong place, you can purchase your life for a thousand marks. Egeon's life, then, depends not on the quality of his soul, nor on the goodness of his actions, but merely on the error of having been born in the wrong place, or come to the wrong place in error, and to lack precisely the money that Cephalus suggests is at the heart of justice. Paying his fine would save his life, having the money to pay, regardless of how gotten, is the guarantor of just treatment for a good man caught up in the error of place.

Solinus gives Egeon a chance to tell his tale of woe, the beginning of which moves Solinus to say, "Nay forward, old man, do not break off so, /For we may pity thee, though not pardon thee" (1.1.96-97). These words recall Othello's tales, the love and pity they occasion. The tales will have their effect by altering the frame of the narrative such that in this case, Solinus will offer a small hope to Egeon.

Egeon's tale includes the births of four babies, two sets of completely identical twins, one a fortunate and happy pair and the other a sad and poor pair whose parents sell their children to Egeon and his wife. There is, then, the comedy of marriage and birth, but also a more tragic tale of marriage and birth that is doubled upon the comic. The intertwining of these two narrative modes runs throughout the play. Birth turns tragic for one pair because of class issues and is comic for the other pair, because they now have servants born at the same time. But the happy purchase of two children who will never again see their parents is interrupted by the storm-induced break up of Egeon's family, seemingly causing this family, too, to lose each other permanently.

Egeon, his wife, and the now four sons are, we find out, on a ship for Epidamnum, a terrible storm arises and the ship sinks. The family is split up, with the mother taking one of each of the twins and the father having the other of each pair. Happy that the master/servant pairs are preserved and the classes mixed and each well-born child has a natural parent, but tragic that the family is split, that the low-born children have no natural parents at all, and that twins are separated and feel the pangs of separation.

Solinus once again interjects, during a pause in the narrative, "And for the sake of them thou sorrowest for, / Do me the favour to dilate at full / What have befall'n of them and thee till now" (1.1.121-123). Solinus's interjections are a mark of the power of narrative to spin, to alter the field of perception, to alter the world and to push the law back toward a kind of sympathetic justice and away from a harsher notion. For the sake of those who are lost, Solinus wants to hear more of the story. One must wonder, of course, if the telling of the tale is truly a memorial for the sake of the lost or is more for Solinus himself who finds himself seduced by the tale. A personification of the Law or not, he is caught up in a narrative that is slowly changing the meaning of "Egeon" from Syracusian interloper in Ephesus to fellow human suffering from a terrible tragedy. Tragic narrative, once enacted, allows the slow shift away from the pure tragic death sentence to a more moderate version of the death sentence and eventually to the comedy that the play's title gestures toward.

At the end of Egeon's tale, Solinus first invokes the law, "Now trust me, were it not against our laws, / Against my crown, my oath, my dignity, / Which princes, would they, may not disannul, / My soul should sue as advocate for thee" (1.1.142-145). All that makes Solinus what he is, the law, and all that he is as prince, keep him from doing what he thinks is just. That is, the narrative that structures him as the embodiment of justice prevents him from enacting that very justice that he is the embodiment of. The tragic paradox of not being able to enact justice when one precisely is justice shows the logic of gesturing past narrative in our understanding of the meaning of "justice." Socrates points past Thrasymachus's performative definition and Polemarchus's performative definitions and Cephalus's performative definition of justice precisely because of this conflict between performance and reality.

Solinus finds a way through his dilemma by delaying for a brief time the unjust imposition of justice on one whose error is mercy-based rather than duplicitous. He says,

Yet will I favour thee in what I can;
Therefore, merchant, I'll limit thee this day
To seek thy health by beneficial help;
Try all the friends thou hast in Ephesus,
Beg thou, or borrow, to make up the sum,
And live; if no, then thou art doom'd to die.
Jailor, take him to thy custody. (1.1. 149-155)

Of course, it will not be easy for Egeon to beg or borrow while he is a stranger in Ephesus, and it will not give him much time, "this day," to raise the money. There is, then, a stern limit to the mercy that Solinus can afford to show. He feels the pity for the tragic errors that Egeon has made, but because he himself is bound by a situation not of his making, he can only offer this very limited route out of the machinery of death. Solinus grants both time and space to Egeon, but only in small supply. The law is not so magisterial, but it certainly can be seduced by a great story.

The class division and sale of two children, the family breakup in a terrible storm at sea, the loss, and Egeon's pending death sentence all suggest the elements of tragedy. And yet, the simultaneous birth of such oddly alike children, the sheer length of Egeon's tale, the delay of the death sentence for a day, and the emergence very quickly of all four children and Egeon in the same place suggest together that the family will likely be re-united and the comedy will arise out of the terrible errors that have been made.

As we have asked, regarding both the *Republic* and *Othello*, just who commits a terrible deed (the eating of one's children for the *Republic*, and the killing of Desdemona for *Othello*), so we will ask, regarding *The Comedy of Errors*, just who commits "errors" and how overdetermined the errors are. Further, we will see if there is really a reduction to a single error that is overdetermined by multiple commissions.

Though scholars of the play tend to treat the sale of the Dromios as something more akin to an adoption or a betterment of the children or a commonplace event that people in Shakespeare's era would not balk at, it is both fruitful and structurally satisfying to take the sale more seriously, to see its parallels with the breakup of the Antipholi, to see it as a kind of fundamental error that sets the moral action of the play in motion. Vincent Petronella's essay, "Structure and Theme through Separation and Union in Shakespeare's *The Comedy of Errors*" is typical of the works that note themes related to family dissolution and yet stop short of singling out the sale/purchase of the Dromios. Petronella does a wonderful job of developing the break ups and reunions, the teleological pressures of reunion. He writes that the "structure in *The Comedy of Errors* is the play's solid base made up of four interlocking levels of reality: family, commerce, state, and cosmos. The last of these does not have as prominent a role as do the first three; nevertheless, it *is* present."[6] This passage shows several points underscoring the sense of the presence and absence of the Dromios' family drama within the drama of the Antipholi. First, Petronella is clearly aware of themes that are mostly absent, as he notes that cosmos is not prominent, but merely present, and still worth noting. He notes further that the "social situation" is underplayed but present, of lesser import than the domestic. That themes can be "there" without being directly and frequently noted suggests that it may well be worth doing things with the Dromios.

Petronella concludes this passage with a gesture toward the reunification of those who have been separated, with the coming together of the society and the family. Despite this gesture, and despite the note that happiness prevails, and despite his noting earlier in the passage that son seeks mother, and father seeks son, Petronella omits even the possibility that the Dromios could seek their parents or that their parents could be seeking them. By absenting even mention of the possibility of the reunification of the family Dromio, one allows for an asymmetry between the sets of brothers, between the sets of parents, and between right and wrong uses of commerce. If the necklace requires rightful placement, and if all of the money that changes hands must need be properly placed, and if the state's demand for money can both be enforced and canceled by the force of the law, then it seems worth thinking through what a reading of the play that takes the sale of the Dromios as seriously as standard readings take the sale of the necklace and the general theme of the disruption of commercial relations. Although historicist readings of this play suggest that there may have been social or authorial tolerance of the sale of the twins, the text of the play gives some room for a suggestion that such a sale might be morally questionable, and at the very least, perhaps there is a gesture toward questioning the act through the absence of symmetry between the sets of twins and the final reunifications.

To add to the sense that the Dromios deserve more attention than they typically receive, Maurice Hunt's essay "Slavery, English Servitude, and *The Comedy of Errors*" is worth considering. Hunt provides an exhaustive account of the scholarship regarding the status of the two Dromios. That they are possibly close to being slaves, that they are beaten and ill-used, that they use punning language to equalize their physical abuse is well-supported by the text and by much scholarship.[7] Hunt writes, "Both critics and editors of the *Comedy of Errors* reveal a notable uncertainty over the social status of the Dromio brothers. Taking their cue from the designations of Shakespeare's text, they refer to the twins sometimes as slaves, sometimes a servants, and occasionally as bondmen."[8] The violence with which each twin is greeted in error, the violence each has been subjected to prior to the start of the action, and the fact that the twins were purchased from their impoverished parents according to Egeon's tale all suggest a less than comic mode of interpretation for this part of the tale.

Hunt delves into English law to help try to figure out the status of the Dromios—contrasting the kinds of employment and use of labor available to people with different amounts of wealth.[9] Laborers did not have liberty, and clearly the Dromios fall under this category at some level. There is risk in reading in too much history to the play, but even a slight awareness of the historical background coupled with the original sale of the children and their treatment over time suggests a less than free life for the Dromios, a less than full concern for their well-being, and a distinctly asymmetrical story when compared with what the Antipholi go through. Hunt concludes his essay by noting that, "Still, providence leaves unaltered the rigid hierarchy of a society in which the Dromios remain slaves and husbands the masters of their wives" (p.1).[10]

Hunt then sees the tragedy of slavery, the hope that servants could be other than slaves, and the Shakespearean preference for a reestablished social order. It is the hope for less than slavery that gives an opening to a reading of the Dromios that veers from complete satisfaction at the resolution at the end of the play. And it is the parallels in family structure that can allow our imaginations to wander to the tale of woe that one could imagine the parents of the Dromios delivering on some other island to some other personification of the law and justice. Two sets of parents, two sets of twins, two classes, and given the doubling, there is an open invitation to compare across the doubles.

For the purposes of this section, then, I will treat the sale of the twins as the originary error that gets the action going. And, with Hunt and Petronella in the background, there is both at least some historical justification and some structural justification. Motivating the error is Egeon's choice to read the birth of his twins as comic, and the choice of the Dromio parents to read their situation as tragic. Two sets of twins, one implicated in a comedy, one in a tragedy. The comic turns tragic for a time, but the tragic does not entirely heal up, even though it is brought, at some level into the comic. The interplay between these modes can make it difficult to re-interpret one's narrative once one is implicated in it. Some of this difficulty can be ascribed to a kind of hysteresis. Once the Dromio twins are marked as tragic, they cannot fully become comic, and once the Antipholi are labeled comic, their trek through tragedy does not fully mark them as tragic. Still, the original interpretive decisions set the characters up for a great deal of suffering.

Assuming then, that the original error of the play is the sale and purchase of the two Dromios, this error functions as the tragic break up of a family with no chance of reunion, and it is this break up that forewarns the further breaking up of the family of Egeus, the break between Adriana and Antipholus of Ephesus, the break between Syracuse and Ephesus, and even the breakdown in commercial relations within Ephesus. The sale of the twins does, though, come after Egeon's loss of his "factor," or commercial sponsor (1.1.41). This initial loss required of Egeon a different travel pattern and a separation from his pregnant wife. These various breakups are commercial in nature, as Syracuse and Ephesus have shipping and piracy conflicts; the breakup of the family Dromio is equally a commercial enterprise, fully dependent upon class and economic distinctions; and of course, the loss of Egeon's sponsor impeded commerce as well. Furthermore, the commerce regarding the necklace affects both the flow of finances for the merchants involved and the "flow" of affections between Adriana and her Antipholus. Without the distinctions between classes and cities, without the breakdown of appropriate commerce, the families would not have been split up and the death sentence would not have been declared.

Egeon has, in the loss of his sponsor and familiar commercial patterns, suffered a quiet moment of shock that sends ripples throughout the play. The intertwining of commerce, familiarity, habit, and domestic space make any shock to the system ripple through the other spheres, and each affects the understanding of the other spheres. Family and commerce, the familiarity of settled relations and the need for money to flow in impersonal ways complicate the domestic simplicity that Egeon and Emilia had likely hoped for. Egeon and Emilia, then, are assuming that they are living out a comic narrative, but commerce, loss, and disruption change the structure of the narrative.

Regarding the intertwining of commerce and family, Curtis Perry notes, "Egeon is similarly despondent when speaking to the duke of Ephesus in the play's first exchange . . . . But by including this earlier instance of near-suicidal melancholy, one that predates the loss of family and so seems instead to have its origins in Egeon's 'great care of goods,' the narrative again exposes the intercomplication of family and economic concerns."[11] The loss of his factor, as Perry notes, is the first disruption, the first cause of Egeon's melancholy. Further, it is worth pointing out, the loss of Egeon's factor is not of Egeon's doing. It is an accident of nature that interferes with commercial relations and stable income. Indeed, were Egeon to have been unable to reestablish commercial relations in some other way, to deal with his "great care of goods," he could perhaps have become as destitute as the parents of the Dromios. This idea is, of course, unsaid in the play, and perhaps such a fall is unthinkable in a system in which class is real rather than a result of luck. But given that accidents do happen and nature does intrude, and further that parallels in the play are deliberate, Egeon's earlier loss and potential destitution function as hints that the personal world can suddenly become impersonal, that gain can become loss, that reversals of fortune do happen. That is, a comic life can become tragic in an instant, the peripety is around the corner, and with it, the discovery that commerce is not as kin.

There will be comic resolution for the Antipholi. They will find their parents, their lovers, and new and good lives. They will return to free commerce, they will be properly known. The Dromios, on the other hand, will not entirely come to comic resolution. They will be left with puns and beatings. And though they will have each other as siblings and twins, and though Dromio of Ephesus will marry kitchen help and so be brought into the realm of proper marriage, and though they agree to a kind of mutual equality with one another as a finale to the play, their stories will not resolve with anywhere near the comfort that the Antipholi will find. They will not, for example, have their parents. Nor will they evade beatings. Nor will they rise above servitude.

The two sets of twins have both symmetries and asymmetries, and where there are asymmetries, there is an opening for inquiry. The symmetry of the twins gives us the comic notion that there could even be two such sets born in the same place and time, gives us the comic space to explore social and class relations, shows us that being in the merchant class or in the servant class does not matter insofar as non-recognition is non-recognition. But at the same time, because there are two different classes involved, only the merchant class ends up entitled to a happy resolution with full family reunification. The Dromios miss out on the complete happy ending. And their missing out on it is linked directly to their having been sold at birth rather than allowed to remain with their parents. Their tale, then, puts a cap on the amount of comic space within the play, a cap that comes because "normal" commerce includes the selling of babies into something like slavery, even if it can be titled "servanthood" instead of "servitude."

Normal commerce in the play is already problematic because of the sale of the children. But there is a further breakdown in commerce as a major error, as well. The conflict over the gold chain sets up a situation in which creditors are not properly paid, commerce is disrupted, and the disruption leads to further suffering. The Second Merchant opens Act IV thus,

You know since Pentecost the sum is due,
And since I have not much importun'd you,

Nor now I had not, but that I am bound
To Persia, and want guilders for my voyage;
Therefore make present satisfaction,
Or I'll attach you by this officer. (4.4.1-6)

Because Angelo, the goldsmith, is caught up in the confusion over the Antipholi, he has handed the necklace to the wrong Antipholus and has not been paid. Because he has not been paid for the gold chain, he cannot give proper payment a merchant to whom he owes money, perhaps for the gold that became the chain. Because the merchant does not have his guilders, his whole enterprise is threatened. That his whole enterprise is threatened will ripple well beyond this small segment of the economy. Angelo will, of course, lose his freedom, but further, all commerce beyond Angelo will be disrupted, and this disruption can be traced directly back to the commercialization of the two Dromios' lives.

The identity of people is clearly an issue, their proper places and names, faces and reputations; but further, there is a concern about the place of commerce at all. That a single sale of a single chain, like a single link within the chain, can hold together such broad relations, or upon failure, can cause ripples far beyond the single sale or link, suggests a profound connection of all events with one another. The meaning of the chain as a token of Antipholus of Ephesus's love for Adriana, as a commercial item that links the merchant with Angelo, that links Angelo with Antipholus, that links the merchant with his further trade in Persia (and all the sailors for his ship), underscores the importance of trade and shows all the more that the selling of the Dromios, their commercialization, can indeed ripple far beyond the most direct relationships.

Wrong transactions and missed transactions are clearly a profound problem. Further bolstering the interrelation is Angelo's response to the Second Merchant:

Even just the sum I do owe to you
Is growing to me by Antipholus,
And in the instant that I met with you
He had of me a chain; at five o'clock
I shall receive the money for the same.
Pleaseth you walk with me down to his house,
I will discharge my bond, and thank you too. (4.1.7-13)

What is striking about this response is first that there is as much of a sense of bond/bondage between Angelo and the merchant as there is between each of the Dromios and each of the Antipholi. The Dromios are bondsmen, "chained" to their masters, and for this moment of debt, Angelo is chained to his merchant—over a chain. Further, there is a moment of freedom in the present such that the two can walk and talk, but are under threat of loss of freedom (Angelo) and loss of money and possibility (the merchant). Angelo's tale of woe is shorter than Egeon's, but is still followed by some space, some time (5 o'clock), and a final threat. The freedom of motion and the coming of gratitude are modulated by this looming threat, and so comic resolution and tragic resolution wrestle with one another. Both tales are linked by a metaphorical and actual chain.

There are two levels of commerce within the play, that of the exchange of money, and that of the exchange of like character for like character. Just as the Dromios are sold by their parents, a monetary/commodity exchange, so they are exchanged for each other throughout the course of the play. One Dromio is mistaken for the other, one Antipholus for the other. These exchanges are as erroneous as is the original purchase of the Dromios.

Richard Henze, in *"The Comedy of Errors*: A Freely binding Chain," works the images of the chain and rope to show that the rending of social ties and their restoration is deeply significant. Ropes and chains bind us, the characters flirt with a kind of liberty they ought not, and so part of the drama is the working out of the proper binding of social ties and then the restoration of those ties. The metaphor of the ropes and chains, then, is indicative of the breadth of the disruption of the social in the play and the concomitant need for deep restoration. Henze concludes the essay, "Such imagery also suggests, however, that throwing off of bonds of society—unbridling of asses—leads to a lower, animal level of existence. Humanity requires society; society requires social restraints. Each Antipholus attempts to reject the bonds, but each only succeeds in getting himself more securely bound."[12]

The uniqueness of a person and the belonging to family and community are lost in the confusion. Shankar Raman writes about memory in the play, "Egeon's hope that the memory of names would spur his son's recognition and thus 'deliver' him gives way to a delusory trust in the memory of faces. Antipholus's insistence that he has never before seen Egeon then evokes a final, equally vain attempt to register identity and presence through the voice: 'But tell me yet, dost thou not know my voice?'"[13] What Raman is discussing here (lines from Act 5, scene 2) is the breakdown in the social system of knowing people. We are only insofar as we are known by those whose actions preserve us. To be unknown, to be mis-taken for another, to be forgotten, to be in a place where one is not remembered, is to be lost for all time. Egeon may well know himself, may well see himself as he is, but if he cannot be known to others as well as he is known to himself, his self-knowledge does not help him survive. Social connection and social memory, family belonging and predictable behavior are all at sea in *The Comedy of Errors*, and with the epistemic blank spaces, errors abound.

Reinforcing the social connections as guarantors of identity, and linking the notion of social identity to commercial relations, Perry notes that a new market often "involved informal credit."[14] The linking together of households Perry describes is clearly an issue in *The Comedy of Errors*, and this very linking together allows the various errors that any one character makes ripple through the whole set of relationships. From the first error of commercializing human relations through the purchase of children through the mistaken identities and the impersonal stance of the law in the person of Solinus, no error is independent of any other, just as no commercial transaction stands alone and no character remains completely isolated from the others.

Social commerce fixes the relationships between people in a place, in relationships, and in transactions. Words are exchanged, looks are exchanged, favors and money are exchanged. All of these exchanges are posited upon a fluid system, a currency, and some amount of familiarity with the medium of exchange. *The Comedy of Errors* details the failures of each of these moments of exchange, and because the moments are in a system, the system as a whole is thrown off by any one external shock. Disequilibrium reigns until the end of the play when stability is reintroduced through the revelations of twinned faces but separate identities, proper ownership of property, merciful law, and proper marriages.

That Antipholus claims never to have "seen" Egeon points to yet another layer of errors, that of the visual. Complicating the visual failures that abound is the scene at Adriana's house when the Syracuse set is inside and the Ephesus set is locked out. Here, there is no visual cue, and yet the visual mistake continues, through a barred door. That so many people so totally fail to see, whether or not they have eye contact, suggests a gap between seeing and knowing. This gap repeats with every mistaken identity, and even describes what happens to Solinus and Egeon in the opening scene. It is not upon seeing Egeon that Solinus decides to enact mercy; rather, it is upon hearing a narrative that Solinus acts.

The identity of all the characters, then, lies more in their narratives and, as Raman notes, in the social memory of those narratives. Being seen is insufficient, and being heard without proper narrative structuring is also insufficient. Though Solinus can tell a tale, Antipholus of Ephesus has a much harder time convincing Dromio of Ephesus that the man outside the door, the man in the wrong place, should be allowed to come inside and be in the right place.

Linked to the fundamental error of the purchase of the twins from their rightful parents is Emilia's unwitting error, described by Egeon: "My wife, not meanly proud of two such boys, / Made daily motions for our home return; / Unwilling I agreed; alas, too soon / We came aboard" (1.1.58-61).

The error here is a smaller one than that of the purchase of the twins, but nonetheless, the excessive pride in her twins, a pride denied to the parents of the servant children, motivates Emilia's desire to leave Epidamnum at the wrong time. They sail into the storm that leads to the breakup of the family.

The storm, of course, is an act of nature and so is less human and more unwitting than is the sale of the children, but the excessive pride in "two such boys" certainly marks Emilia as needing some level of humility and some denial of parenthood, both characteristics marking the unnamed parents of the Dromios. It is, then, indeed an error of pride as well as an error of space and of time, that Emilia commits, and that leads to the opposite result from the one she most likely wanted. She, unlike her husband, is denied any parental connection with her child or with a servant, as it turns out that after the initial separation of husband and an Antipholus/Dromio set, and wife and the other Antipholus/Dromio set, the wife loses her set to "rude fishermen of Corinth" (5.1.357).

The suggestion, then, is that though selling children is an originary error that instigates the human drama of the play, excessive pride is a companion sin, and excessive pride coupled with the cruel treatment of the Dromios and their parents is indeed terrible. Emilia's tragedy is the loss of her family, a loss she has lived with for the first eighteen years of the children's lives, and for the following five years as well. As Egeon says,

My youngest boy, and yet my eldest care,
At eighteen years became inquisitive
After his brother, and importun'd me
That his attendant, so his case was like,
Reft of his brother, but retain'd his name,
Might bear him company in the quest of him;
. . .
Five summers have I spend in farthest Greece,
Roaming clean through the bounds of Asia,
And coasting homeward came to Ephesus,
Hopeless to find, yet loth to leave unsought
Or that or any place that harbours men . . . (1.1.124-136)

Egeon has wandered searching for his son who is searching for his other son. The aimless wandering among the Greek islands and Asia, that is, being in no place and in no time, is the collective punishment Egeon bears for both his and his wife's errors. Emilia, meanwhile, has become an abbess, and is in only one place, but still, it is the wrong place. She is penitent, as an abbess should be, and her husband wanders the world in an odyssey-like journey.

Adriana is, as well, an error-prone character. From her shrewish unacceptance of her Antipholus to her acceptance of the wrong Antipholus, from her argument with her sister Luciana to her argument with her mother-in-law Emilia, Adriana fails to know what she sees, to see what she should know, and to be properly married within her proper marriage. She fails, then, to enact her role at every level.

In the first interaction between the sisters, Adriana expresses frustration and Luciana counsels patience and knowing one's proper place. Given the motif of displacement that runs throughout the play and undergirds many of the errors, Luciana is expressing a proper concern and Adriana is improperly aggressive.

Luciana: Perhaps some merchant hath invited him,
And from the mart he's somewhere gone to dinner.
Good sister let us dine, and never fret;
A man is master of his liberty;
Time is their master, and when they see time,
They'll go or come; if so, be patient, sister.
Adriana: Why should their liberty than ours be more?
Luciana: Because their business still lies out o'door. (2.1.4-11)

Luciana, here, explains to her sister that men are governed by commerce and time, that commerce and time have their own external place, and that place, time, and merchants' concerns are proper to men, whereas domestic space is proper to women. The women could simply dine together in their own proper space and time and "never fret."

Adriana, on the other hand, wonders why men should have more liberty. Luciana answers that all animals live the same way, with male dominance, and Adriana quips in response, "This servitude makes you to keep unwed" (2.1.26). This line is ironic in that Adriana, though married, is at some level unwed as well. Her husband is elsewhere and she is frustrated. Her frustration leaves her all the more impatient, so that in a single scene she chastises her sister for being too pure, Dromio for bearing ill news regarding her husband, and her husband for making her more unattractive by his absence and her need to be shrewish.

In each case, Adriana has mistaken the proper role she should play as sister, mistress of a servant and as wife. Though contemporary readers may well balk at some of the conventions of proper wifely behavior, within the context of the play Adriana's comportment toward her husband is problematic. Her hardness is, in a way, its own punishment as she is occasionally self-aware. She says that she does indeed have "defeatures" and "decayed fair," though, again, "A sunny look of his would soon repair" them (2.1.98-99). Her shrewishness, then, chases her husband away, and in turn his absence chases away her beauty and increases her shrillness. Who will be the first to change course in deep forgiveness so that she again is desirable and desired in turn?

Adriana's errors regarding her proper role as proper wife are made worse when she espies Antipholus of Syracuse and confuses him for her Antipholus. One might allow for master/servant confusion as the two exist in such different strata, and one might forgive parent/child confusion given the changes that time works on us all, and one might well forgive merchant/customer or citizen/citizen confusion or courtesan/customer confusion, but the husband/wife confusion that Adriana suffers from seems to be a worse error than the other mistakes of identity. As readers, we must either accept her mistake as natural, or perhaps wonder if it is a mistake that stems from the lack of intimacy between her and Antipholus. After all, Antipholus fails to recognize his father, and Emilia and Egeon need to be introduced. Characters who do not have recent history together fail to recognize one another, and so perhaps, again, there is some suggestion of the distance between Adriana and her husband. The depth of the sense of things being amiss such that no visual or behavioral cue at all can help Adriana distinguish between her husband and his visually exact, but not at all behaviorally exact, twin is both a farcical element and a tragic one. She does not know her own husband, but without some kind of visual cue, she is not allowed to know him, even as the audience is cued in. She says, in the scene of the confusion,

Ay, ay, Antipholus, look strange and frown,
Some other mistress hath thy sweet aspects;
I am not Adriana, nor thy wife.
The time was once when thou unurg'd wouldst vow
That never words were music to thine ear,
That never object pleasing in thine eye,
That never touch well welcome to thy hand,
That never meat sweet-savour'd in thy taste,
Unless I spake, or look'd, or touch'd, or carv'd to thee.
How comes it now, my husband, O, how comes it,
That thou art then estranged from thyself? —
Thyself I call it, being strange to me,
That undividable, incorporate,
Am better than thy dear self's better part. (2.2.110-123)

In this long passage, Adriana unwittingly speaks a partial truth, that she is not Antipholus's wife, but this partial truth is coupled with much that she gets wrong. For she most certainly is Adriana, and she most certainly has had a deeply intimate and physically intense relationship with someone who looks a great deal like the man to whom she is directing this speech. But "thou" art only estranged from himself, in that he has come to Ephesus to lose himself in order to find himself, that he is one drop of water separated from his twinned drop. Though she thinks she senses something amiss in this Antipholus, she can only fit the strangeness into a pre-existing narrative of marital infidelity, in the same way that at first, Solinus can only fit Egeon into a pre-existing narrative of the role of the law.

Because the existence of an exact twin is not at all within Adriana's epistemic sensibility, she is left with psychological theories of madness, strangeness, and magic as explanatory mechanisms. Adriana, then, suffers both from a mistaken sense of familiarity and a mistaken narrative she has constructed to explain the strangeness of the familiar. That the other and the same, the strange and the known, are equally odd does indeed make it hard for Adriana to be properly faithful, but that she should be more aware of her husband's identity and more aware of her own identity ("I am not Adriana") shows the many errors she is committing on the way to re-engaging in a proper marriage at the end of the play. One wonders what Occam's Razor would suggest here. What, really, is the simplest explanation for the sense of strangeness that Adriana notes. Magic? Madness? Profoundly exact twins being confused with one another? Farce may be that which turns Occam's insight upside down and has us look for odder rather than simpler answers.

Antipholus of Syracuse responds to Adriana in an aside, wondering,
To me she speaks, she moves for me for her theme;
What, was I married to her in my dream?
Or sleep I now, and think I hear all this?
What error drives our eyes and ears amiss?
Until I know this sure uncertainty,
I'll entertain the offer'd fallacy. (2.2.181-186)

Beyond the Cartesian dream/waking confusion and the desire for certainty over uncertainty that is explicit here is a far more disturbing notion. Antipholus of Syracuse is willing to engage in the dream/uncertainty situation, even while acknowledging the "fallacy" of it all. That is, he knows that there is something odd and disturbed and disturbing about Adriana's conduct, and yet he decides to give in to the insanity rather than to go to a quiet room and, say, meditate for a week and try to figure out what is more real, and what is most certain. He has already lost his identity in order to find it again, he has felt bereft of the other drop of water, he is fairly sophisticated as a reader of his own situation, and still he is willing to engage improperly, even if only for a brief time.

Antipholus ends the scene and the act with the following admission, even more damning than that above,

Am I in earth, in heaven, or in hell?
Sleeping or waking, mad or well advis'd?
Known unto these, and to myself disguise'd,
I'll say as they say, and persever so,
And in this mist at all adventures go. (2.2.212-216)

To "go native," as it were, were one in heaven, one might fare well. But to do so in hell is not well advised, and to do so not knowing who one is or what is really going on is especially ill-advised. That Antipholus is willing to go along despite his sense that all is wrong, that he is dreaming or mad, that he is undisclosed to himself, suggests a particularly wicked error. To engage with a woman who thinks she is married to him when he is unclear if he is married to her suggests an ignorance of what marriage is about.

Neither of the Antipholi, then, entirely knows how to be married, and Adriana is unclear as well. They are as estranged from their proper roles as they are from one another, and as they are from themselves. The endless levels of estrangement are at every moment fraught with incredulity. Every encounter with self, other, and role, is wrongly engaged in. To have so much go so wrong, morally, in terms of self-identity, in terms of social and marital relations, is all closer to tragedy than not. And yet, for all the oddity of the relations and for all the discomforts that the characters undergo, they continue with a sensibility that is closer to the comic than to the tragic, and by enacting comedy, they preserve the possibility of the comic resolution at the end of the play. Were they, any of them, to interpret their situation tragically, the end of the play would look far more like the end of *Othello*. Death would be meted out for law breaking, for jealousy's sake, and for all the mistakes of identity.

The final push toward Antipholus of Syracuse's acceptance of his new, and completely incorrect role is Adriana's declaration:

Come, come, no longer will I be a fool,
To put the finger in the eye and weep
Whilst man and master laughs my woes to scorn.
Come, sir, to dinner; Dromio, keep the gate.
Husband, I'll dine above with you to-day,
And shrive you of a thousand idle pranks. (2.2.203-208)

Adriana, again, commits more errors. She declares herself no longer to be a fool at her most foolish moment. She refuses her tearful role at home and becomes the aggressor, but is completely wrong in directing her aggression toward Antipholus of Syracuse. When she has Dromio bar the gate, she is actually going to be locking out her rightful husband, and her forgiveness of his "thousand idle pranks" will be directed at the wrong man. She cannot forgive Antipholus of Syracuse for the wrongs of Antipholus of Ephesus, and she cannot forgive Antipholus of Ephesus for her own wrongs.

In a kind of twist on the scene between Adriana and Luciana, that between Adriana and Emilia starts with Emilia's recommending that Adriana ought to have chastised Antipholus of Ephesus for finding "some love that drew him oft from home" (5.1.56). Emilia suggests not only chastising but being even more rough than Adriana has been. Of course, Adriana has been harsh to both her Antipholus and herself. Either Emilia is encouraging Adriana to confess her jealousy, or is pointing out that Adriana has taken the jealousy too far. Adriana's admission of being rough on Antipholus both in private and in public leads Emilia to chastise Adriana,

And thereof came it that the man was mad.
The venom clamours of a jealous woman
Poisons more deadly than a mad dog's tooth.
It seems his sleeps were hinder'd by thy railing,
And thereof comes it that his head is light.
Thou say'st his meat was sauc'd with thy upbraidings;
Unquiet meals make ill digestions;
Thereof the raging fire of fever bred,
And what's a fever but a fit of madness? (5.1.68-76).

Emilia's harsh harangue does three important things here. First, it suggests in no uncertain terms that Adriana's error is that of disturbing her husband with her jealousy such that he ends up not eating well, becoming feverish, and developing a fit of madness. The madness that Antipholus of Syracuse notes is not merely his own but also his twin's. The madness of displacement and loss of identity would seem to be all in the family.

The second task these lines perform is to unite Emilia and Antipholus of Ephesus in anticipation of the mother/son relationship that will soon be disclosed. Emilia is, technically, though not-yet-revealed, Adriana's mother-in-law. This taking to task of the daughter-in-law for the ill-treatment of the son is in keeping with the in-law relationship. Emilia has an instinctual preference for the son she hardly knows over the jealous wife she has never met as daughter-in-law. Furthering this not-yet-disclosed relation is Emilia's history of excessive pride in her sons. Excessive pride may well lead to an excessive fault-finding of an in-law, and an excessive excusing of the son.

The final task here is to unite the two sisters after their earlier dust up over how to be proper wives. Luciana responds to the harangue by saying, "She never reprehended him but mildly, / When he demean'd himself rough, rude and wildly; / Why bear you these rebukes and answer not?" (5.1.87-89). Luciana, here, allies herself with her sister, but undermines her own alliance by noting that normally, Adriana would not at all bear such rebukes. Though the sisters are allied, just as mother and son are allied, the truth is a little bit different from the narrative that is used to formulate the social bonds.

The final set of interchanges in the play shows a dramatic turn from the errors of unrecognition and partial narrative and improper alliances to the sorting out, adding up, and problem-solving interweaving of the various tales. The fantastical and magical are explained away by the stitching together of individual perspectives, and the law, in the person of Solinus, forgives all.

On the way to the resolution of all errors, to complete forgiveness, and epistemic clarity, Adriana exclaims "I see two husbands, or mine eyes deceive me" (5.1.331). And the two Dromios state "I, sir, am Dromio" (5.1.335-336). The Duke says, "These two Antipholus', these two so like . . . " (5.1.347). And the Abbess says,

Renowned duke, vouchsafe to take the pains
To go with us into the abbey here,
And hear at large discoursed all our fortunes;
And all that are assembled in this place,
That by this sympathised one day's error
Have suffer'd wrong, go, keep us company.
And we shall make full satisfaction.
Thirty-three years have I but gone in travail
Of you, my sons, and till this present hour
My heavy burden ne'er delivered.
The duke, my husband, and my children both,
And you, the calendars of their nativity,
Go to a gossips' feast, and joy with me,
After so long grief, such felicity. (5.1. 393-406)

The clarity of the doublings, the undoing of the errors of a lifetime, the apology to all who have suffered for the error of a day, and of thirty-three years (scholars note the error in the dating)—all of these elements have both comic or farcical strains and tragic strains as well. A lifetime of error, while it is ongoing, is tragic, but it ends in felicity and so is comic and joyful. The apology is necessary for the errors, and is more humble than Emilia's original pride. She still gets to show off her wonderful sons, as such, many years later, and with far more of a sense of their flaws. Antipholus of Ephesus has not been the best of husbands, and Antipholus of Syracuse has been willing to play along with the fantastical. Everyone is older, perhaps wiser, and certainly more full of suffering after years of separation.

Chain, ring, ducats, and life are all returned to their rightful places, and the commercial world retreats even as the characters retreat into the abbey to hear a dilated discourse of all the events that have befallen the characters for the last twenty-five or thirty-three years.[15]

The comedy of the play is comprised of a series of tragic errors, mistakes in judgment, wrong perceptions, commercial incursions into family life, and at the heart of it all, the sale and purchase of the Dromios. That original tragic decision to separate a family, to turn the Dromios into slaves or servants from the earliest moments of their lives, and to see this transformation as comic rather than as tragic, is in the end, what all the characters must overcome through their journeys and separations and reunions.

The Odyssean and Socratic elements here abound. Separation, growing up without proper family, journeying in an attempt to reconstruct a fallen life, war between islands, misreading the proper boundaries between commerce and social life, and finally, thinking you are in a comedy and missing the tragic, thinking you are in a tragedy and missing the comic—all of these play a role in the workings out of the plot. Each of these causes a range of moments of incredulity in the face of loss and at the moment of discovery and peripety. The correction of mistaken impressions, the person who is other than one thinks, the loss that is re-found, the recasting of one's perceptions—these all come about in moments of shock, and they come about in the face of tragic and comic confusions.

A Cartesian look at the action of the play would note that indeed the uncertainty inherent in pride, in the identity of twins, and in a kind of assumption that the way the world has gone is the way it must go, that error is not always lurking. There is room for a kind of skepticism throughout, especially at the moment of the adoption of the Dromios. The Derridean counterpoint, though, is that twins are indeed twinned and that being skeptical rather than open to the familiarity would be problematic. The community must function with a kind of communal knowledge, and there would be no way to be properly skeptical of the friendship one feels for someone so familiar. The Dromios are the same, the Antipholi are the same. To offer friendship to the one you see is a kind of necessary social gesture.

Where the worst of the tragedy could be headed off, it turns out, is in the original taking of the twins. It is this act, an undemocratic, unkind, unthinking, unanalyzed act that causes the problems. If Egeus does not grab from every dish, as it were, he would not be deprived of his family, nor would he suffer. It is the outsized desire for these additional children, these young servants, that causes the near tragic outcome. The proper place for skepticism, then, is not in perception but rather in the initial desire. Once that has been set up, though, the acts of trust throughout the play are more appropriate.

NOTES

1. Northrup Frye, "The Argument of Comedy," in *Shakespeare: An Anthology of Criticism and Theory 1945-2000*. Edited by Russ McDonald (MA: Blackwell Publishing, 2004), 93.
2. Frye, "The Argument of Comedy," 94.
3. Frye, "The Argument of Comedy," 94.
4. Frye, "The Argument of Comedy," 97.
5. Martha Tuck Rozett, "The Comic Structures of Tragic Endings: The Suicide Scenes in Romeo and Juliet and Antony and Cleopatra," in *Shakespeare Quarterly* 36 (2) (Summer 1985): 153.
6. Vincent Petronella, "Structure and Theme Through Separation and Union in Shakespeare's *The Comedy of Errors*," in *MLA Review* 69 (3) (July 1974): 481–482.
7. Maurice Hunt, "Slavery, English Servitude, and *The Comedy of Errors*," in *English Literary Renaissance* 27 (1) (December 1997): 31–56.
8. Hunt, "Slavery, English Servitude and *The Comedy of Errors*," 31.
9. Hunt, "Slavery, English Servitude and *The Comedy of Errors*," 44.
10. Hunt, "Slavery, English Servitude and *The Comedy of Errors*," 56.
11. Curtis Perry, "Commerce, Community and Nostalgia in *The Comedy of Errors*," in *Money in the Age of Shakespeare*. Edited by Linda Woodbridge (New York: Palgrave, Macmillan, 2003), 42.
12. Richard Henze, "*The Comedy of Errors*: A Freely Binding Chain," in *Shakespeare Quarterly* 22 (1) (Winter 1971): 41.
13. Shankar Raman, "Marking Time: Memory and Market in *The Comedy of Errors*," in *Shakespeare Quarterly* 56 (2) (2005): 180.
14. Perry, "Commerce, Community and Nostalgia in *The Comedy of Errors*," 40.
15. See note 400 in *The Comedy of Errors*, Foakes, edited, for the issue of dating or timing the action in the play.

Part II

POLITY, ECONOMY, AND SOCIO-STRATEGIC CHOICE

Prologue
The Republic, *Polity, and Economy*

The basic notion underlying social contract theory is that we are, for a variety of reasons, better off cooperating with one another in some organized scheme than we are fending for ourselves. There are political/moral versions of the worth of cooperation, such as the improvement of our souls or the development of human excellence through cooperation, and there are structural arguments about the worth of working together, such as the provision of non-excludable and non-rival public goods, the elimination of free riders, corrections of market failures, and the mitigation of risk. Each of these sets of problems has both economic and political analogues. Coordination and cooperation can require a certain amount of coercion which is more readily available under some kind of political contract than it is under other public forms. Crucially, contract theory also posits the two-sidedness of rule—those governed consent to the governing system. With there being two parties to the contract, and with the contract's being there to improve on pre-contractual circumstances as a backdrop, this section will look at ways that the balances between these political and economic forces that underpin social relations can be misused and misunderstood, and it will sketch out the consequences for the misuse of the categories of the polity and the economy.

While neither Plato nor Shakespeare is working in an explicitly democratic framework, and indeed the *Republic* is, in part, a sustained attack on the horrors of democracy, both authors explicate the obligations rulers have toward the people, and the obligations people have toward the state. If not explicitly contractual, then, the ruler-ruled relation is thick with obligations, and when those obligations are not met properly, chaos results for both rulers and the people.

This section will argue that the two sides, the political, or what I call the "polity," on the one hand, and the public goods and risk mitigation, or what I call the "economic," on the other hand, are inherently intertwined and cannot at all function without each other. That is, we have both a deep responsibility to one another's betterment, and a deep need to provide public goods and mitigate risk. Choosing only one of these tasks, without seeing the need for both, lands us in the same predicament as we see in part I when comedy and tragedy are at issue. Siding with one term, seeing only like a polity or only like an economy leaves us open to the same frustrations, pains, moments of incredulity, bad action, and self-fulfilling prophecy as does choosing either comedy or tragedy.

"Polity" here is painted with a rather broad brush. Like its original Greek form, *politeia*, it refers to just about anything state-related. The Greek name for Plato's *Republic* is "*politeia*," and so it seems well within the proper boundaries of "polity" to include the moral, social, and human-connectedness issues that arise in the *Republic*. "Polity," then, will be concerned with the most direct human needs and responsibilities that we take on in a state.

The purpose of the polity in the *Republic* is defined in Books I and X almost as bookends to the workings of the polity in the middle books. From the very beginning of Book I we learn that the passing of the torch is a crucial metaphor with both the literal passing, on horseback as a novelty, and the figurative passing as Cephalus gives way to Polemarchus even as Cephalus has himself been handed two generations worth of metaphorical torches.

This passing of the torch, or the handing off, or down, of whatever knowledge has been built up is precisely what education must be concerned with, and so polity encompasses all that has to do with education, with soul turning, with value. Socrates' goal in the course of the dialogue is to try to keep polity separate from other concerns even as the interlocutors push back and demand money, couches, pastries, and other luxuries, along with honor and status. The tensions are such that polity, in the *Republic*, breaks down in Books VIII and IX and gives way to the concerns of money, allocation of goods, and status as measured by accumulation. That money can win out, along with honor and strength, suggests that Socrates' vision fails to deal with the tensions inherent in human preference schemes. This chapter will look at the relations between polity, on the one hand, and economy, on the other, and will show how economic concerns frequently disrupt the proper concerns of polity and lead to numerous moments of incredulity rather than appropriate balance.

"Economy," for the purposes of this work, will encompass notions of transactions between people qua transaction, and not qua people. Economy is concerned with the flow, measurement, and allocation of scarce goods and services, the more impersonal relations of a complex system of flow, and of course, the proper flow of money. Further, economy deals with notions of markets, market failures, and risk. Risk should be thought of as concerned fundamentally with the preservation of, and increase in, one's own status, acquisitions, and futurity.

Working through the concerns about money in the *Republic*, *The Merchant of Venice*, and *Pericles*, I will sketch out a description of economy as a central tool in risk mitigation. The phrase "time is money" will be turned around so that we see that, in fact, money is time; that is, money comes closer to guaranteeing futurity, more time, easier time, better times, than social relations do. Money can buy services that trust cannot guarantee. But, when money is misused, when the economic sphere is brought to bear on the polity, the consequences are swift and severe. Characters suffer horribly when they make improper translations between the two modes and when they make improper transactions. Economy is used, in the two Shakespeare plays especially, as a tool for psychic coping, in what can be termed a "libidinal economy," and as such is deeply problematic. Risk is courted rather than mitigated, systems of repetition, demanded by psychic need are imposed both in the polity and in the economy and wreak havoc in the lives of many of the characters. Finding the proper uses of the economic and the political is central for the functioning of the state and for the imposition of a stable order in which contractual relations can work well and to the benefit of the people.

Because money has a time-sense, it takes on an import that sets it apart from other human activities, becomes an end in itself even as it is the means to the end of futurity. That is, the money/time equivalence makes us value money in itself because valuing money is equivalent to valuing time. Hoarding money is synonymous with hoarding time, and so when an estate is settled, it is done only when time is up, when time is out, when there is no reason left to hoard.

The economist Michael Spence has written about "systemic risk" and notes that, "Systemic risks drive most crises . . . . First, they are not easy to detect with confidence, and are even more difficult to prove. Second, predicting the exact timing of a break point . . . is, and will likely remain, beyond our ability. Finally, crises are highly non-linear events."[1] What Spence points to here is the likelihood that the very system we set up to mitigate risk ends up carrying with it its own risk. Spence limits his discussion to periodic moments of instability of the sort that the economist Hyman Minsky has theorized about.[2] Overconfident traders, feeling the successes more than the failures, end up taking on increasing levels of risk until the system collapses under the failure of mitigation. Risk mitigation, after all, is not risk elimination.

The result of these periodic moments of turmoil can be better managed or worse managed depending on how the political system handles the parties to the collapse and depending on how intertwined the systems of risk are. If my hedging is your risk, and your risk collapses, then my hedging collapses as well and I have been drawn in to your collapse, a dynamic that affects

Ephesus in *The Comedy of Errors*. The more intertwined our systems of risk mitigation are, the more ripples our system will encounter. Spence's note that these moments of instability "impose high social costs on those with the least to do with causing them" reminds us that, indeed, our economic decisions impact our polity and require, therefore, political regulation.

There is, then, a kind of layering of polity upon economy, and economy upon polity such that actions is one sphere have broad implications for other spheres. In the *Republic* we can see this layering effect in the way that the father/son relations devolve, in the way that function matters, and in the way that Socrates insists that the whole must be harmonious rather than the parts being individually happy. Socrates is pushing back at a kind of individualist utilitarian calculus and for a broader notion of justice that looks at the system and not merely at the parts.

If any one of the important parts of the system fails to hedge its risks properly, the system collapses. For Socrates, this collapse is periodic, related to cycles of fertility (546a-547a), to the mystical notion of the need for the destruction of what has been created.[3] Minsky and Spence seem to be not so far from this point of view as there is a sense in their work that stability will inevitably lead to instability.

The accumulation of wealth that can happen within an economic system, the hedging of risk and the buying of time, end up creating a second layer of the economy where it is precisely the dynamics of accumulation that lead to downfall. As is suggested throughout the *Republic*, we run into failure points when we are not fully attuned to truth. The more confident we are in what we think we know, the greater the instability that results from our false confidence in our stability.

The greatest hazard of being born is, of course, the inevitability of dying. Part III will deal with this issue more explicitly, but this section will look at what the risk of death does for our relationships to one another on both the moral and economic fronts. Because death is the ultimate threat, the undoing of the familiar, the last thing we ever do, we find ourselves both drawn into a risk pool (social cooperation) and drawn away from that very risk pool (because we overestimate our ability to manage without others.)

This section will discuss the conflicts in the *Republic* that arise from the tension between the interlocutors' relationship to money and to the polity. Cephalus is quite specifically concerned about money issues as his estate is soon to be handed down; Thrasymachus conflates money, power, desire, and the ability to use money and power to achieve desire; and of course, Socrates explicitly forbids the guardians to have any contact with gold at all. Socrates loses this battle in the long run, in that the collapse of the polity is hastened by the privatization of money, the concerns about estate, and the desires that can be satisfied through the use of money.

The section will turn next to Shakespeare's *Merchant of Venice* to show the layering of concerns about money and concerns about family. Shylock seems to confuse the two, and Antonio seems to reverse the confusion so that we see the overvaluation of money on one side and its undervaluation on the other. Although Shylock is condemned within the play for overemphasizing business relations and underappreciating the beauty of love and proper marriage and charity, the fact remains that the conflict to which he is responding is one over a dowry—the payment of money for love. Money, then, underlies proper marriages, and yet goes unrecognized as such.

The second Shakespeare play to be considered is *Pericles,* which deals explicitly with the psychological reading of economic-like relations. With *Pericles*, we will see a clear working out of libidinal economy, the proper uses of wealth, the perversions which wealth can allow, and the ways that these perversions affect political rule. The key term in this section will be risk. Since both the political system and the economic system are designed, entered into, and encouraged to evolve to help us deal better with risk management, we will consider, for each text, who undergoes risk, and how that risk is managed, mitigated, and how it ends up serving psychic structures.

If *The Merchant of Venice* focuses more on economic issues and their intrusion into the polity in order to help satisfy psychic needs, *Pericles* works the other way and focuses more on the polity and its intrusions into the economic, with a similar range of psychic issues including repetition compulsions. Both texts deal with all three terms, the economy, the polity, and psychic structures, but there is some difference in the emphasis, and this difference will be highlighted to show the importance of balancing the concerns among these domains and avoiding improper boundary crossings. The misuse of either the polity or the economy, the abuse of either for personal psychic gain, causes incredulity in each text.

The twinned notions of hedging risk by enlarging risk pools and the concomitant interdependence we create through this hedging will be developed. If an economy is hyperlocal, say, lodged within one family or one small town or village, and a disruption emerges (weather-related, supply-related, labor-related) the economy can be devastated and those dependent upon it end up destitute. A more complex economy with broader geographic dispersion and with non-family member laborers can more likely withstand an external shock.[4] There is, then, a push toward greater complexity of relations to help deal with the shocks of disruption. Shakespearean drama typically keeps the economy hyper local, and any disruption tends to affect all of the major characters in significant fashion. *The Comedy of Errors*, discussed in part I, has this structure, as do *Merchant* and *Pericles*. Because the economies are small, any one character's misstep, any accident of nature, any stoppage in the flow of money ripples through the whole system and uses significant harm to all the characters.

The *Republic* is also aware of the concerns of the spread of harm from external shocks. What Socrates does to deal with this problem is to think through what it might mean simply to have no economy. This part of the thought experiment is as much a failure as the other parts. There must be exchange, risk must be spread, the political and the economic must run together, but it is not until the end of the work that it becomes clear that the individual is the sole risk bearer. It is his own soul that is at stake. Yet the quality of the society matters, too, as a polity must make space for the study of philosophy. It is always better not to execute Socrates, better to examine one's soul, better to study philosophy. Those who study philosophy, who care for their souls, will be better able to make the ultimate decision about how to live, to the extent possible.[5]

Some of the questions this section will address are: What do we gain or lose or trade off in our attempts to mitigate the risks of being in the world? How do time and materiality affect our notions of risk? This section will include some discussion of recent works in the psychology of risk-evaluation, along with some discussion of some very basic, non-technical economics.

Cephalus's pride, in Book I of the *Republic*, is his fortune. He says, in response to Socrates,

> As a businessman, I am somewhere between my father and my grandfather. The grandfather for whom I am named inherited slightly less than the estate I now have and made it many times as great; my father Lysanias made it less than it is now. I will be glad if I leave my sons here not less, but at least a little more than I inherited. (330b)

Cephalus touches on several major themes of the work in this passage. First, he notes his position with regard to his progenitors not as a genetic or generational position, for were he to be generational, he would note that he is third in line after a grandfather and a father. He locates himself, in fact, in the middle between two elders. He is better than his father, he hopes, and his father is lesser than the grandfather. Cephalus has a preference, then, for outdoing his own father, at least in terms of inheritance.

The issue of outdoing is of profound importance in the notion of justice that Socrates develops in the *Republic*. It is Thrasymachus, the tyrant, who at first thinks outdoing is the preferred strategy, and it is only Socrates' correction that moves Thrasymachus away from this notion, though whether or not Thrasymachus' blush is evidence of his moving away from the desire to outdo is unclear. Thrasymachus does, though, agree that one does not outdo when it comes to instrument tuning, so he has either been moved or has realized that he has been in error in his thinking.

Not only does Cephalus wish to outdo his own father, even if not his own grandfather, and not only does he place himself above his father, he also worries about what he will leave his own son. He thinks of this remainder of himself in monetary terms at this point, though he will add to the inheritance soon.

We have, in this small passage, then, an introduction to generational location and to the proper remainders of a life. Outdo your father, leave more than you got, and perhaps be true to your namesake, if not to your father. Julia Annas, in *An Introduction to Plato's Republic*, notes that this tendency to wish to outdo is termed *"pleonexia,"* "the state of always wanting to have more (*pleon echein*)."[6] *Pleonexia* is the wanting of more than what is yours, more than is proper, more than is your due. It can be thought of, for the purposes of this section, as the desire for an inappropriate return on risk, return that is more than you deserve. While Annas looks into the narrowest confines of Socratic arguments and finds them often wanting, it is still worth thinking about the more general sense of proper place, proper amounts, proper returns on investment, and a complete understanding of what happens when we desire reward for our risk, rather than merely accepting the terms of risk as such.[7]

Socrates responds to Cephalus on the notion of outdoing and Cephalus's reaction to his money,

> I asked because you do not seem overly fond of money, I replied. That is generally true of those who didn't make it themselves; those who did are twice as fond of it as other people. Even as poets love their own poems and fathers their children, so businessmen care about money as a work of their own, and of course for its usefulness, as others do too. (330b-c)

Socrates' response, which garners Cephalus's assent, is equally crucial for setting up a reading of the lines from economy to polity and back. The concerns of money makers are circumscribed by their money, just as any craftsperson has a preference for what he has created. If a father creates both children and money, the father may have a hard time preferring the child over the money, and the preference for the money may outdo the preference for the child, a structure we see in *The Merchant of Venice*. Thus, Cephalus's grandfather, Cephalus, may have raised Cephalus's father with less concern than Cephalus, Jr.'s father raised Cephalus, Jr. Cephalus, Jr. hopes to leave more money for his own children, and thus perhaps has a little more regard for money than did his own father, but he has less regard for money than did his grandfather.

The familial regard for money is central to the development of the monetization of social relations that we will see in Shakespeare's work. At this point, though, it suffices to note that makers of money love their money, just as makers of things and works love their things and works, and makers of people love the people whom they make.

The standard Socratic notion of one function per soul jumps out at this point and we quickly realize that one cannot both love the money one makes and love the child one makes. Choices will be made, and when those choices place money above people, when economy takes over from polity, we lose the proper excellence of the state, which is to care for the citizens and not for wealth.

Cephalus returns to the topic of the value and purpose of money,

> It is in this that I assume the greatest value of having money consists, not perhaps for everyone, but for those who are decent and well-ordered. Not to have cheated or misled anyone even unintentionally, nor again to owe sacrifice to a god or money to a man and then depart to that other world in fear—the possession of money in large part makes this possible. (331b)

Here, Cephalus is enlarging on his sense that the aged spend many sleepless nights doing accounting work, making lists, and checking them multiple times to see if they have harmed or cheated anyone, have committed large or small injustices. The having of money is a kind of insurance policy against the risk of doing injustice and facing punishment in the afterlife. Indeed, having money, and living in a well-ordered society, would seem to be the prerequisites of being just to one's children and one's fellow citizens.

We know from Book X of the *Republic* that, in fact, Cephalus has this point backward. It is precisely the well-ordered nature of the society and the ease of being just that lead people to mishandle their most important decision. What is owed is not some sum of money, but rather some kind of soul. Because Cephalus misreads his duty, misreads the purpose and value of money, misreads his duty to his son, because he reduces human relations to accounting tactics, he is inexorably headed in a direction he will regret.

Julia Annas reminds us that, "Plato was writing for an audience that knew that the security based on wealth which Cephalus had spent his life building up, and which is so much stressed here, was wholly illusory: only a few years later, when Athens fell, the family was totally ruined, Polemarchus executed, and Lysias driven into exile."[8] One of the fundamental categories Cephalus gets wrong then, and one that will be taken up multiple times in this section of the book, is that of risk and risk management or mitigation. Cephalus sees risk inherent in human relations that require debt to be taken on, and he sees these relations as inherently monetized rather than as political or familial in origin. The risk is that one could die indebted to another for some transaction or some deed or some object, and the debt could be visited upon one's soul in some version of the afterlife. Cephalus, in poetic form, imagines such an afterlife as a transactional time in which accounts are squared, punishments are meted out, and he puts in a good word for hope that such accounting will come up properly even. Even his poetry, then, is the creation of an accountant's mind, and his hope as well is an accountant's hope.[9]

Cephalus's checkbook justice works in his favor, so he thinks, because it is what he already does in his life. He has given up bodily pleasures because it is easy to do when one is old, he has defined justice as what he is doing now, paying debts, and in these definitions he has conjured, Cephalus has eased his mind, mitigated the risk to his soul, and made the life of his children easier. In short, he has done everything he could think of to deal with the single biggest risk of being alive—doing injustice and being punished for it.

But because Cephalus improperly identifies justice as an economic or transactional entity, he has mitigated the wrong risk and has actually put his soul in more jeopardy than he realizes. Not only is his own soul at risk, of course, but so are the lives of his children, if we are to read the Myth of Er as descriptive of Cephalus's future.

Stanley Rosen writes of the transactional notion of justice, "[J]ustice is not a transaction between an art and its material, such as medicine and the body, but between human beings. There are two kinds of justice, corresponding to public and private transactions. One of the most difficult questions about justice is whether political justice is the basis for private justice or vice versa."[10] What Rosen is suggesting here is that there are nuanced senses of justice running through the *Republic*, a notion that might push back some at what the theory of Forms tries to get at and which seems to suggest that the doing away of the entire private sphere is a wrongheaded move on Socrates' part. If there is a preservation of a private sense of justice that we use despite Socrates' preference for a formal and substantive notion, then much of the *Republic* is misargued. Further, if there is still a transactional notion of justice that is preserved, then Cephalus's and Polemarchus's positions are less wrong-headed than they seem.

There is room for a part of what Rosen is arguing for, in the end however. What gets preserved, and what I will deal with in part III of this book, is a non-transactional obligation of service to the other. This non-transactional notion of justice is not really private (in Rosen's sense of Socrates' doing away with the private sphere) nor is it really public (in the sense of the requirements of the city). Rather, it is a condition of humanity, especially of philosophy, to serve the world regardless of any return on investment. It cannot be thought of as "the fair or equitable" as it is not at all related to comparisons to the duties or fulfillment of duties of others. It is not a fair return on investment, as there is no investment, and as the expectation of return is what gets us in trouble in the Myth of Er.[11]

If Cephalus misunderstands the category of the economic, he partially compensates for this misunderstanding by bequeathing not just money to his son, Polemarchus, but also a discussion with Socrates. For one's soul, there may be nothing better than going toe-to-toe with a barefoot philosopher. But Polemarchus is an indifferent, confused, muddled student who does not end up benefiting from this inheritance. Polemarchus engages more in the discussion than does his father, but the engagement is not fruitful. Socrates' investment, and Cephalus's bequest, end up losing value. Polemarchus's stated agreement to "join the fray" to defend the help friends/harm enemies notion of justice ascribed mistakenly to Simonides, or Pittacus (336e).

Underlying Polemarchus's changing views here are first, a notion that there is anything due a just or unjust person, a friend or enemy. That we are to "pay" one another based on the state of our souls or that we should help or reward, harm or punish, is a restatement of the transactional notion of justice that Cephalus espouses and that Polemarchus has inherited. Though Polemarchus changes his view on the help-and-harm-are-due-friends-and-enemies definition of justice, he has kept this very notion and merely changed it so that he is willing to harm those who say that Simonides says that harm is due to those who are our enemies or those who are unjust. Benardete notes that Polemarchus's move is to go from a "neutral" sense of debt to a more particularized notion.[12] Debt is owed in particular ways to particular people, and is paid, seemingly, transactionally.

Reducing justice to the transactional is to turn human relations into economic relations and thus to miss a layer of debt that is not at all transactional, but is social or political. As a father, Cephalus owes Polemarchus truth and philosophy, not money. As a philosopher, Socrates owes all of his interlocutors good arguments in favor of truth, and a communicative strategy that works. He may well owe poetry along with argumentation. Rosen notes that poetry, like money, is a thing we make and therefore that we love.[13] Our love is triggered by things we make and therefore is a kind of self-love. Self-love, or the love of one's own products, is precisely what Socrates wants to move beyond, and so poetry, money, and even eventually children, must be stripped from the guardian class. But, perhaps contradicting Rosen, it may be that Socrates needs a communicative strategy replete with poetry, that Socrates owes poetry, that Cephalus with the right kind of poetry is a better father than Cephalus without poetry. If poetry can aim us in the right direction, as creation aims the soul in the *Symposium*, then, as a step on the ladder up, poetry may well be something owed. The text is in tension with itself over this issue, as it clearly uses poetic images to gesture beyond itself even as it argues for concerns regarding the status of poetry.

The status, then, of the debt, is perhaps more complex than Rosen's gesture here.

If poetry is something owed, at least by Socrates, and maybe by Cephalus, it is a kind of "soul debt," not a monetary debt, and it is paid through the polity, and through the relation of the parts of the soul to one another, and through the relationship between soul and truth. Materiality, money, and transactions as such play no proper role in the Socratic notion of justice, and yet these are precisely the things that lead to the downfall of the beautiful city Socrates draws.

Socrates' purity, then, is as much a problem for the city and for justice and for our souls as is Cephalus's and Polemarchus's transactional justice. Justice, then, cannot simply do away with transaction, nor can it be only transaction. Rather, transactions must be done justly. Combining any action with justice is the specific function of the soul's guidance.

After Thrasymachus's lunging, beastlike, into the conversation, money comes up as a topic, but is diverted momentarily by Socrates. Thrasymachus challenges Socrates, "[W]hat if I indicate a different answer about justice beside all these, and better than they are . . . . What penalty would you pay?" (337d). Thrasymachus, here, is suggesting that he has an answer about the nature of justice that will outdo the answers Socrates has suggested Thrasymachus would not accept. And not only does Thrasymachus boast here that he has a better answer than any such thing, he further boasts that Socrates will have to pay a penalty to Thrasymachus as the reward for a wager.

Underlying the plot-level issues here is first the idea that money should transfer from Socrates to Thrasymachus because Thrasymachus has a truthful definition of justice. Thrasymachus, then, keeps a sense of justice as transaction; in this case, though, the transaction is an exchange of truth for money rather than a Cephalean exchange of money for harm done. Thrasymachus seems willing to keep silent if he is not paid for his wisdom, while Cephalus would pay in order to avoid the harm of inappropriate silence or voice.

Further, Thrasymachus is trapped in the help/harm, reward/punish notion of justice that is, itself, transactional. What is owed is money to Thrasymachus and truth from Thrasymachus, but it is a truth that must be paid for in the money economy rather than a truth that must be granted through the obligations of the polity.

Socrates suggests a counter-punishment (of the sort he offers in the *Apology*) and suggests that he might pay the penalty of the ignorant, "to learn from one who knows" (337d). This counter, though not monetary, and therefore not at all what Thrasymachus wants, is a play on the notion of payment, duty, and reward. If you do not yourself know, you are obligated to learn. If you do know, you are obligated to explain. Not-knowing is a more painful state than is knowing, and so there is an incentive built into this non-monetary transactional system that makes the burden of knowledge more bearable than it might otherwise be.

Glaucon, pragmatically, offers actual money for the transaction, and in doing so, shows that he fails to understand Socrates' challenge to Thrasymachus. "Speak for the money, Thrasymachus: we will all contribute for Socrates" (337d). The goal, as we noted in part I, cannot be the reward for deeds. The transactional definition of justice is, in itself, problematic, and in itself leads directly to the eating of one's own children presented in the Myth of Er. The reward we seek is not the reward we should seek, and upon gaining this seeming reward, we experience the originary moment of incredulity.

The following interchange between Thrasymachus and Socrates further develops this theme:

> So this is the wisdom of Socrates! He refuses to teach, but goes around learning from others and offers no thanks in return.
>
> . . .
>
> It is true that I learn from others, Thrasymachus, I replied, but you are wrong to claim I do not pay thanks. I pay what I can, but I can only pay in praise, because I do not have money. This I do eagerly, if I think someone speaks well, as you will very soon learn when you answer; for I am sure you will speak well. (338b)

Again, there is an issue of transaction. Socrates is taking from others, and in Thrasymachus's account, is not even decent enough to offer thanks. Socrates promises a laudatory response even before Thrasymachus speaks. There is, in Socrates' note, an interesting challenge to what would otherwise be a game theoretic impasse. Socrates is publicly pre-offering to avoid a situation in which Thrasymachus is not assured he will get a return on investment, and given that Thrasymachus is overly invested in his own self-regard, he is willing to offer the following, "Listen then, he replied. I say the just is nothing other than the advantage of the stronger. Well, where is your praise? You won't give it!" (338c). Though Thrasymachus agreed to his side of the transaction or bargain, and though Socrates pre-agreed to hand out praise to a good argument and to the one who delivers it, Socrates has failed at the instant to perform as Thrasymachus thinks has been contracted. Thrasymachus risks his self-regard, Socrates pre-promises to praise that very self-regard's foundation, and all in an instant, the transaction is not completed, the economy has hit a wall, and Thrasymachus replies to Socrates, "You are disgusting, Socrates. You understand me in the way you can best hurt the argument" (338d). If the argument is the enemy, clearly, helping friends and harming enemies is a part of justice.

What happens if, indeed it is the case that arguments can be enemies, that one can accurately identify friend and enemy arguments, and that it is right to harm enemy arguments? At some level, this doing of harm to enemy arguments is the Socratic method. He may outsource the actual harm-doing to the one who offers the enemy argument, but he is the origin of the harm to the argument.

If the argument is part of the man, if it is taken personally, if it is part of one's identificatory structure, then to harm the argument is to harm the man, so constituted. But, of course, harming the enemy argument may leave room for a friend argument to move in and become constitutive of the man. Our souls are better off with true arguments rather than with false ones, and so we should be grateful for the help Socrates offers. He does not charge much, he cleans up our souls, helps us destroy bad arguments, and leaves us in a better place.

Unless he does not actually do any such thing. Thrasymachus will soon find himself blushing (350d);[14] the argument will restart with less combativeness, and the result will be that "injustice is never more profitable than justice" (354a). On the way to this conclusion, Socrates says,

> Thank you again, my friend. But tell me this: if it is the work of injustice to introduce hatred wherever it is present, will it not when it comes to be present among people, whether free men or slaves, cause hatred and faction among them, and render them incapable of acting in common with each other? . . . . If it should come to be present in two people, won't it set them at odds? They'll be enemies and hate both each other and those who are just. (351e-352a)

The reference to "my friend" is significant for suggesting that the man, Thrasymachus, is a friend and ought not to be hurt, in contrast to any argument in defense of injustice, which argument must be destroyed. Such an argument will divide people, make the performance of functions both socially and internally to the person unworkable, and will cause a social breakdown such that justice itself becomes hated.

At the same time, though, any argument that frustrates Thrasymachus, that does not give him the respect he feels he demands, is going to have a similar effect. If the argument and the man cannot be entirely separated, if what Thrasymachus is, is his arguments regarding how he should live, then Socrates is doing harm both to a friend and to the very society he is trying to defend.

There are, then, two levels of incredulity in dealing with Thrasymachus. The first level is Thrasymachus's own incredulity that his argument was not part of a properly concluded financial transaction in which the rules, as he understood them, were followed as he saw fit. The second level is Socrates' incredulity when he realizes that in the name of helping he may very well have harmed.

Because the discussion between Thrasymachus and Socrates is transactional, and even financial, the two end up with a kind of tension that can cause profound social division. Further, because the transaction does not follow quite the pattern Thrasymachus expects of such exchanges, Thrasymachus has room to feel unjustly treated. He concludes with a more charitable line, "Let this be your feast at the Festival of Bendis, Socrates" (354a). But if all Thrasymachus has gotten out of the exchange is a well-fed, or even gluttonous guest, as Socrates describes himself at the end of Book I, then clearly Socrates has failed to help and harm as he needs to, and the whole transactional underpinning of the argument has failed.

Because transaction is only a partial model of social interaction, and because it is an economic model rather than a polity-oriented model, it leaves us very much in the wrong place, with the wrong goals, and susceptible to incredulity. Thrasymachus, in Book I, assumes that polity itself is transactional and that the tyrant wins all transactions. Further, he assumes all discussion and definition are transactional and that he, feeling his own self-worth, will beat the odds here as well. He, like the thieves who need to be just among themselves if they are to succeed, must also try to overcome some of the transactional behaviors in his interactions with Socrates. He gives up one kind of power game during the interchange, that of the "stronger," and he further gives up payment for his answer despite feeling that he deserves the reward, and in the place of these he becomes the magnificent and generous host of a feast and celebration in which a torch is passed.

The Thrasymachus who is a generous host may not be any better at torch-passing than the Thrasymachus for whom justice is the advantage of the stronger, especially given Socrates' self-confessed boorish behavior at the banquet of words and gods. A generous Thrasymachus may be generous only strategically, in which case Socrates has truly had no success in his time going down to the Piraeus.

The *Republic* begins with the problem of engaging in conversation, notes that the passing of the torch on horseback is an unusual sight, and is not really the right way to pass the torch. Cephalus, too, fails to pass the torch, for his torch is more financial than not, and Thrasymachus has failed with regard to the torch. He suggests payment for teaching; that is, a transaction or reward for helping his friends come to know the truth. He only helps his friends if they help him, and they are only his friends insofar as they are helping him. If friendship, truth, justice, and all social practice are transactional, then we will be limited by all the considerations of profit, self-interest, error, risk-bearing ability, risk aversion, and the gloss of seeming truth that profit seems to paint on human action and human thought.

The glistering objects of Thrasymachean fancy are not the kinds of objects that will bring about a just state, but are instead more likely to bring us to a point where we cry havoc and blame the gods for our unfortunate banquet. And though the ultimate horror is, as we have noted in part I, the feasting upon one's children, Book I ends with Socrates' banquet of words, a seemingly less risky dinner choice. Words, though, do have significance and the risks of arguing the wrong way, or for the wrong position, or in a way that incites wrong action are part of what Socrates risks as he fulfills his obligation.

To the extent that Socrates can be taken as a figure equivalent to language or argument, to the extent to which he is a personification of philosophical discourse, he can be read as a kind of cannibal at the banquet of words in Book I, a nice parallel with what happens in the Myth of Er in Book X. Devouring in both sections, certainly, and then one is led to ask precisely what Socrates is in his devouring. Does he eat his own children, the children of others, himself, an imitation of himself, or perhaps an imitation of philosophical arguments at an imitation of a banquet? Without pushing too hard here, we can still note that the parallels in imagery and the ring structure of the dialogue together link these scenes in interesting ways.[15]

Book II of the *Republic* is taken up with what might be termed a cost/benefit analysis of the practice of justice. Is it worth being just? Is justice profitable? Does it pay to be just? The answer to each of these questions rests on a notion that one should receive benefit for right action, that one should be rewarded, that something should come from both the effort of being just (for it is not fun), and for the cost of being just (for there are significant opportunity costs in any just action.)

The story of the Ring of Gyges, the magic ring that turns you invisible when you turn it around on your finger, is part of the working through of the costs and benefits of just actions. Gyges, a shepherd, and suddenly a grave robber, takes the ring from a mysterious body that is in a mysterious underground chasm and he puts the ring on, discovers that he is invisible and launches a career of crime (359d-360d). In imagining an unjust man like Gyges, the grave robber with the ring and a just man with a second such ring, Glaucon suggests that,

> No one would be of such unyielding strength, it would seem, that he should abide in justice and submit to keeping his hands off the belongings of others and not touch them, when it was possible for him to take without fear whatever he pleased from the marketplace, and enter houses and have intercourse with whomever he wished, kill or release from prison anyone he wished, and otherwise act among men as equal to a god. (360b-c)

Clearly, Plato wrote this all long before the e-ring of anonymous internet file sharing. Aside from all the music and movies that travel across the web, the timeless quest for material goods, sex, murder, prison release, and playing god seem to be as potent for Glaucon as they ever are for anyone. It is pretty convincing, at this moment, that an inviso-ring is a tempting thing for anyone.[16]

Adeimantus tag-teams with Glaucon to strip away any reason for being just so that the unjust man has the reputation of being just, the just man has the reputation for being unjust. The cost for being just, then, becomes nearly infinite. Can anything that bears nearly infinite cost ever be said to be "worth it," or is the cost so great that no one would willingly bear it for justice?

If justice were to come with such grave risk that it no longer seemed worthwhile to practice justice, then we may have come to the limiting case for social organization. A society that "prices" justice so that it is not worth it, that allows Thrasymachus's desires to determine the worth of justice, that rewards the unjust for their seeming justice, that suggests that justice is transactional and so only the wealthy or those with means can practice justice cannot, definitionally, be a just society. It is only in a society in which,

> [J]ustice is among the greatest goods, which are worth possessing for their consequences but much more for themselves alone—like seeing, hearing, thinking and being healthy, and all other goods genuine in their own nature rather than by appearance—please then praise this very thing about justice: how justice in and of itself benefits him who has it, and injustice harms. (367c-e)

Adeimantus, here, asks that justice be removed from the transactional and defended in itself. It has instrumental value, but its chief value is intrinsic. Asking as he does next that "rewards and appearances" be left out, that the wages of justice be left out, that good and evil themselves be the main determinant is precisely to take polity away from economy, to take the soul and its relationship to itself, to other souls, and to the gods as the chief concern and to omit any thought of exchange, profit, instrumental good, bargaining power, or any other economic notion.

The one telling mistake Adeimantus makes here is to preserve a sense that perhaps the gods know if you are being bad or good. He lacks the strength to be good solely for the sake of the good and retains some desire for recognition. A proper defense of the just life is one that would take no account of the notice of gods or men, but Adeimantus is not able to give up all sense of reward for being good. The desire for any reward at all is, as we have noted in part I, a significant contributor to the moment of incredulity that the first soul to choose ends up experiencing.

The beginning sketch of the city starts with Socrates' noting that "we are not each self-sufficient, but lack many things" (369b). Our incompletion means that we are at any moment economic as well as political beings. There are, clearly, transactions that must take place among providers of food, shelter, and clothing (369d). And since people do better at one task than at many, the exchanges make for better provisioning.

What matters at this stage are two underlying issues. The first is that there is an instrumental underpinning to the state—we actually use the division of labor so that we have a better material life, we are not at all independent from one another—and second, at the lowest level of the economic, there is a moment that is transactional. The transactional will be surpassed, though, by the notion of debt that goes beyond providing roofs in exchange for shoes or grain in exchange for minimal clothing. It is worth remembering that Socrates recommends nudity in the summer, and the most basic of foods, nothing that could be likened to the banquet at the end of Book I. All material provisions, in the first telling of the state, are hyperminimal.

The hyperminimal economy gives way quickly to a somewhat thicker telling, with imports, exports, seamen, merchants, craftsmen, shopkeepers, and laborers who all seem to provide bodies for money. There are, then, minds, on the one hand, and, on the other, there are movers, people who mark time in the market, bodies and muscles, and they all come together to make a mildly complex city, but one that might seem to satisfy many of our desires in a somewhat complicated way. There are many moments of transaction, many points at which non-compliance or non-performance could ripple through the system and cause significant problems for others.

Glaucon counters that even this more complex system is fit for a "city of pigs" and not, apparently for a city of people (372d).[17] He wants his "couches" and his "tables" and his "relishes and desserts" (372d). The addition of comfortable furniture, comfort foods, and customary accoutrements adds a new round of producers and consumers, transactions, wealth and all that goes with wealth—the need for territory, guardian soldiers, private space, additional complexity, and ever more emphasis on the material rather than on the relational or abstract space between subjects.

The progression from a hypersimple economy in which justice is easy to implement and monitor, in which transactions are direct, local, face-to-face, and carried out with known implications to a far more complex economy in which the impersonal other provides satisfaction of all of one's desires, in which labor is hidden, in which the conditions other people live in disappear in the face of material provision is the progression from a city in which justice can take root to one in which injustice is the natural product of social relations (372e).

And it is precisely this progression away from simple face-to-face transactions carried out with the face of the other immediately present to the transaction that makes injustice most likely. It is always worth remembering, of course, that the laborers are not recognized as faces and souls so much as muscle groups, and so there is, as ever, reliance on non-participants to ease the lives of those most implicated in a system of justice. The more impersonal the transaction, the easier it is to dismiss the other party's worth as a soul, and the more likely it becomes that injustice will result.[18]

Because of the territorial needs of a complex and desiring society and the need for internal protections from fellow citizens, this present version of the city requires an entire social class of guardians, or soldiers, whose job is to protect without threatening, to keep without using, to be useful when things are useless and useless when things are useful, to know what they know and what they do not know such that they only attack the unknown which, by definition, is inimical to the peace. They are to be dog-like, though not pig-like, even though they are guarding something of a piggish city. They are trained to avoid strong emotions, to think anything that might make them attack their own kind, to value anything that might make them have private rather than public purpose. The guardians, then, are the keepers who need not be watched as they have fully internalized their disdain for all things material. They are philosophic in temperament and as such they value the abstract over the concrete. They have no use for actual gold, and so they will not rob the keepers of the national treasure. Socrates describes them,

> First, none to have any dwelling or storehouse not open to anyone who wishes to enter. Provisions needed by temperate and courageous men in training for war to be received from other citizens as pay for being Guardians, in the exact amount needed for the year. Common meals, and living together as though on campaign. They are told that they always have in their soul divine gold and silver from gods and no need of the human kind in addition, that it is impious to sully possession of the former by mixing it with mortal dross, because many unholy things are occasioned by the popular currency, but what is present within the is undefiled. (416d-417a)

There is no privacy or space for being unknown or unpublic. Without space, so it would seem, we cannot develop fantasies that would turn us away from the good of all, nor can we devise secret transactions or the even the mere desire for such a transaction. There is only one set of books, as it were.

The guardians are paid for by the rest of the citizens, so the debt incurred on either side is satisfied year-to-year, with no additional debt that might require private transactions, and no chance of an unpaid debt that might create the desire for private space and secret dealings. Because the guardians have abstract gold in their abstract souls, they can turn away from the concrete variety and stay separate from the common run of man who are ever desiring a return to the gold standard. The standard in the *Republic* is that of abstract value. Not being allowed to touch material gold, and even being taught that material gold is unclean, ruinous, helps preserve the guardian class as guardians. As long as the gold around them is useless to them, the guardians can be useful to the state. Should gold become useful to the guardians, the state is lost.

Returning to Cephalus's value system here, we see that his set of concerns has been turned upside down and inside out. While he expresses the certitude that money is what makes justice possible, Socrates has shown that in fact, money is what makes justice impossible. Only there are some modifications here. The fact is that the guardians will need upkeep, and that upkeep will come from taxation, and that taxation is dependent on precisely the commercial transactions that the merchant class engages in. There is, then, a distanced dependence on defilement. We will see a similar pattern in Shakespeare's *Merchant of Venice*.

Cephalus expresses the sense that money hedges risk. It is money that allows us to live just lives because with money we are never in a position in which lying, cheating, stealing or other property or promise breaches are necessary for the preservation of our lives. We have time precisely because we have money and we have life, liberty, happiness, and the like also because we have money. The hazards of life are all mitigated by the addition of money, hence money is the ultimate hedge. Except, of course, it does not ever hurt to go to sacrifice and commit oneself to religious belief in conjunction with money. You never know what you do not know, and so it can be a good policy to hedge the hedge, just in case. And if you are not quite right about money and about religion, you can always leave things to the next generation, too. Thus, Cephalus has a triple hedge in the hopes that he will have a more peaceful soul after death.

If Socrates is right, though, money defiles, the gods are crazy, and the next generation will devolve. It is only through philosophy that we can properly hedge the looming disaster, and what philosophy does at its finest is to destabilize everything we think we know. The comfort of couches and pastries, the purchase of time through money, the certainties we walk around with are all misdirected attempts at balancing the forces of risk and anxiety, and they all need to be disposed of.

Books VIII and IX of the *Republic* show the problems with the attempts to hedge risk and create a private space in which private concerns over longevity and personal power and status lead to precisely the opposite outcomes from what the great hope suggests. It all starts with this passage from VIII,

Difficult it is for a city so founded to be moved. But since all that comes to be admits destruction, not even this kind of foundation will abide for all time, but will suffer dissolution. Its dissolution is this: not only for plants in the earth but also for animals upon it, there comes fertility and barrenness of soul and bodies, when the revolutions for each complete the circumferences of their circles, short for the short-lived, oppositely for the opposite. As for your own kind of propitious birth and barrenness, wise though the leaders of the city whom you have educated may be, they will not the more by calculation combined with perception hit upon them, but miss, and sometimes will beget children when they ought not. (546a-b)

The suggestion here is first, that nothing lasts forever, and so the attempt to hedge the ultimate risk by building a city in which nothing can go wrong is simply an empty fantasy. The city cannot be built because the city cannot fulfill its function for more than a brief time, however long that time is. It will always be more brief than the totality of human time and so it will always fail. If the soul is immortal, every soul will end up at the fail point, and so at some level, the actions of humans matter less than they might seem to.

The second issue here is that the cycles that lead to the failure of human society, and plant life and animal life for that matter, will lead to the births of children who cannot fit into the proper slots the society has created. A child who does not fit in to the social system is still a child who is loved by a parent, and that child will give rise to a push for private wealth. Not everyone will agree to infanticide or to limited fertility or to the notion that a child is not equivalent to money.

The child who is not exposed in infanticide, who occasions the move toward private family life, in whose name private fortunes are to be amassed, is the child who ends up nearly synonymous with money. When Shylock confuses his jewels and his daughter, when the Dromios' parents sell their sons, when Dionyza has Marina killed because she upstages her own daughter, there is a clear sense that money and shiny things are being conflated with people. In each case, the parent wants very much to preserve his or her own child, and in each case the parent ends up worsening the condition of the child rather than improving the condition.

Thrasymachus's relationship to the economic in Book I comes largely through his sense that justice involves the garnering of all scarce resources for the ruler, and any weakness on the part of the ruler, any distribution of resources that benefits others at the expense of the ruler is improper. When pushed, Thrasymachus backs off of this argument a piece at a time. We can see from both Thrasymachus's initial preferences and his (perhaps) changed views that proper rule requires that a ruler not rule for himself and not rule from the vantage point of the economy. The polity, the sphere of human value, needs to guide all other preferences.

When the values of the polity are transferred to the economy, when justice becomes mere transaction, when reward becomes the goal, the political system falls toward tyranny. The trajectory of the *Republic* is precisely this fall from a philosophic state that abides as polity to a material state that abides as economy. Polity may well need moments of economy, as there are some transactions that are part of the basic maintenance of life, but this economy is a restricted one that is guided by the demands of the polity.

As the fall of the state snowballs, more and more parts of human life become bound by economic concerns. Doctors become money makers, just men become unjust, desires and the inner beast come to rule. People steal from their parents, tyrants refrain from no food or deed, and eventually everyone is potentially a cannibal, mutual devouring becomes the rule.

We will see, in the sections on *The Merchant of Venice* and *Pericles*, how the misuse of money, the confusion of polity and economy, and even cannibalism all come together. Money oversteps its boundaries and the economy is made to serve the polity in improper ways, even as the polity is made to serve the economy improperly. Further, the psyches of characters end up in a kind of libidinal economy in which sex, cannibalism, melancholy, and repetition compulsions all flow. The misuses of economic and political structures to satisfy psychic desires repeat the kinds of structures Thrasymachus would put in place were he to rule a state.

Where the *Republic* resolves these tensions through the fall of the state and the retreat for a time of the philosophic soul into his own private space, the Shakespeare plays resolve the tensions by recasting the boundaries between the spheres. The most irredeemable characters are lost, and there is some suggestion of some repetition in cycles not unlike what happens in the *Republic*.

NOTES

1. Michael Spence, "Can We Regulate Systemic Risk?" Project Syndicate, 13 August 2010, accessed 12 January 2017.

2. Minsky notes that periods of stability lead to overconfidence and that very same overconfidence can cause a period of instability. This period of instability after a period of stability has been termed a "Minsky moment." See Hyman Minsky, *Stabilizing an Unstable Economy* (New York: McGraw-Hill, 2008).

3. Sallis links miscalculation and fertility. It is interesting to push this miscalculation a little further. Not only do the rulers make math mistakes, after a fashion, so too does Polemarchus when he fails to calculate who properly is a friend and who properly is an enemy. Cephalus, as well, miscalculates debts, and makes accounting errors of a sort as he measures his father, his grandfather, their wealth, and their worth. Thrasymachus miscalculates the chances he could be wrong. Socrates miscalculates his diet. See Sallis, *Being and Logos*, 452. John Sallis, *Being and Logos: Reading*

the Platonic Dialogues, Third Edition (Bloomington, IN: Indiana University Press, 1996).

4. Partha Dasgupta, *Economics: A Very Short Introduction* (Oxford: Oxford University Press, 2007).

5. Tad Brennan reads the tripartite soul as a set of mediations between the otherworldly nature of reason and the completely world-bound nature of body. Spirit helps appetite and reason communicate, as it were, and allows reason to inhabit the body. He writes, "Spirit, then, can be seen as the necessary bond between two things that would otherwise lack unity." (Brennan, 123) In this reading, all of the layers of risk mitigation we see in the state, and in the Shakespeare plays discussed in this section of the text, also likely appear within the soul. Spirit may well be charged with keeping reason and appetite in a right balance, just as polity and economy must be kept in right balance. See Tad Brennan, "The Nature of the Spirited Part of the Soul and Its Object," in *Plato and the Divided Self.* Edited by Rachel Barney, Tad Brennan, Charles Brittain (Cambridge: Cambridge University Press, 2012), 102–127. See also Mary Margaret Mackenzie, *Plato on Punishment* (Berkeley, CA: University of California Press, 1981), for another nuanced look at the tripartite soul in Plato, and Plato's moral psychology.

6. Julia Annas, *An Introduction to Plato's Republic* (Oxford: Oxford University Press, 1981), 50.

7. Harry Berger, Jr. develops a reading of the *Republic* as largely motivated by concerns over outdoing, or *pleonexia*. He locates this concern in Thucydides' *The History of the Peloponnesian War* as well as in the *Republic,* and he suggests that Plato's overarching concern is the problems that *pleonexia* raises for a society. Berger uses a broad sense of *pleonexia* that includes desire and that is body-based. Certainly desire is a central concern, and the desire for more (which sets up the need for the non-minimal state and the couches and pastries) is important in the *Republic.* Even as Socrates allows the discursive inclusion of more and more into the state, he strips all of the excess and all of desire out of the lives of the philosophers. There is thus something akin to an overstuffed city running parallel to a city on a diet. As the fall of the city progresses in Books VIII and IX we see that the very desire that has been stripped out of the philosophical city is returning one generation at a time. And important concern to think through with this notion of *pleonexia* as foundation in both Thucydides and Plato is the extent to which the "more-ness" is a structural problem rather than a problem of desire. Competition for survival rather than cooperation for survival may contribute to the perceived need for "more" and once there are separate cities (as in *The History of the Peloponnesian War*) or separate people (as Thrasymachus describes the world), or separate parts of the soul (as Socrates suggests), there is room for competition, room for distrust, and thus, room for a structural demand for "more." "More" is life and security and enjoyment, and competing others provide the occasion for the arising of thoughts of "more." We can, then, wonder if the internal philosophical city that Socrates gestures towards at the very end of the text is sufficient for overcoming the problems Berger rightly sees with *pleonexia*. We can, further, wonder if philosophy itself suffers from a need for more—more understanding; or whether philosophy in Socrates' sense of the discipline can be modest and accept less, or even nothing. See chapter 2 of Harry Berger, Jr., *The Perils of*

Uglytown: Studies in Structural Misanthropology from Plato to Rembrandt (New York: Fordham University Press, 2015) for his full and fascinating discussion of this concept.

8. Annas, *An Introduction to Plato's Republic*, 19.

9. Again, for the issue of debt justice, see Shalini Satkunanandan, *Extraordinary Responsibility: Politics Beyond the Moral Calculus* (New York: Cambridge University Press, 2015) and G.R.F. Ferrari, "Glaucon's Reward, Philosophy's Debt: The Myth of Er." In *Plato's Myths*. Edited by Catalin Partenie (Cambridge: Cambridge University Press, 2009), 116–133.

10. Stanley Rosen, *Plato's Republic: A Study* (New Haven, CT: Yale University Press, 2005), 32.

11. See Part I for a full discussion of this issue.

12. Benardete, *Socrates' Second Sailing*, 17. Seth Benardete, *Socrates' Second Sailing: On Plato's Republic* (Chicago, IL: The University of Chicago Press, 1989).

13. Rosen, *Plato's Republic: A Study*, 27–28.

14. As noted above at note 27, a possible reading of Thrasymachus' blush here is that it is a gesture towards a Homeric battlefield victory altered for the purposes of philosophical competition. If Socrates can be said to have "outdone" Thrasymachus, and thought of as having drawn "blood" with the dagger of words, then the moment can be seen as a kind of Socratic appropriation of the Iliadic hero, and a gesture toward the notion of the proper kind of outdoing. One does not outdo a just man, but one may very well outdo an unjust man. One ought not to harm friends, but bad arguments do, indeed, need to be defeated. The cost of being defeated is a blush rather than death.

15. Sallis provides two schematics for the ring structure. See Sallis, *Being and Logos*, 320 and 455.

16. Tangential to the issues raised by the Ring myth are concerns regarding *akrasia*, incontinence. Can we turn down the temptations to overextend, can desire be limited. Just as we must worry about *ataraxia* as a desire for "more" in general, so we must be concerned about *akrasia*, the condition that allows us to want more. Christopher Bobonich addresses the issue of akrasia as stemming from the tripartite structure of the soul in Plato. See Christopher Bobonich, "Akrasia and Agency in Plato's Laws and Republic," in *Essays on Plato's Psychology*. Edited by Ellen Wagner (Oxford: Lexington Books, 2001), 203–237.

17. McCoy provides a reading of the gendering here. The phrase "city of pigs," is a city of "sows," and this term is slang for female genitals. McCoy's suggestion is that Glaucon is dismissing the simple city because of gender anxiety. She notes, as well, that Socrates uses feminine imagery to describe his task as a midwife, and to describe the ascent in the *Symposium*. See Marina McCoy, "The City of Sows and Sexual Differentiation in the *Republic*," in *Plato's Animals: Gadflies, Horses, Swans, and Other Philosophical Beasts*. Edited by Jeremy Bell and Michael Nass (Bloomington, IN: Indiana University Press, 2015), 149–160.

18. Nightingale discusses the issue of the "banausics," or workers, mechanics. See Nightingale, *Spectacles of Truth*, 121–123. Andrea Wilson Nightingale, *Spectacles of Truth in Classical Greek Philosophy: Theoria in Its Cultural Context* (Cambridge: Cambridge University Press, 2004).

Section 2

Melancholy and Risk Analysis in *The Merchant of Venice*

The proper and improper uses of money are at the heart of *Merchant of Venice*. This section will look at the circulation of money and risk and will show that when money is used to combat melancholy or to substitute for love or to extract political revenge, there are consequences. Just as the *Republic* is concerned with the proper place of money, so, too, is *Merchant*; and just as errors regarding the nature of money cause moments of incredulity in the *Republic*, so too do such errors cause shock in *Merchant*.

Antonio's melancholy at the start of the play, Bassanio's love for Portia, the subplot of the caskets, Shylock's treatment of both Antonio and Jessica, and the subplot of the rings all point to the range of errors that *Merchant* deals with. In each case, the misuse of money and the confusion of the boundaries between polity and economy cause the characters to stumble and to suffer.

The soft boundaries between polity and economy are precisely a major source of the problem in the play. The characters do not have easy ways to determine how to proceed at the boundaries of affect, desire, or need and so they all make mistakes in applying the rules of polity and the rules of economy. The miscues, misuses, mistakes everyone makes regarding the proper roles of money and human relations cause moments of incredulity as characters confront death and loss and falsity even as they are expecting to find life and gain and truth.

Antonio begins the play with a simple plaint, "In sooth I know not why I am so sad" (1.1.1). The mystery of Antonio's melancholy and what he does to diagnose and cure it drive much of the action in the play. He notes that "It wearies me, you say it wearies you," suggesting that the melancholy and the complaints are longstanding, and that there is a kind of meta-level set of problems here (1.1.2). Not only is Antonio melancholy, he is tired of the feeling and he has worn out his friends with the complaint. The melancholy itself is tedious, but even more tedious is the endless complaining about the melancholy. There is room for a kind of infinite progression here in which complaining about the complaining about the complaint . . . becomes ever more tedious. The possibility of infinite complaint, then, is a threat to the social order. Relations break down in the face of the infinite chain of dissatisfaction. Clearly an intervention is called for from these first lines, and Antonio will indeed find some excitement to relieve his boredom.

The "Sallies," Salarino and Salanio offer diagnoses of Antonio's melancholy, but both diagnoses seem to miss the mark. Salarino assumes the melancholy comes from the potential loss of wealth from a merely possible shipping accident. If the winds blow unfavorably, if chance and nature are against Antonio's ships, Antonio risks losing everything. For Salarino, this worry would seem a sufficient cause of deep melancholy.

Antonio denies the worry, though agrees that if he were to lose everything he would be sad. But, he notes, "My ventures are not in one bottom trusted," (1.1.41) meaning that he has a diversified portfolio and everything is completely safe. As Antonio concludes, "Therefore my merchandise makes me not sad" (1.1.44).

Salanio chimes in that if it is not money that makes Antonio sad, "Why then, you are in love" (1.1.45). Between them, the Sallies have hit on the two major concerns in the play, economic security and the social security that comes from the fulfillment of desire in a love relationship. Antonio denies that he is in love, and thus the two diagnosticians of Antonio's melancholy have missed the mark completely. It is not financial insecurity and it is not emotional insecurity that lead to Antonio's psychic pain.

Antonio's sadness is a mystery of some sort. He has no detailed explanation for why he is melancholy. It is not a money problem because he is fully hedged against disaster and has properly diversified his investments, and it is not a love problem unless, as some critics suggest, he is in love with Bassanio. But were he in love with his friend Bassanio, his sadness would not be a mystery to him. And further, it is not a problem with being too concerned about the world, nor is it entirely new. As long-standing as it is, it is still misunderstood.

There is a clue in the line that both he and his fellows are weary of his melancholy. It would seem that Antonio's expressions of sadness have a long history such that everyone is pretty sick of him, including himself. Given that he is wealthy and his wealth is diversified and his merchant and shipping business goes well, we can see right from the outset that there is a hint of a split between the human and the economic, or between polity and economy. Antonio is fully economically well-positioned, a time-consuming endeavor, and yet he has long been deeply melancholy. Money, clearly, does not buy happiness, at least so far. The diversification of his estate up to this point is spatial and temporal, as his has more than one ship, more than one place, and more than one year's savings to keep him going. And yet he is melancholy.

It is possible that his melancholy is temporal in nature. That is, though his future space in his body and his future time are secure, and secured, by the breadth of his diversification, his present circumstances are not going particularly well. We find out soon enough that he has limited present means but great future means; limited local ability to help a friend in need but great ability to garner credit. He can call upon his far-flung wealth to help him generate better local conditions, but indeed he does not have instant comfort.

Two other, related, diagnoses suggest themselves here at the outset of the play. First, despite his broad diversification across space and time, Antonio realizes the structure of wealth demands ever more and is ever insufficient, thus rendering happiness impossible, and second, that even if there were some way to have infinite and infinitely increasing returns, Antonio still could not be made to be happy from merchandise, for "merchandise makes me not sad." And if it is not the source of sadness, fixing it cannot be the source of happiness.

Antonio's melancholy, then, may be both related to the need for infinite return on investment, and separate from it, in that no amount of return can really buy what he wishes for. Indeed, he does not even know what he wants, though he does know what he has. And though one might suggest that his melancholy is a kind of foreshadowing, the fact that he notes that he has long been this way and that he and everyone else is a little sick and tired of his affect means that foreshadowing is not at all the operative term. Rather, it seems, melancholy is a condition of his version of modernity—an economy of plenty with seemingly all the risk hedging one needs, and no reason for the anxiety that Salarino and Solanio express. Antonio, then, reads his situation as overly safe, and that very safety causes his melancholy, and yet he is in fact on the edge of a cliff, or more precisely, on the wrong end of a knife.

In his book *The Hour Between Dog and Wolf*, John Coates, schooled in both economics and neurology, a former Wall Street trader and currently a neuroscientist, looks at the dopamine receptor system in our brains to try to explain what happens in Wall Street manias. While the vocabulary is that of contemporary neuroscience, the basic insights Coates has dovetail nicely with Antonio's experiences in *Merchant*. Safety and certainty are less thrilling than anticipated rewards. Coates writes, "[T]he amount of dopamine released into the nucleus accumbens does not depend on the absolute amount of reward an animal receives, but on how unexpected it is. This further suggests that we enjoy and crave environments in which we receive unexpected rewards; in other words, we enjoy risk. Put another way, dopamine spikes with information."[1] The insights here are several. First, unexpected rewards are far more enjoyable than the ones we already know about. If we are promised a particular reward, or a return on investment, we enjoy it less than if we suddenly get an unexpected reward. To the extent that Antonio is well-hedged and feels that he can predict the future, he has set himself up for little or no dopamine or greater melancholy to use Shakespeare's language. Antonio is not gambling on his wealth and so cannot derive great pleasure from the gambling. If he is to enjoy anything, then, with regard to his money, it will have to be doing service to Bassanio. His relationship to Bassanio, then, need not be that of lover so much as that of benefactor with some uncertainty. The uncertainty, at the moment of anticipation, will give Antonio a shot of dopamine. Thus, on Coates's reading, it is not the risk of loss that worries Antonio, but rather is the loss of risk. He is too safely invested, he is too sure of his relations; he is too set on a path to have any kind of enjoyment at all.

Second, the issue of information comes up. Coates defines information as that which we do not already know. If we know something, it is not informative to tell us that item.[2] What Antonio craves, then, is information or novelty that will increase his sense of pleasure in the world. Having it all worked out already so that there is nothing that is unknown, nothing new or surprising, is simply tedious. The kind of melancholy Antonio suffers from is precisely this, for him, there is nothing new under the sun.

Third, the notion that an unpleasant experience might lead to pleasure in the end, dovetails with what Antonio is going to face eventually in the course of the play. He will be under great threat of pain and painful death and even that pain may be something of a source of a dopamine rush in the end. Pleasure and pain, then, are inseparable feelings, as we will see in the course of the play. We may come to enjoy that which is truly awful, even if "enjoy" is an uncomfortable term for, say, the threat of losing a "pound of one's flesh."

Drew Daniel, in his essay "'Let me have judgement, and the Jew his will': Melancholy Epistemology and Masochistic Fantasy in *The Merchant of Venice*" suggests that Antonio's melancholy, "is not only an illness—it is a discourse, a field of study, and one whose daunting curriculum (etiology, source, transmission, substance, and origin) mocks exhaustion."[3] The notion that Antonio's melancholy spans such space, and further, that the melancholy can be traced to Antonio's masochistic fantasy suggest that there is much to be said about what motivates our economic and political behavior. If, underneath Antonio's boredom (my term), there is a layer of masochistic desire that will generate the excitement Antonio wants, then the polity and the economy need to provide moments of this kind of excitement in order to satisfy him and anyone else who has this psychic structure. It could be argued that any desire for excitement that comes with any understanding of a potential for loss has a moment of masochism, but it requires that the potential for loss be understood rather than denied. If Antonio recognizes that there is a chance his flesh could be taken and used for fish bait, as Daniel notes Shylock suggests, then indeed the reading of masochism into the text is well-taken. If, though, Antonio honestly feels well hedged, and does not really think there is a risk of loss, then perhaps "masochism" is too strong a term, and indeed there are other operative terms here, including dream logic. Later in this section, I will discuss resignation as a complement to incredulity and will suggest that Antonio is resigned more than anything else. It is not the loss of flesh that will satisfy him, but rather the fantasy that he has undertaken risk and shaken up his certainty while simultaneously maintaining it.

Daniel notes that, "Antonio's melancholy functions as a discursive switch point that allows it to 'carry' any or all of the multiple, overdetermining explanations his behavior solicits: merchant capitalist anxiety, Christian heroism, unrequited homoerotic desire, moral masochism."[4] What is interesting in this passage is the broader reading of Antonio's melancholy as stemming from a panoply of potential causes. Indeed, it would seem that Antonio cannot be anything but melancholy given the position he occupies in Venice, as if it were almost comically overdetermined and perhaps caught up in some kind of libidinal economy. Antonio "desires" his melancholy, desires its resolution, and desires the repetition and intensification of the cycle. If melancholy is overdetermined and structurally bound at the same time, then indeed both economic and political institutions and structures must take account of this response among the array of actors within these realms. If melancholy can cause a range of wreckage, including the disruption of proper marriages, the function of the law, and the proper movement of money, it must be dealt with. And if melancholy can be broadened by one more term, boredom and the behavior toward risk, then all the more must economic and political structures respond.

A second and opposing kind of conflict is that which Shylock experiences. If Antonio needs financial risk to feel alive, Shylock seems to need to avoid the very risks that Antonio seeks. Shylock, by trade, lends money, risks loss, but is supremely loss-averse. He monetizes all human relations, and he values the monetization over the human. Neither character has any kind of balance between risk and loss, money and relationships, excitement and variations on dread. And each character stands in opposition to the other in important ways. If safe investment, Antonio's practice, is tedious and is the source of his melancholy, he still invests safely and diversifies. If, on the other hand, Shylock is deeply risk-averse, he still invests with risk and makes a living off of risk. Antonio is socially accepted as a Christian in a Christian society, and Shylock is socially marginal as a Jew in that same society. Antonio and Shylock are also in tension over love and law. Despite these tensions, the two are drawn together through the Christian dependence on Judaism, through generosity's dependence on money-making, and through the fact that Antonio, as an individual, needs to borrow money from Shylock. Thus, across polity and economy, the two are pulled apart and pushed together, bitter enemies and yet mutually dependent. They will misunderstand each other, as they must, and the misunderstandings will cause each of them to risk significant loss. A pound of flesh or a set of identificatory structures and meanings, a casket or what is inside the casket, each will have to come to terms with dependence and value, polity and economy.

The third strand, entwined with Antonio's melancholy and Shylock's anxiety about loss, is Portia's marriage story. The caskets, with differing outward appearances and inward value, are another way of characterizing risk, human relations, and value. Numerous suitors get the terms confused and pick outward show for internal value. Each of the mistaken suitors loses, terribly, in the marriage game that Portia's father devised. And each of these mistaken suitors is one more character who does not understand the balance between polity and economy. Bassanio, though, is successful, and his success, dependent upon the risky generosity of Antonio, is noteworthy.

Bassanio precisely does not know how to spend money "properly" and so his willingness to choose the least worthy-seeming casket is both properly in-character for him, and odd, since his original attraction to Portia is based on her wealth. Somehow Bassanio lucks into success, somehow he manages, as if through a gift from the gods, to choose virtue despite not having lived long as a virtuous character. Accidental correctness is clearly a Platonic theme. Correct as it is, it requires knowledge to be a workable way of life. Thus, Bassanio must come in to a kind of knowledge or be ever dependent on the luck of the draw.

Antonio, then, is pressed by Bassanio for money so that Bassanio, who has overspent his inheritance, can woo the wealthy Portia. Bassanio describes Portia as, "a lady richly left, / And she is fair and, fairer than that word, / Of wondrous virtues" (1.1.161-3). She is, first, rich. Then she is fair. And only then is she of fair virtue. This hierarchy of value shows that Bassanio, like Antonio and Shylock, has some confusions regarding the proper place of value. That the money comes first, and the virtue last, is problematic within the play. Bassanio corrects this mistaken hierarchy by the time he chooses a casket. But at this instance, as he is trying to woo Antonio to provide help in the wooing of Portia, he starts with the least essential characteristic (wealth) and moves to the least visible characteristic (virtue.)

The two devise a sort of Willie Sutton plan—to go "where money is" in order to find a way to help pay for love (1.1.184). The dependence of love on money, like the dependence of Christianity on Judaism, like the dependence of Antonio's wealth on his cargo, and like all dependencies suggests that a certain measure of risk is inherent in social relations. Getting the level of risk, the use of risk, and the mitigation of risk correct is, for the play, the main task.

When Antonio and Shylock meet, Shylock describes, in an aside, his chief grudge against Antonio. Antonio "lends out money gratis, and brings down / The rate of usance here with us in Venice" (1.3.40-41). The conflicts here lie in the sense of the purpose of money and the proper way of life in Venice. For Antonio, money, or the economy, serves the purposes of human relations as social, freely giving, and loving. One gives freely to those one loves, and when one gives so freely, sometimes the recipient starts out like Bassanio, wasting money and becoming increasingly more indebted. Antonio's Venice is one of having a freely giving economy in which the money flows seemingly effortlessly. If money flows this way, ever effortlessly and ever without risk of loss, as the fantasy would have it, the results are, first, the kind of melancholy that Antonio struggles with, and second, the kind of wastefulness that Bassanio engages in. Neither one is doing well at the outset of the play, and Bassanio's initial inversion of values shows that he does not do well in this kind of free economy of flow.

Shylock, on the other hand, overvalues money and bears a grudge not merely against Antonio but also against generosity itself. His vision of Venice is one in which money is as dear as possible, and loss is as unlikely as possible. The tension here is clear—money that is never lost carries a low risk premium and therefore comes with a low rate of usance. The flow of money is constrained to drive up the interest rate, and the punishment for non-payment is such that it simply will not happen. On the other hand, seemingly, the equilibrium point will be at a lower rate than what Shylock wants. Dear money, no risk of loss, limited flow, and no generosity all work together in Shylock's vision, but not, perhaps, within the logic of economics.

Clearly these two visions and these two men cannot coexist. Money cannot both flow freely and be constrained; generosity cannot both flourish and be non-existent. The working out of the tensions here is crucial for the resolution of the plot. Proper generosity, proper flow of capital, a proper kind of risk balanced against a proper kind of security—all of these must be established for a city to flourish.

Ironically, Shylock has to borrow from Tubal to raise the full three thousand ducats, suggesting that the Willie Sutton plan was not carried out properly. Had Antonio and Bassanio done their research, perhaps they would have gone directly to some other money lender and perhaps they would not have run in to Shylock's long-standing battle with Antonio over respect and decency and the interest rates. As Shylock complains, "You call me a misbeliever, cut-throat dog, / And spit on my Jewish gabardine" (1.3.106-107). There is no single worldview on which these two can be made to have concord. And yet, they need each other.

The deal is finalized on the legal promise that if the debt is not paid in full and on time, the "forfeit / Be nominated for an equal pound / Of your fair flesh, to be cut off and taken / In what part of your body pleaseth me" (1.3.144-147). Bassanio does not want this to be the bond, but Antonio responds, "Why fear not, man, I will not forfeit it" (1.3.152).

Antonio's body, in part, in whichever part Shylock takes pleasure, is the object at risk. Not money, not cargo, not even Bassanio. The symbolism here is thick, as there are sexual overtones, hints of the casket subplot, and of course, the psychological intensity as now Antonio has something very real at risk, something essential to his life. The risk has him say to Bassanio, "fear not," because in fact, fear is not at all what Antonio feels at the moment. He is excited about the possibility of the risk, and yet he still "expect[s] a return / Of thrice three times the value of this bond" (1.3.154-155). There is risk, expectation of safety, but not certainty. And there is his body at stake; or, rather, some unknown part of his body.

Asking for a body part as a bond is inappropriate. Agreeing to the bond is inappropriate. Bassanio sees the wrong here, but is, at some level, the cause of the wrong, for the bond is made to benefit him in his quest for marriage. The sacrifice of, potentially, Antonio's genitals for Bassanio's future marriage is inappropriate at every level and it shows how misguided are the motives of each of these characters. No marriage should occur on these terms, and no loan should be offered or accepted on these terms. The economy does not exist to support this kind of excitement, and the polity should not make a demand like this either.

Because, however, excitement is central to the avoidance of melancholy, to the satisfaction of marriage, and therefore to the perpetuation of civil stability and order, both polity and economy need to create some kind of space for enough excitement to soothe, and not so much excitement that destruction ensues. Disciplining both the flow of money and the flow of marriage, then, becomes the proper work of polity and economy. Both spheres are tasked with balancing forces and boundaries so that the results work to the benefit of dynamic stability.

Both the casket and ring subplots work to this end. Both are similar to the mystery of Antonio's ships and cargo, in that there is containing and something like unknown conditions; but where Antonio's cargo is so well split among ships as to be a near-guarantee of safety, the casket system is a gamble with certain ends for the losers and uncertain means for all. The depth of sacrifice for choosing the wrong casket is the loss of all love, the freezing of feeling, the excommunication from the human. The reward for choosing correctly is all love, all money, all feeling, all polity, and all economy. The casket system was set up by Portia's father as a way to guarantee her a good marriage in his posthumous absence, so the caskets are the ghostly presence of her absent father. Suitors come to town, choose a casket based on outward appearance and then are fated by the inner meaning. Gold seems the safest bet, silver a middling bet, and lead seems the worst of all. The parallels with the Myth of Er are striking. The choice is both clear and not, and it comes with all peril. Bassanio has figured out how to choose, how to dismiss appearance and focus on reality, how to dismiss the outer and find the inner, how to go where the money really is. And so when he chooses, he picks the lead casket because in fact the money is not where the money is.

Portia offers comfort to the first suitor, Morocco, as she describes her situation. She says, the "lott'ry of my destiny / Bars me the right of voluntary choosing" (2.1.15-16). Were she able to choose freely, she would be able to look past the "shadowed livery" of his skin (2.1.2). Portia, then, declares herself able to look past the outer appearance to find the next layer down. She will not let the "nice direction of a maiden's eyes" be the only guide to a worthy suitor, but she does have the ghostly presence of her father to deal with (2.1.14). That she would be willing to look past the "complexion" of Morocco, though, is not matched by Morocco's looking past the complexion, as it were, of the casket. He goes for the showy gold one and what rhymes with "gold" is "cold," and that is Morocco's fate. He must "Never to speak to lady afterward / In way of marriage" (2.1.40-41).

Love requires risk, and the risk it requires is the willing sacrifice of all to gain all, the willingness to look past what is outside and find what is inside, and the willingness to shed false belief and choose what is true. Love that finds no risk is not love; love that sees only the outward appearance is not love; love that is too easy is too unstable.

Portia's absent but ghostly father resides in each casket and chastises the failed suitors as they misdirect their attentions.[5] If Morocco chooses the one that is too cold, Arragon chooses the one that is too hot, the silver casket, and Portia comments "Thus hath the candle singed the moth" (2.9.78). The seeming light and seeming correct temperature turns out to be deceiving. The true light is not as it appears, the true temperature not what it seems, the true balance between desire and reality requires more insight than instinct.

When, finally, Bassanio chooses, he picks the least appealing casket by outer appearance and it turns out to hold a pale likeness of the actual Portia. The appearance is never what is real, the container is never what the contained is, and we are bound to wager, risk, guess, attempt, and thrill as we choose. Excitement wards off melancholy, uncertainty leads to excitement, the basic distinctions between appearance and reality or the outer and inner or the container and contained structure our experiences so that there will be uncertainty. What Portia's father has done with the casket-marriage ritual is to formalize the gaming around uncertainty. Just as a suitor could not know what Portia's father would say regarding a marriage proposal—were Portia's father alive, so the suitor could not really know what is in the chosen casket until the moment of the reveal. Keeping this structure of mystery in place, keeping the thrill and risk of the loss of everything for the gain of everything is central, then, to the success of a marriage relation.

This basic structure of uncertainty that undergirds marriage can be broadened to that which undergirds all social relations. The task of a social and political order, then, is to design institutions that manage the tensions between proper thrill and going too far. Portia's absent father is the one character who seems to have a proper understanding of the use of uncertainty and of the balancing of polity and economy. The suitors want both the thrill and the financial gain, and the casket system functions to balance these pressures against each other. A suitor cannot gain financially without understanding social, moral, and metaphysical concerns. And a suitor needs as well an understanding of the finances of courtship. Bassanio gets something of a financial education from needing to borrow money (he has to figure out where money is) and he gets something of a moral education as he sees what his friend Antonio is willing to sacrifice to help him. These put together allow him to make the right choice, to go where money is, and to value what is worthy of value.

Portia's father, again, is the only one who actually understands the balance between polity and economy. The tension between Antonio and Shylock shows what happens when these spheres are misaligned, when one side misuses the other side, when the understanding of how to balance these forces is absent. The absent father, then, is more properly present than the present father, Shylock, or father-figure, Antonio.

At the plot level, of course, Antonio borrows money from Shylock because that is where money is (even if it turns out not to be the case, as again, seeming and being diverge), because he wants to help Bassanio's wooing of Portia, and perhaps because he is, himself, in love with Bassanio and is attempting to woo indirectly. On a more psychological read of the borrowing, Antonio is attempting to treat his melancholy by adding some risk to his life. And on a kind of social level, Antonio may be going to Shylock to show Shylock, the Jew, how a Christian deals with money. The text is explicit on the question of religious identity and how religious identity guides relations to money. Christians are generous in a way that Jews are not, Christian money is different from Jewish money, and Christian family is different from Jewish family. Critics all struggle with this material as it has its offensive side.[6] There is, though, a way through this morass that highlights Shakespeare's very clear inversions in the texts and works both to rescue the play, after a fashion, and to show the kinds of misuses of money and polity that are at work in the text.

If Antonio's borrowing from Shylock shows that Christian use of money is a better use than Jewish use, that usery is wicked and that pure generosity is preferred, and that Antonio's relationship to money is completely other than Shylock's, then this trope fails. Antonio is as dependent on Shylock as

Christianity is on its precursor; Antonio's ships are as much part of the money system as is Shylock's money; and though Shylock views his daughter as equivalent to money, money is still implicated in all love relations throughout the play. Shylock is reported second hand to have run around crying, "My daughter! O, my ducats! O, my daughter! / Fled with a Christian! O, my Christian ducats! / Justice, the law, my ducats and my daughter! / A sealed bag, two sealed bags of ducats." when he found out that his daughter Jessica had run off with the money to marry Lorenzo (2.8.15-18). But then, Bassanio needs money to woo, and woos to get money; and Jessica is quite comfortable with taking her father's money so that she can marry Lorenzo. Thus, money is part of every relationship, and Shylock's take in only one variation on the theme.

The language here, the equivalence of daughter, ducat, law, sealed bags, and the betrayal through the fleeing with a Christian shows precisely what Shylock is concerned with. The sealed bags, like the sealed house, and the caskets, and Antonio's ships, and Antonio's chest are all packages with something inside that is not quite what is expected. The Jewish daughter in a Jewish house with Jewish money from sealed bags turns out to be Christian inside. The law, which should support Shylock's claim to his property, will equally not be quite what he expects.

What Shylock fails to understand is that his daughter is not money, his money is not the law, his house cannot seal off his daughter from the world. He cannot have the safety of sealed bags and no losses whatsoever. It is mere fantasy to think that money can stay in a sealed bag, the daughter can stay in a sealed house and be a sealed virgin. If Shylock is going to lend money at interest, he will lose control of his money and nothing at all will be sealed up, safe with the meanings he ascribes.

In a similar manner, when Antonio agrees to the use of his flesh as bond, he does not expect the bond to be called. But his ships go down in the ocean, it is reported, and he readies himself to pay the bond through his flesh. He speaks what he expects to be among his last words, "Commend me to your honourable wife; / Tell her the process of Antonio's end, / Say how I loved you, speak me fair in death, And, when the tale is told, bid her be judge / Whether Bassanio had not once a love" (4.1.269-273). Of course, Portia, in drag, is actually the judge, and she knows well that Bassanio once had a love, though perhaps she does not realize the depths of Antonio's love for Bassanio.

Antonio expects the money he has loaned to substitute for his unrequited love of Bassanio, and he hopes that the money will purchase a good posthumous tale. Where Portia's father's posthumous actions are indirectly money-related and meant more to teach a lesson about how little money and appearance matter and how much love and inner worth matter, Antonio's posthumous hope is that he will be remembered, and that his love will be fulfilled indirectly. He has a kind of dramatic false ending here that casts him as a hero, gives him a rush of dopamine, allows him to make the same kind of sacrifice for Bassanio's love that the failed suitors made for Portia's hand. The loss of all, the heat of blood and the cold of lovelessness will be Antonio's fate.

If Shylock thinks that money can guarantee security, that he can lend with no loss, that money and love are equivalent, then Antonio thinks not so differently that money equates with love, that total loss can be redeemed through posthumous storytelling and world-spinning and the indirect requiting of love, and that money can be made to be things it is not. Neither character at all understands the proper role of money or the proper role of love. If the anti-Semitic characteristics given to Shylock are paired with the less attractive characteristics of Antonio, then their equally being wrongheaded and wronghearted helps mitigate some of the unsavory imagery in the text. It is not a perfect rescue, but it is in keeping with oppositions and inversions in the text.

Shylock's insistence on the paying of the bond rather than having his monetary debt doubled, trebled or more, shows, again, that he is using money in incorrect ways. Portia even offers, indirectly, a doubling of the original amount, a doubling of that and a trebling of that much. Shylock insists again and again that his bond be paid, that flesh be given over, that money is no substitute for the promise of the bond.

There is a kind of inversion here, for what Shylock is demanding in the courtroom scene is the non-equivalence of money and justice. It is not the money that is at stake at this point, it is the bond. And the bond is a summation of all social and religious resentment, all social pain, the loss of his daughter, all humiliations suffered because of religious intolerance. Shylock stops being a moneylender in this scene and becomes obsessed with restitution and with honor. He turns to the polity to restore what the economy has not provided, and he refuses the economy's offer of an incredibly high rate of usance. That he has blamed Antonio for lowering the interest rate and now refuses the much higher one suggests either that Shylock has changed his views or that his grudge has nothing at all to do with Antonio's lowering of the rate of usance.

If it is not really the money for Shylock, and it is not really the money for Antonio, then clearly each character is using the money economy for other purposes, purposes that money is not well designed to satisfy. Because it is not money that either wants, neither one can be made whole and well through the use of money. Indeed, the turn to money as a substitute for love, justice, excitement, security, social or economic supremacy is a false turn that turns Venice topsy-turvy for the duration of the play.

The settlement in the courtroom, mandated by a non-impartial judge (Portia disguised as Bellario), strips Shylock of all of his property and his identity, grants Antonio half of the money and the state the other half of the money. Shylock loses everything because he risked everything. He, like the failed suitors, misunderstands the proper workings of money.

Antonio is made whole again, but one assumes that his melancholy will cycle. His ships turn out to be safe, he has half of Shylock's money, and Bassanio is married to Portia. He has had quite a rush, a brush with bankruptcy, loss of identity, and death, and the subsequent dopamine rush may well carry him awhile, but it is not clear that he has changed his character so that he will never again need a thrill.

Antonio, again not exactly a disinterested party in the matter, demands as a final set of terms of settlement, that Shylock convert, that Shylock's money go to Jessica and Lorenzo upon Shylock's death. Antonio's conditions here show that he is still unaware of the debt that Christian money has from Jewish sources, and that Christian identity has from its Jewish precursor. The handing over of money negates its origin, the changing of identity negates its source, and together they act as a repressive tactic to hide the Jewish sources of Antonio's identity.

Not only, then, does Antonio not recognize the causes of his own melancholy, he also does not recognize the sources of his identity and the underpinnings of the economy he depends on for his own wealth. That he would repress rather than accept suggests, again, that the repressed will return, the melancholy will strike again, and Antonio will seek once more some grave risk to give him purpose; and, of course, it is explicit in the text just how risky his next wager is. At some level, the diagnoses of the Sallies are correct. Antonio is worried about both money and love, but not in the way that either of them thinks. Because this worry, rooted in his melancholic desire for excitement, is ever unrecognized, Antonio repeats the whole cycle of risk, but the second time through he wagers not his body but rather his soul.

Because Antonio misuses the polity and economy to satisfy the psyche, he can neither diagnose nor cure what ails him. That he turns again to the court for the satisfaction of his psychic need to repress suggests that he still cannot understand what ails him. Because Shylock turns to money and to the courts to satisfy his fear of loss and his sense of social humiliation, he, too, cannot be satisfied. Neither man has figured out what money is for and what the polity needs to do. Compared to Portia's father, both Antonio and Shylock come up short in ways that harm their children.

The ring subplot is a repetition of the basic structure in this play of using the techniques of the polity within the economy and the techniques of the economy within the polity. The inappropriate boundary crossing causes pain and incredulity, and then there is a kind of resolution through the re-establishment of proper boundaries. Where Portia's father separates money from value in the casket system, Portia fails to make this separation in the ring cycle.

She insists upon the gold as a kind of faith, both for marriage and for justice, and she has set up a kind of tension between Bassanio's love for Antonio and Bassanio's love for her. Demanding the sacrifice of the token of marriage to Antonio suggests that Portia does not entirely understand what it is her father wanted her to know about love. Bassanio has already sacrificed everything to win Portia. He should not have to sacrifice his friend to keep her or sacrifice her to honor his friend. Because Portia is the author of the whole subplot, she is in control and could easily set different terms for settlement.

Briefly, the ring subplot starts with Bassanio's offer of payment to Portia/Bellario, the judge. Bassanio wants to turn the favor of justice to a monetary transaction, an inappropriate response to the good that Portia/Bellario has done. Portia turns down the money, saying, "He is well paid that is well satisfied" (4.1.411). But the offer of money gives Portia/Bellario the idea of demanding the marriage ring given to Bassanio, and Bassanio, egged on by Antonio, agrees.

Of course, because Bellario is Portia, the ring never actually leaves its proper circle, and because Bellario is thought by Bassanio to be a man, there is no gender crossing that could endanger the marriage. But inappropriate giving, receiving, asking, encouraging, the wrongful use of exchange as payment for justice all work together to create yet another moment of incredulity. Not only can Portia not believe that she has been betrayed (though she is the one to devise the subplot), but Bassanio cannot believe that Portia has discovered the missing ring.

The plot is repeated at the servant level with Nerissa and Gratiano, and again, the ring cycles to the wrong-yet-right person. Gratiano rightly describes the ring as "a hoop of gold, a paltry ring" suggesting that the ring is not love, that money is not life (5.1.147). And Nerissa counters that when she gave Gratiano the ring, he promised to "wear it to the hour of death" (5.1.153). The ring, then, is not merely a paltry thing but rather is indeed life. The two disagree about the status of gold, the ways that gold intrudes into polity. Nerissa uses gold, an economy function, as a promise, a polity function. Incredulity ensues.

The women, who of course have the rings, go on strike as it were, with Portia's declaring, "By heaven, I will ne'er come into your bed / Until I see the ring" (5.1.190-191). The ring, then, becomes virginity, sex, love, promise, fidelity, and all marital social relations. The economy has fully crossed into polity and has become more than what it is.

Bassanio and Portia trade poetic lines about what the ring really is. For Bassanio, it is a thing given for the life of Antonio. "Sweet Portia, / If you did know to whom I gave the ring, / If you did know for whom I gave the ring, / and would conceive for what I gave the ring, / And how unwillingly I left the ring, / When naught would be accepted but the ring, / You would abate the strength of your displeasure" (5.1.192-198). And Portia replies, in the same music, "If you had known the virtue of the ring, / Or half her worthiness that gave the ring, / Or your own honour to contain the ring, / You would not then have parted with the ring" (5.1/199-202).

Here it is clear that on one level, the ring means different things to these two lovers. For Bassanio, it is the gratitude to Bellario for the life of Antonio, and for Portia, it is virtue, worthiness, and honor. It both had to be given and could not be given. The ring, then, shows the impossibility of separating polity and economy and yet the need to keep the terms distinct enough that one sphere is not used to bring about ends in the other sphere. Bassanio should not have offered money for gratitude and Bellario should not have asked for the ring instead. These are both improper uses of exchange. In reality, of course, Bassanio does not exactly part with the ring, because in reality he gives it to Portia. In appearance, in the outer sense, he does part with it. The appearance/reality, outer/inner structure, then, is repeated here. Bassanio gets the right casket, but does not quite understand the proper use of money and the proper way to express gratitude.

Even more troubling for these characters though, is Antonio's promise:
I once did lend my body for his wealth,
Which but for him that had your husband's ring,
Had quite miscarried. I dare be bound again:
My soul upon the forfeit, that your lord
Will never more break faith advisedly. (5.1.249-253)

Antonio's repetition here, his willingness to use his soul as a bond, in contrast with his prior willingness to risk a pound of his own flesh—his body—suggests that the drama of the courtroom has not had much of an effect on him. Dopamine or melancholy, he seems to have a choice. And he chooses dopamine. If his soul is ever at risk, he can never actually be entirely safe. He can always conjure a scene of an unfaithful Bassanio and a courtroom in which his soul is demanded and thousands of ducats are insufficient payment. His ships are generally safe until they are not, but then they are. His soul will be safe in the keeping of Portia, until it is not, and yet will be.

Shylock is an interloper of sorts; he is the seeming locus of money, and money intrudes in love temporarily. And yet, the ring cycle suggests that it is not really Shylock who is the interloper. Portia and Bassanio and Antonio manage well enough without Shylock's demands. It is Antonio's offer to Bassanio that causes them to seek out money, it is Bassanio's spending habits that cause him to need the money. Further, it is the entire history of denials of Shylock's humanity that embitter him and cause him to use the economic system to gain justice, and then to refuse that very economic solution and demand instead something so beyond justice that the justice system cannot contain it. No courtroom could allow the extraction of a man's flesh for a small monetary debt, a debt that could be paid in money. If the entire system is a fault for the incredulity suffered by the individual citizens, then a systemic intervention is needed.

Portia's father's genius is first to set up a dopamine-delivery system to help keep her marriage going, and second to keep that dopamine exchange system outside the economy. There is no gold in the correct casket, no direct monetary value. The money is secondary and comes only after money is foresworn. The risk is intense, the loss is the loss of everything. But all of this risk and loss is carried out outside of the money system. If Bassanio had been able to woo without money from Antonio, he would have been able to avoid a fair amount of the drama. Bassanio's money problems, then, are replicated in his wooing of Portia. It is incumbent upon both Venice and the people in Venice to find ways to generate dopamine rushes while keeping matters of polity and matters of economy in their correct spaces.

Given that Antonio does not have this figured out, given that Portia sets the conditions for a crisis even as she is resolving a previous crisis, there does not seem to be much room for these characters to keep straight the proper separations between the polity and the economy. They will lurch from crisis to crisis.

Antonio's desire to wager his soul is a dramatic coming together of the peripety/discovery/hysteresis cycle. He should have been cured of his need to use his person as bond once the courtroom peripety was resolved. The turnaround, coming with the discovery that his circumstance was not what he thought, coupled with the fast peripety/discovery that his body was not at risk, should be enough to satisfy his melancholy and to shock him into a better frame of mind. But hysteresis rules, and he returns almost to his original state, with the slight change where he actually intensifies the risk. This final round of wager, again, is for his soul. If the wager is safe, like his ships, he clearly will not have a way out of his melancholy, and if he needs a scene in a courtroom with a more ultimate judge than Portia/Bellario, he will have yet another moment of world-shaking incredulity. The repetition compulsion, with escalation as the mark of hysteresis, may be too strong a force for lessons to take deep hold, and may instead cause a cycle of intensifications of risk. One likely ought not wager one's soul, though, even if it is exciting to do so.

NOTES

1. John Coates, *The Hour Between Dog and Wolf: Risk Taking, Gut Feelings and the Biology of Boom and Bust* (New York: The Penguin Press, 2012), 149.

2. Coates, *The Hour Between Dog and Wolf*, 133.

3. Drew Daniel, "'Let me have judgement, and the Jew his will': Melancholy Epistemology and Masochistic Fantasy in *The Merchant of Venice*," in *Shakespeare Quarterly* 61 (2) (Summer 2012): 206.

4. Daniel, "'Let me have judgement,'" 216.

5. Alex Schulman notes the Freudian themes here regarding fathers, daughters, civilization and its unifying powers. See Alex Schulman, *Rethinking Shakespeare's Political Philosophy: From Lear to Leviathan* (Edinburgh: Edinburgh University Press, 2014).

6. See Janet Adelman's discussion about "Christian supercessionism" and the difficulties with scholarly encounters with *Merchant* in *Blood Relations: Christian and Jew in 'The Merchant of Venice'* (Chicago, IL: The University of Chicago Press, 2008), 1–37. Schulman also discusses Judaism in the context of *Merchant* in *Rethinking Shakespeare's Political Philosophy*. See especially chapter 6, "Shakespeare and the Theological-Political Problem."

Section 3

The Economy of the Sea in *Pericles*

Shakespeare's *Pericles* delves into the psychological, political, and moral implications of proper political rule, proper desire, and the proper use of money. The characters he develops work through repetition compulsions, cannibalism, and various kinds of risk as they falter along the division between what can be called polity and what can be called economy. The proper bounds of each are violated routinely as characters struggle with internal psychic drives, and the restoration of the proper balance between polity and economy come only after great cost.

In brief, the plot of *Pericles* deals with Pericles's attempts to marry well, rule well, grieve for his father, and have some youthful travel adventures, and the bumps along the path to completing his list of tasks. His first attempt at a good marriage comes as he answers a riddle only to discover horror in the answer; his second attempt at a good marriage works out better as he enters a knightly contest and wins the hand of the maiden, in a way that complements the action in *Merchant*. Unfortunately, a shipwreck gets in the way of his marital bliss and happy fatherhood and the family is separated, much as happens in *The Comedy of Errors*. In between the finding of horror and the momentary happy marriage is a brief travelogue in which he finds more horror. Though there is a comic reunion at the end of the play, it is only through tragedy and horror that the characters reunite and the disrupted family, polity, and economy are made whole. The underlying questions that this text raises for the purposes of this book include the role of risk-taking in the satisfaction of desire, the intentional and unintentional act of eating our children and the risk that having children always courts, and the question of what is owed to the children we have risked all to meet and/or eat.

After the prologue from Gower, the poet, the action starts in Antioch with Antiochus and his unnamed daughter. Antiochus proposes a riddle and the suitor who answers it correctly will marry her. Failing to answer the riddle correctly will result in a beheading, and the subsequent display of the suitor's head on a stick. Of course, success in answering the riddle leads to the same outcome, as the answer leads to incredulity.

Just as the contest for Portia, in *Merchant*, requires the risking of all for the gaining of all, and just as failure is met with a kind of death-by-exile-and-cold-isolation, so the suitors in *Pericles* risk all and lose all. In both plays there is a kind of riddle. In *Merchant*, the riddle is both physical, in that there are three caskets to choose from, and intellectual, in that the goal is to come to understand what has true value and how interior value differs from exterior ornament or show. In *Pericles*, the analogue is a riddle which says one thing but means another, and the answer to this riddle says something very different about the father and daughter from what might be expected by a suitor. The play on expectations of inner and outer meanings shows up in both plays, but the underlying horror in *Pericles* is a twist on this theme.

Pericles, at first starstruck by the beauty of the daughter waxes,
See where she comes, apparelled like the spring,
Graces her subjects, and her thoughts the king
Of every virtue gives renown to men;
Her face the book of praises, where is read
Nothing but curious pleasures, as from thence
Sorrow were ever razed, and testy wrath
Could never be her mild companion. (1.1.13-19)

The words here are all sadly backwards, as the daughter has no virtue at all, as the spring that dresses her is more akin to cold winter and as her father has far more than curious pleasures. Further, sorrow and testy wrath are her constant companions. Pericles is not yet aware of just how incorrect his analysis of the game is, but he soon readjusts his expectations. That he can manage this risk and flee at just the right moment suggests that he has something on the other suitors, none of whom seems to have gotten away safely.

The riddle, which Pericles reads out loud, runs thus,
I am no viper, yet I feed
On mother's flesh which did me breed.
I sought a husband, in which labour
I found that kindness in a father.
He's father, son, and husband mild;
I mother, wife, and yet his child.
How they may be, and yet in two,
As you will live resolve it you. (1.1.65-73)

The seeking of a husband and the finding of that "kindness" in a father is the clearest statement of the incestuous relationship that this riddle testifies to. Add to that the line that the daughter is "mother, wife, and yet his child" and there is no doubt at all what the relationship is.

There are several curiosities here. First off is why Antiochus feels it necessary to display his incestuous relationship with his daughter in a screamingly obvious riddle.[1] What kind of risk-taking does he need to gain satisfaction? Is there some horrific relationship between his sexual attraction to his daughter and the stream of suitors whose deaths he arranges? What has his odd desire done to his daughter, and how does his arranging this contest differ from what Portia's father does?

Clearly, there is an analogue in the two contests. Both are designed by fathers, both are meant at some level to attract appropriate suitors, and both lead to bad outcomes for a line of suitors. But Portia's father is dead and so is absent from the game, and he is not in an incestuous relationship with his daughter. He clearly has been obsessed with Portia's marriage, though, for the casket system is a fairly elaborate set up to have designed. The father's desire is there, but channeled far more appropriately in the case of Portia than it is in the case of Antiochus's daughter.

That Antiochus is present during the contest is striking. He can watch the various suitors, watch as they either figure out he is committing incest and must kill them for the knowledge, as some readers of the passage suggest, or that they fail to figure out the riddle and he must kill them as per the rules of the game. Either way, he gets to watch and to kill. The courting of risk Antiochus engages in is a game he feels he cannot lose because he is safely hedged through the killing of all players. The titillation of publicity of his secret can be replayed over and over in an odd libidinal economy of repetition, as long as there are suitors willing to risk all to gain all. At some level, then, Antiochus is both risking all through the discovery of his secret and risking nothing as all discovery will be dealt with in summary fashion.

The other oddity in the risk that Antiochus takes is why he would bother at all to offer up his daughter in this contest. Not only, then, is the riddle too obvious, but the fact of the contest at all suggests a variation on the notion of risk-taking. Antiochus clearly feels a need to pretend that his daughter is marriageable and not tainted or polluted by the incest. There is a public display to be maintained here, and he has turned that display into a sexually laden game that ends in murder. One could speculate that each suitor's attempt to marry her returns her to her spring-like garb, her freshness, and her unsullied original beauty, and so there is a huge sexual payoff for Antiochus to risk the offering of his daughter in this contest, and a simultaneous thrill in the repeated solving of the riddle which sends his spring-child-wife into winter. The repetition of the riddle, the line of suitors, the unbroken sameness all suggest that Antiochus's risk-taking is motivated by a deeply disturbed psyche.

Pericles responds to the realization that Antiochus is incestuously involved with his own daughter, and Pericles's fantasy bride, with appropriate incredulity. His errors in judgment, in hoping that the outer beauty of the daughter would match inner beauty, that a king would properly respect boundaries, that his own fantasy would match the external world leave Pericles almost as shocked as the first soul in *Republic* X. Pericles's fate is not yet to eat his own child, but it might have been to marry a devoured child, and it certainly was to love where no love is appropriate. Pericles should be fated to the cold exile of a failed lover in a contest, and indeed he does exile himself for much of a lifetime in order to compensate himself for this failed fantasy.

Suzanne Gossett suggests that much of Pericles's fraught adventures can be seen as Neptune's capriciousness. Neptune, of course, is the sea, and Pericles's daughter Marina will be shown in this section to be, at some level, the sea. Marina, though, will be a more stable version of the sea than Neptune seems to be. Gossett notes that Neptune wavers in his treatment of Pericles, at times allowing travel and at times intervening.[2] Gossett emphasizes the traditional characteristics of a romance, rather than the fantasy misdeeds of a character who then deserves his punishment and redemption, though she does note later in the introduction that "all members of the family are reunited after undergoing suffering, purification . . . and miraculous renewal."[3] At the same time, she also suggests that Neptune "seems especially hostile to Pericles."[4] There may be some reasonable tension in reading the text between seeing Pericles as something of a victim of forces beyond him and someone who has chosen his fate over and over through improper desire. Indeed, it is this tension that makes him a compelling character. He does have flaws that he fails to correct for, and he does have very human desires that he fails to control. Unlike the first soul in Book X of the *Republic*, Pericles does not inhabit a world in which all of his choices will come out right. He is not in a well-ordered city, and he is not at all ready for a one thousand year-long celebration of his wonderful ability to choose properly. Pericles chooses badly, has a life that is more down and to the left than he might want, and comes out better than he would have in a well-ordered city.

Lynda E. Boose suggests that "The punishment meted out to Pericles throughout the play has no such obvious cause, and it seems in fact so basically causeless that it makes him appear almost Job-like. The implicit 'cause,' however, is rooted in the matter of Antioch that begins and ends the play and that Pericles' actions unconsciously mirror."[5] While Boose sees the roots of Pericles's problems, she suggests that they are buried in some unconscious sense and that somehow Pericles is more a victim than an actor in his fate. The text may point to more than an implicit cause. Indeed, Pericles's inappropriate desires are quite explicit, as is his swaggering and risk-taking and adventurousness.

W.B. Thorne points out that, "Though the play does not on the surface discuss the extent of his involvement in the sin of Antiochus, the following action indicates that Pericles has been 'tainted' by the incest with a stain which he must eradicate through his own behavior."[6] Boose notes further that "even his proximity to the incestuous evil has infected him."[7] Thorne's sense that Pericles must be punished for his having had inappropriate desires stands in contrast to Jeanie Grant Moore's sense that "Pericles remains a victim of misfortune,"[8] and in contrast to views that see Pericles as an Odysseus-like victim of a battle between Diana and Neptune.[9] Pericles is flawed as a king and a father. Moore notes that "Pericles abandons his kingdom as well as his daughter."[10] Further, Pericles is deeply flawed as a man who desires inappropriately, who takes inappropriate risks for that desire. The abandoning of his roles stems from the deeper issue of his fantasies and desires for risk.

He says in reaction to the horror,
Sharp physic is the last. But O, you powers
That gives heaven countless eyes to view men's acts,
Why cloud they not their sights perpetually
If this be true, which makes me pale to read it? (1.1.73-76)

The sharp physic, the medicine that both cuts and cures, is the eye-opening knowledge of what he is encountering—the bursting of a fantasy bubble, the outcome of a poorly chosen risk. That heaven would allow this horror, that heaven would allow it and continue, unlike Oedipus, to be sighted, is all the more shocking. Pericles cannot yet fathom the disturbance of normal relations, the destruction of what he expected his return to be on his investment. He is bankrupt at a fantasy level just as Antiochus and his daughter are bankrupt at a moral level.

He concludes his musing by saying to the daughter, "Good sooth, I care not for you" (1.1.87). The fantasy of her beauty and spring-like being, the glory of the challenge of wooing and winning, the sense of futurity that Pericles feels at the beginning of the scene have melted away, along, perhaps, with all of the dopamine. When a fantasy of time, space, beauty, worth, wealth, and sex evaporates or bursts or in whatever metaphorical way simply stops shaping perception, the result is a profound sense of loss that leads directly to the moment of incredulity. Pericles says out loud his interpretation; Antiochus denies it and offers a second chance interpretation. Pericles exits, knowing he is likely to have risked his life because of his knowledge. Pericles flees, and Antiochus sends Thaliard to kill him.

Pericles is not the only one with a moment of incredulity in this scene. Antiochus, too, seems shocked that he has been found out. It is not clear from the text whether or not Antiochus is merely repeating the shock he always feels every time a suitor names his crime, or if Pericles is really the first suitor to have figured it out. It seems a fair reading, given the obviousness of the riddle, that the whole scene is simply a repetition of Antiochus's crime for the nth time. Not only does Antiochus, on this reading, then, need to have his daughter displayed, offered, refreshed routinely, he also needs to have his crime named again and again, and then he needs to kill the namer of the crime again and again, as if to cleanse his soul of what the heavens should have dealt with already but have not gotten around to thus far.

Antiochus says, right before assigning Thaliard the task of killing Pericles,
He hath found the meaning, for the which
We mean to have his head.
He must not live to trumpet forth my infamy,
Nor tell the world Antiochus doth sin
In such a loathed manner;
And therefore instantly this prince must die,
For by his fall my honour must keep high. (1.1.144-150)

Given that Antiochus is named as one to lose his head, it seems likely that his "crime" is precisely that of the other suitors—naming the sin rather than failing to solve the riddle. That Antiochus both sees his sin, in this passage, and continues to think he has anything like "honour" left "high" suggests that he really does have some kind of doubled sense of himself in which he sins, confronts, and then feels restored after murder in a repetition of the same. The incredulity is part of that repetition, as is the cleansing of the daughter and the endless re-commission of the sin.

Antiochus's incredulity has something of the Book X moment in it, in that in *Republic* X there is repetition as souls are immortal and have made these choices for all time, over and over again. Shock that comes from repetition is an interesting phenomenon. At some level, there is really no reason to expect a different outcome, and yet somehow, when choices are made, we really do feel "this time is different" rather than "this time is going to be the same as all other times." Like Lucy and Charlie Brown and the football, like every financial crash, like every suitor who names Antiochus's crime, the repeated repetitions still fill us with both a hope that it is all different this time and the horrible recognition that in fact, it is the same.

Hope, or foolishness, keeps us going in these situations. Our souls do not turn, and our moments of incredulity repeat. To set up social and economic institutions to deal with the obsessive repetition of patterned foolishness or evil and realization, to balance the economic versions of repetition and the socio-political versions such that both domains function well and do not, upon failing, contaminate one another, is the underlying challenge that all of these texts present us with. Our hopes in both domains may be part of our problem in the end.

After a brief return to Tyre and advice from Helicanus, Pericles continues his journey. Pericles names Tarsus as his next destination. Tarsus is an island in great distress from famine. Cleon, the governor, says to his wife,

Dionyza,
Who wanteth food and will not say he wants it,
Or can conceal his hunger til he famish
Our tongues our sorrows do sound deep,
Our woes into the air our eyes do weep,
Till lungs fetch breath that may proclaim them louder
That, if heaven slumber while their creatures want,
They may awake their helps to comfort them
I'll then discourse our woes, felt several years,
And, wanting breath to speak, help me with tears. (1.4.10-19)

He says not much further down,

Those mothers, who to nuzzle up their babes
Thought naught too curious, are ready now
To eat those little darlings whom they loved.
So sharp are hunger's teeth that man and wife
Draw lots who first shall die to lengthen life. (1.4.42-46)

These two passages, both from Cleon, testify to the sheer misery of Tarsus, to the intensity of hunger, the terrible things it does to people. Hunger may start as a feeling that is expressed in language, that is brought to the public notice by cries and complaints, but it quickly becomes something far worse, cannibalism and the hope that one's wife or husband will be the one to die in order to lengthen one's own life.

What should sustain us, the love of parents and children, of husbands and wives, becomes as corrupt in Tarsus as does the love between Antiochus and his daughter. Sustaining love becomes consumptive love because some quality or object is missing from the world. The boundary crossing in both Antioch and Tarsus is one that lurks just under the surface of human relations. Absent a proper economy, we turn to eat one another. Absent proper love, we devour where we are most forbidden to devour.

Gossett notes the link between goodness of the soul and generosity with money, or, one could say, a proper balance between polity and economy. She notes the goodness of the good, the economy of plenty, and the giving of food and armor in this economy of generosity.[11]

Generosity, an economy of plenty, giving without need for overt return, though perhaps hoping for return as Pericles does when he leaves his daughter in Tarsus later in the play, these all suggest that the risks of giving should be minimized through a sense of good behavior so that the economic deed is met with the politically correct response. And politically safe relations should be met with proper generosity rather than with the removal of heads or the eating of children. (The theme of proper gift giving will be taken up again in the discussion of *Timon of Athens*.)

Gossett contrasts the good people who manage an equilibrium of generosity and political balance with those who fail to do so.[12] It is, then, perhaps the most important issue to deal with in setting the proper boundaries of polity and economy—how do we stop ourselves from eating one another (Gossett identifies the theme of cannibalism in the play) when either desire or money outstrips the other? Tarsus has run out of money, Antiochus cannot manage desire.

While Pericles could do nothing for Antiochus and his daughter, for desire had already taken over in improper fashion, there seems to be an opportunity to respond to the crisis in Tarsus. Pericles offers ships full of food, helps calm the political and economic problems, and seems to have righted the place. Because of Pericles's intervention, Tarsus becomes monetarily prosperous.

Cleon, in gratitude, says to Pericles,
The which when any shall not gratify,
Or pay you with unthankfulness in thought,
Be it our wives, our children or ourselves,
The curse of heaven and men succeed their evils!
Till when—the which I hope shall ne'er be seen—
Your grace is welcome to our town and us. (1.4.99-104)

Cleon, with these words, curses his own wife in advance of her deep unthankfulness, a feeling that will be expressed not merely in thought but also in deed before the end of the play. It would seem that those who contemplate or support or find reason in the devouring of their own children do not really overcome the passion or the lack of moral bearings that leads to the idea. Cursing, here, is a speech act with far more risk than Cleon realizes. And trusting one who has cursed this way will come back to damage Pericles. Neither character has a solid understanding of the power of words to change circumstances.

Though Pericles has already experienced the problems that a riddle can cause, the problems that his overriding sense of his own worth can cause, he fails to heed the warnings of this curse and assumes that the curse means that the result that has been suggested will not come about. The curse, here, is not going to forestall a terrible fate but rather is predicting or perhaps causing that fate.

Act II opens with a nearly drowned Pericles, washed up on a beach in Odyssean fashion, lamenting his fate and his state. Pericles likens himself to a beaten tennis ball, declares that he is a frozen and nearly dead man, and one who wishes for pity, and if not that, at least a decent burial. His thoughts are of his own death and suffering along the way to that death. It is significant that he is in the company of fishermen as he describes himself, both because of the Neptune/Marina connection and because, as one of the fishermen notes, Pericles will starve if he cannot fish, "for here's nothing to be got nowadays unless thou canst fish for't" (2.1.67-68). If you cannot work, you cannot live, and if the sea does not provide you cannot live, and the state will not provide, therefore you must.

Fishing, casting for food, is an act of risk-taking, in that the result is uncertain; fishing boats can go under, storms take fishermen, and the food supply is never really guaranteed even if the boat returns safely to shore. While Pericles has, thus far, courted risk for mere excitement, the lives of the fishermen suggest that risk-taking can have a much more immediate effect. If you cannot fish, you cannot eat. The economic side of risk-taking has a very significant political side in a way that differs from what Pericles is accustomed to.

Pericles learns from the fishermen that he is in Pentapolis, that Simonides is king, that Simonides has a daughter, that the daughter is to be married to the winner of a "joust and tourney" (2.1.106). This contest, unlike that for Antiochus's daughter, is a knightly joust. There is a physicality to the game that Antiochus's set up lacks, even if there is a common purpose in having suitors compete for the love of a princess.

Just as Pericles has washed up out of the sea, so does a seeming fish that turns out to be rusted armor. But the rusted armor is not simply any old rusted armor washing up for no good reason at all and interfering with the day's actual fishing. Instead, by chance or luck or narrative necessity, the armor is from the shipwreck and it belongs to Pericles's father. Symbolically, it is Pericles's father. The armor is there to protect Pericles, to help him with his melancholy, to give him hope and to cloak him for the tourney. The armor is the blessing of Pericles's father for the wedding that will come in part because of this blessing.

To the extent that what the fishermen fish out of the commons of the sea belongs to the fishermen, the armor is theirs, as Pericles realizes. He once again has to beg of the fishermen that they help him by giving him the rusted husk. The second fisherman also realizes the debt and says,

Ay, but hark you, my friend, 'twas we that
made up this garment through the rough seams of the
waters. There are certain condolements, certain vails. I
hope, sir, if you thrive you'll remember from whence
you had them. (2.1.144-148)

The lower-class fishermen have a few advantages over Pericles for the moment. They hold the knowledge of how to fish, for as they note, you have to have some kind of skill in order to get anything at all. Pericles has no ability to fish, even if he can solve riddles and joust with the best of them. His riddle-solving did not come out so well, and without the fishermen's ability to fish, his jousting might well have been equally useless. There is a whole social and economic network with varying kinds of risk-taking that together underlie Pericles's life and livelihood.

The armor covers his top half, a fisherman supplies cloth for covering Pericles's bottom half, and another fisherman agrees to escort Pericles to court. The mixing of classes here is part of Pericles's journey, even as his physical travels include going between islands. Pericles has to become, has to take on a wide array of roles in order to see what is really at stake in risk-taking behavior. His cavalier attitude toward contests needs to be tamed.

The scene shifts to the jousting and tourney. Unlike the previous contests we have discussed, this one is not terribly risky. The losers do not end up exiled and alone, or dead with head on a pike. Simonides does not threaten any of the suitors with imminent death, in part because he is still alive and thus able to watch over his daughter's suitors, and in part because he is a good king rather than a deeply corrupt one. The risk inherent in choosing a mate with either absent or inappropriate parents is what leads to Portia's caskets and Jessica's elopement in *Merchant*, and the riddle that Antiochus presents to his daughter's suitors.

The risk, for Pericles, then, is mitigated both by his father's ghostly, if rusty, presence and by Simonides's actual presence and true kingship. It is not that there is no risk, as there is still a contest, there are still contestants, there is still some kind of prowess to display, and there is at least the risk of humiliation from losing. And further, it is not the case that Simonides is a perfect ruler, as Moore notes, "Many have seen Simonides as the ideal father and the ideal king . . . . but the picture of the ideal king is undercut by the fishermen in the preceding scene."[13] Thus, though there is a decided improvement in rule, and Pericles can certainly see that Pentapolis is better-ruled than are the two previous places he has visited, Tarsus and Antioch, he still will not have seen a properly ruled city from which to learn how to rule his own, currently abandoned, city, and it is unclear if the tourney is any better a way to marry off a daughter than, say, a riddle guessing contest. Though certainly, having the daughters finish growing up rather than being served for dinner is a big improvement.

Instead of riddles handed from father to suitors, Simonides's contest has the suitors' coats of armor and shields with foreign language phrases, each of which is read by Thaïsa and translated by Simonides. The intellectual game, then, is still present but is played very differently in this contest from how it is played in the others. The risk is not played out linguistically at all.

The jousting happens off stage, as we find out from a stage direction, "enter knights from tilting," and we get confirmation of Pericles's victory as Thaïsa hands him a "wreath of victory" (2.3.9). And she says, later in the dinner scene, "By Juno, that is queen of marriage, / All viands that I eat do seem unsavoury, / Wishing him my meat" (2.3.29-31). Gossett points out what is clear from this passage, that Thaïsa is expressing a desire for cannibalism.[14] There is, again, a risk in using language this way, and in conjuring even well-sublimated desires for what is at base very disturbing or immoral. Parents should not devour daughters and wives should not devour husbands, and really, no one should be suggesting inappropriate hunger. If Thaïsa makes a mistake that leads to her fate, if she errs in her categories, it is here more than anywhere else. Her appetite here is not properly disciplined and so she expresses what should not be. She risks the realization of her desire to eat what should not be eaten.

In the midst of the banquet, there is a swift, and awkward, cut in scene back to Tyre where we learn first that Antiochus,

When he was seated in a chariot
Of inestimable value, and his daughter with him,
A fire from heaven came and shrivelled up
Their bodies even to loathing, for they so stunk
That all those eyes adored them ere their fall
Scorn now their hand should give them burial. (2.4.7-12)

The difference between appearance and reality, or inner and outer, or reputation and reality, or worth of vessel (the chariot) and worth of what is contained (inveterate sinners) is made clear in Helicanus's description of the demise of Antiochus. That a "fire from heaven" or lightning or the wrath of a deity is responsible for this sudden end suggests the beginning of putting the awry world back into order.

When it comes to issues of risk and worth, the relationship between polity and economy, it can be a comforting thought that something ultimate comes in occasionally and puts things to right. Antiochus certainly deserves his bizarre death, and though one could meet this death with a certain amount of dramatic incredulity, indeed it is such a fitting death, one Antiochus probably knew was coming eventually, that the incredulity for the reader, and perhaps for Antiochus, is limited to the sense of cheesy theatrics rather than genuine shock at an event.

The chariot, "of inestimable value," the daughter, of no name, and the father, of no worth at all, are destroyed in a blast that leaves those left behind with a greater degree of incredulity, though. For it is the survivors who are left to refigure the value of their king, the stench on their hands, and the realization that what they valued (the king and the king's chariot) are of no actual value at all. In fact, the smell of the hand, the perhaps unwashable smell, is of greater significance. And here, it may be worth mentioning that the fishermen of Pentapolis would prefer the smell of fish on their hands to the smell of the burnt body of a sinning king. Lowly fishermen of good soul outdo high kings who commit incest, and walking escorts are better than chariots of inestimable value.

It is clear from this scene that the overvaluation of economic position is deeply problematic for a healthy society, and that some kind of comeuppance is due those who fail to set proper boundaries around the institutions that are inscribed in polity and economy. Antiochus uses his political and economic power to satisfy a sick fantasy of sin and confession and destruction and repetition. He fails to balance power against the good, even as his people allow the incest to continue, and even as young enterprising and adventurous men provide the material for the repetition.

The second piece of news we learn in this odd interruption is that Tyre needs its own king back. There is unrest and Helicanus is merely a regent, not the actual king. So even if we are momentarily happy to see the end of the bad king Antiochus, and even as we see that Pericles is now safe to return, we also are privy to the notion that Pericles is not necessarily himself the best of kings. He has risked his own people's well-being for some adventures, he has been on the run, and his return has been delayed enough that he is causing some problems. That these problems are co-incidental with a party in Pentapolis is notable, even if awkwardly expressed in the text.

Somewhere between the end of Act 2 and the beginning of Act 3, Pericles and Thaïsa are wed, she is pregnant, or, as Gower the poet narrates, "A babe is moulded" (3.0.11), and Pericles has received a letter telling of Antiochus's death by fire from heaven, and that Tyre is undergoing political upheaval. It is time, to the extent that we are in narrative time, for Pericles to return to Tyre. Journeys by sea are fraught, Pericles is still not quite done with his punishment for being attracted to that which must be burned by the heavens—if the hands of those who had to bury Antiochus were covered with uncleanable stench, and if those so charged would n'er be clean, and if incredulity has marked their psyches, Pericles is in worse shape for he had been prepared to woo and wed the source of the stench. Those before him died for their desire, a fate Pericles avoids. But he must come close to death, and must face the worst of losses in order to compensate the world for his courting of risk. Thaïsa, too, is going to suffer for her metaphorical cannibalism, as noted above.

There is a terrible storm at sea, Thaïsa gives birth to a baby girl with the help of a nurse, Lychorida, and to pacify the sailors on board the ship, Thaïsa's body has to be buried at sea because a dead body on board will make the storm worse. In short order, Pericles's life is wrecked once again, and his wife is denied a proper land burial. Just as in *The Comedy of Errors*, the family is broken up by the wide and wild sea. The sea, then, is the container of a significant amount of risk, a container that sometimes appears to be peaceful and therefore often courts risk-takers.

The fishermen Pericles encounters in Pentapolis take risks for their livelihoods, and they respect a kind of economy of the sea and its trove. The sea gives them food, and it even gives Pericles the armor that allows him to win his wife. But just as the fishermen deserve repayment, so, too, does the sea. The economic exchange, coupled with a moral overlay, is central to the development of Pericles's character and understanding of the society he is to govern.

Family separation in romances, designed to foster growth and settle moral scores, requires some kind of reunion, and so Thaïsa's death turns out to be temporary. Her casket, with jewels inside, washes up on shore, just as the armor of Pericles's father washes up, and just as fish do. The sea takes and gives, punishes and rewards and exchanges. Cerimon revives the dead-but-not-really-dead Thaïsa, and she spends years living in a convent where she has washed up, unknown to Pericles and not knowing that she has a child and a husband somewhere.

That somewhere turns out to be Tarsus, which has recovered quite well with the very generous help provided by Pericles. There is a debt that Cleon and Dionyza owe Pericles, there is a standing offer of help that Cleon has made, and there is a need for that help. Pericles turns his baby girl over to Cleon and Dionzya, with Lychorida as a nurse, and Pericles returns to Tyre to rule. It is unclear how immoral or unacceptable or totally justified this abandonment, or foster-parenting, of Marina is. Is the debt, the need for a wet nurse, or perhaps Pericles's own melancholy sufficient excuse for this act? Moore characterizes Pericles as abdicating his role.[15] And Gossett notes discomfort with both the abandonment and the lack of contact for fourteen years.[16]

The baby girl, Marina, of the sea in many crucial ways, is raised by Cleon and his wife and the nurse, alongside Dionyza's daughter. Dionyza, despite have a profound debt to Marina's father, decides that Marina, now much older, is a threat to her own daughter and needs to have her killed. The debt that Cleon feels he owes, a very real debt, is payable only to the point that paying it is destructive of Cleon's family, or so at least is how Dionyza thinks through the issue of debt. And certainly, it is crucial to try to come to understand what debt is, how it works, how much there can be, and what happens if repayment is destructive or if it is merely infinite.

The sea gives and takes in a circle of debt. It gives armor, fish, transportation, life. It takes back life and property. Pericles loses ships and family, finds himself washed up on a beach, and yet finds himself drawn to seafaring both for adventure and for grieving. He is given to and taken from. Dionyza, sea-like but not in a moral way, takes from Pericles, gives some back by taking care of Marina, but then decides to destroy that which she has been given rather than protect her charge. Her decision is based on jealousy rather than on moral desert, and so there is nothing properly economic in the exchange. She is given, she repays, but then takes immorally. Notably, the only reason Dionyza has not eaten her own child is that Pericles provided food and wealth for the people of Tarsus. That Dionyza would return the favor by "dining" as it were on Marina is all the more wicked, then.

Although Dionyza schemes to have Marina killed, Marina, like the sea, is a force of moral economy, the union of polity and economy, and the model that the play presses. She describes, and defends, herself to Leonine, a not entirely lion-like would-be executioner,

As I can remember, by my troth,
I never did her hurt in all my life.
I never spake bad word, nor did ill turn
To any living creature. Believe me, la,
I never killed a mouse nor hurt a fly.
I trod upon a worm against my will,
But I wept for't. (4.1.70-76)

The issues of debt and deserving, of risk and compensation, are clear in this speech. She has been careful her whole life, risking nothing save the untimely death of a single worm, for which she has wept. Her life is one of doing no ill, save for one deed. She has compensated the world for that one misdeed by weeping. And yet, she is, simply by the fact of her existence, in some kind of debt the repayment of which seems to be death. (The theme of the relationship between birth and debt will be taken up in part III of this book.) At this point, the issue is that she has lived in moral rectitude and yet has become the locus of an immoral and improper repayment that she has inherited from her father, Pericles.

Just as the sea gives Pericles the armor that allows him first to win the love of Thaïsa and to create the life of Marina, so the sea comes to Marina's rescue in the person of a band of pirates who grab her from a not-so-brave lion. That pirates could be saviors is surprising only if we fail to see that Marina is the sea, and is part of the economy of taking and giving. Marina does it always with justice and morality, while the pirates are only unwittingly helpful.

Marina is taken by the pirates to Mytilene where she ends up being purchased by a brothel in need of fresh women. Pander, one of the brothel proprietors, says of the poor finances of this brothel, "We lost too much money this mart by being too wenchless" (4.2.4-5). In the brothel, flesh is synonymous with money rather than with humanity, and yet basic or base human desire is what is at stake in a brothel. The overlay of what is most human with what is most inhuman in the structure of a brothel is yet another kind of sexual relation that the play deals with. Fathers and daughters, husbands and wives, semi-adopted stepdaughters, prostitutes and johns, these are all relations that hinge on something sexual and on something financial, but that must be properly mediated by the moral dimension. The characters in the play, thus far, have failed in their attempts to mediate these relations.

Marina is, for the play, the epitome of the proper union of polity and economy. Where she has erred, in killing a worm, she has wept as a way to repay the world for the loss, and for the cost of her suffering, the redemption of those characters deserving of redemption will be purchased. Marina encompasses, sea-like, the economy of proper balance, give and take, and the true relationship between money and matter. Moore comments on the passage about the worm, and on Marina's goodness in general, "Marina's goodness is never in question; in fact, she is too good to be true."[17] Moore notes that there is a comic or ridiculous side to the goodness here.

It may be worth granting more to Marina's confession than mere audience laughter or the mocking of romantic convention. While it does not seem like much of a sin, the killing of a worm, it does suggest that even the best among us is not perfect, though the imperfection may be trivial. There may also be a subtle reference to the lives of fishermen here, in that Marina killed that which might be used as fish bait. If this reading is acceptable, then there is some sense here that even small transgressions may end up spiraling through the human world. Marina is not separate, then, from all others, and in her connection to the wider world, she may affect things in untraceable ways. For that possibility, even Marina will suffer something. We could read further into this passage a reminder from the *Republic* that it is insufficient to make only correct decisions in a well-ordered city, that in fact, we need a deep knowledge of the truth, and that we may need to suffer along the way to coming to understand the truth. Marina, then, like all philosophers, must suffer along the way to gaining philosophical knowledge sufficient to guarantee good decisions under all circumstances, regardless of desire and regardless of the condition of one's city.

Pander, one of the brothel proprietors, says, of his own moral situation,

> O, our credit comes not in like the commodity, nor the commodity wages not with the danger. Therefore, if in our youths we could pick up some pretty estate, 'twere not amiss to keep our door hatched. Besides, the sore terms we stand upon with the gods will be strong with us for giving o'er. (4.2.27-32)

He means that he realizes that the way that the brothel makes money is through an immoral use of flesh and desire, a use that the gods disapprove of. Pander expresses a wish here to have enough money so that he can escape the life of selling flesh. There is, though, no sense that Pander feels a need to weep over his pandering of flesh. He would like to be out of the trade, though, for the risks are significant, and the moral worth of the proprietors is not great, given how they make their money.

That Pander can see his immorality would seem to put him a step above Antiochus, but just as Antiochus confesses, but then repeats, so Pander confesses his sin here, and yet repeats his desire to stay for a little while longer in the trade. Antiochus is motivated by desire for his daughter and by desire for maintaining his status. Pander has no status, yet desires money. In both cases, the result is the gross misuse of both female flesh and male desire for that flesh. The suitors lined up for Antiochus's daughter, and for Thaïsa, are not so far from the customers at a bawdy house, the text seems to suggest.

Marina, unlike the other characters who accept their places in the risk and venture system, who are willing to sin for the satisfaction of desire, who are internally complicated by economies of melancholy and risk, is single-mindedly focused on virtue. Her sorrow is that she has not been killed and that she is pretty (4.2.59, 63) Not having been killed puts her in the position of having been kidnapped by pirates and sold to a brothel, and being pretty has put her in the position of almost having been killed and being sold to a brothel. She is the thing that men desire, and as such, she suffers. She gives the invocation, "If fires be hot, knives sharp or waters deep, / Untried I still my virgin knot will keep. / Diana, aid my purpose!" (4.2.138-140). Here, Marina gives tautological proofs of her virtue. The proper qualities of things are inherent in them. There is no cold fire, nor a knife we would call a proper knife that is not sharp. In the same way, there is nothing we would call "Marina" that is not a virtuous virgin. It is her most proper quality, and to lose it would be to cease to be what she is.

She calls on Diana for help, but what helps her most is her own identity, and the sense that if a thing is what it is, it cannot be what it is not, and the risk relations shift in a significant way. There is, it would seem, no risk that

that which we call "Marina" can be anything other than what she is. Her identity, then, like that of the full and proper economy, and like that of the sea, encompasses proper relations between flesh and money, between virtue and a female body, between father and daughter. She cannot be purchased.

Immediate upon Marina's promise to keep her virginity, we are presented with Dionyza's line, "Why, are you foolish? Can it be undone?" (4.3.1). Though most directly, this line is spoken to Cleon and refers to the purported death of Marina, but its place in the text suggests that it is a question for Marina as well. Can her promise to keep her virginity be undone, can her virginity itself be undone? If what we are most properly can be undone, we are not that thing most properly. Fire is hot, knives are sharp, water is deep, and Marina is a virgin.

There is, then, underlying all of the properties of characters and events a sense of deep reality. Thaiïsa, seemingly dead, becomes undead, and, therefore death can be undone. Marina, also seemingly dead, will turn out to have been undead. But these characters have a constitutional "aliveness" to them that allows their deaths to be purported or temporary or localized but not global and most real. They each return to their real state eventually, having been chastened for a minor misdeed.

And because Marina is a figure of the sea and of the economy of moral give-and-take, she most of all must return to life. To answer Dionyza's question, then, yes, it can be undone, but only under certain circumstances. When it is done, but not really done, when it is done improperly, when it is seemingly done, when its done-ness is merely local, when the sea coughs up what is done, when moral balance demands undoing, it can, indeed, be undone. And, interestingly, the birth of a child to a mother can be undone by the mother's eating of that child, something Dionyza has spoken of.

For Cleon and Dionyza, for now, and for this place, though, it is done and seems not to be that which can be undone. Cleon repents for his wife's deed,

Were I chief lord of all this spacious world
I'd give it to undo the deed. A lady
Much less in blood than virtue, yet a princess
To equal any single crown o'th'earth
I'th' justice of compare. O villain Leonine,
Whom thou has poisoned too,
If thou hadst drunk to him 't'ad been a kindness
Becoming well they face. What canst thou say
When noble Pericles shall demand his child? (4.3.5-13)

Just as Emilia, in *Othello*, would wish for the whole world so that she could undo whatever it has taken to gain the world, so that she could sin and unsin, so that killing could be unkilled, or at least so that she could change the rules so that sin becomes unsin through a new definition, so Cleon would wish to have the power to undo the deed.

This power comes with a terrible responsibility, though, as we have seen that at some level, Antiochus actually has the power to undo, or to redefine, or to confess and unconfess and confess again, and he has used that power to the limits of horror. Dionyza has, as well, used the power to undo. She had a debt to Pericles which she has had undone by ordering the murder of Pericles's daughter as a way to discharge, or undo, the debt. She has murdered Lychorida, a nurse whose job it was to guard the life of Marina, and she has murdered Leonine, whose job it was to guarantee the death of Marina.

In response to Cleon's question, Dionyza replies, "That she is dead. Nurses are not the fates. / To foster is not ever to preserve. / She died at night. I'll say so. Who can cross it?" (4.3.14-16). There is both a kind of honesty in this answer to the question, "What canst thou say / When noble Pericles shall demand his child?" and a kind of dishonesty and a kind of world-spinning as if one could undo what has been done. Honestly, at least to the best of Dionyza's knowledge, Marina is dead. Of course, she is not really dead, only locally so. Indeed, "nurses are not the fates" and so Pericles erred greatly in thinking that Lychorida could preserve his daughter, that the debt that Cleon and Dionyza owed would be enough to guarantee Marina's life, that life comes without death. Indeed, "fostering is not preserving" and so what grows under proper tending can just as easily die. "She died at night. I'll say so. Who can cross it?" The very language is a seizing of the world, a changing of its terms and as long as there is no witness to testify to a very different death, falling off a cliff into the sea, say, then the world that Pericles inhabits will simply include the death of his daughter, however it is that Dionyza's words describe the death. The "event" here is really Dionyza's language and not really Marina's death.

Many Shakespeare plays reject, for us, a world in which events exist only in language. There is always something real, something human, and something divine that language is grounded on and that corrects the errors of human perception, human deception, and human desire gone awry. Most directly then, what will undo Marina's death is the fact that it exists properly only in Dionzya's language, and not in the world.

Annette Flower, in "Disguise and Identity in Pericles, Prince of Tyre" emphasizes this issue of language and storytelling. She notes that the whole tale is told by Gower, that Antiochus fears tale telling, that Cleon has concerns about tales, that Marina and Pericles tell each other their tales at their reunion, that Diana requires that Pericles tell his tale.[18] Language, then, is used both for rendering the world and for deceiving the world. When it is deceptive, though, the world stands as a correction to the language, even as the gods stand in correction to human misdeeds, and even as the sea corrects for fortune and misfortune. There are economies and balances of risk in the use of language in the play.

To mark the "death," the one that is merely in language, Dionyza says that, "Her monument is almost finished, and her epitaphs / In glittering golden characters express / A general praise to her and care in us / At whose expense 'tis done" (4.3.42-44). We know from Marina herself that gold is an unacceptable medium of exchange for flesh, and so the placement of golden characters on her monument is as wrong a use of material as is what Hamlet complains about, that the funeral meats are being served at the wedding feast. Some things simply do not belong together, and golden monuments falsely equating the material with the worthy, falsely praising a murderer for care and expense—this is a complete breach of the acceptable, a complete betrayal of a debt deeply owed, and a complete misstatement of equivalence.

Marina suffers a double entombment for a time, both in the grave Pericles sees as Gower narrates and in the brothel. Just as her "dead" body cannot be priced by golden tributes on a monument, so her living body cannot be purchased by gold, even as a number of gentlemen try to buy her, and Pander and the Bawd try to sell her.

The second gentleman says, "Come, I am for no more bawdy / houses. Shall's go hear the vestal sing?" (4.5.6-7). And the first gentleman replies, "I'll do anything now that is virtuous, but / I am out of the road of rutting forever" (4.5.8-9). The Bawd comes on stage and incredulously says,

> Fie, fie upon her. She's able to freeze the god Priapus and undo a whole generation. We must either get her ravished or be rid of her. When she should do for clients her fitment, and do me the kindness of our profession, she has me her quirks, her reasons, her master reasons, her prayers, her knees, that she would make a puritan of the devil if he should cheapen a kiss of her. (4.5.12-18)

The two gentlemen's comments come into clear focus after the Bawd's description of Marina. They are, neither one now, willing to pay a prostitute or be immoral or have sex outside of a proper marriage. Without illicit sex, the illicit sex trade will go bankrupt financially, though it is always already bankrupt morally. The Bawd's speech suggests a kind of debt that Marina should owe, both to clients and to the Bawd herself. Further, there seems to be a debt of sorts to the profession of prostitution, and Marina should feel obligated at that level as well.

Debts of this sort, debts to an immoral system, are not, for Marina, debts one can be held to. Her higher debt is to morality and to prayer. The Bawd thinks more of "hire" debt, that she has hired Marina, or purchased her, which is the same thing here, and that therefore, Marina owes as the Bawd sees fit.

These two kinds of debts, one to employment for hire and one to a purpose that is higher, create in both Marina and the Bawd, significant moments of incredulity. Neither can reckon the debt as the other defines it, both need to find a way out of the incredulity, a labor that defies melancholy and resignation and leads to a greater functioning. Marina's plan is to have Diana help her convince clients that morality is a better path, and the Bawd's plan is to have Marina raped so that she becomes docile, has nothing left to defend, and ends up resigned to her fate as a prostitute.

The deep corruption of Mytilene is evidenced by the next "guest" at the bawdy house, Lysimachus, the governor of the city. He comes in a mask, is introduced as "an honourable man" (4.5.55) and the Bawd adds, "He will line your apron with gold" (4.5.63).

We know, of course, that no "honorable man" will "succeed" with Marina, though a truly honorable man may very well succeed. Further, we know that no amount of gold is at all equivalent to moral flesh, and that the economy of Marina, the sea, will only make proper exchanges based on the higher values. It is not gold she deals in.

Lysimachus, making awkward small talk at the start of the encounter asks how long Marina has been at this trade, and then cannot speak the name of the trade. He says, "Why, I cannot name't but I shall offend" (4.5.73). Marina claims to be unable to be offended by the name of her trade, for in her view, her trade has nothing to do with prostitution, while in Lysimachus's view she is most essentially a prostitute, perhaps even since she was five or seven years old.

The true trade, rather than Lysimachus's fantasy of the trade, is always speakable. What Marina is, can be spoken, for she is proper. The proper can be put into language, and cannot offend. Further, the fact that Lysimachus both is aware that he cannot speak the word, and yet is ready to do the deed, suggests a divided soul, one that Marina can convert, and one that is, indeed, in need of conversion.

Cleon, too, has trouble speaking of immorality, and Dionyza does not. But Dionyza's reason for being able to speak is that she is completely corrupt. She is unconcerned about offending, and she is unconcerned about lying. Lysimachus, though, worries about offending, and is not trying to lie, though he is trying to have sex with a prostitute. His fantasy of Marina's age at the start of her trade is striking. If she really has been a prostitute since age five or so, then he carries less guilt for his desire for her. After all, what she most profoundly is, in this fantasy, is a prostitute. Her trade defines her, and simultaneously exculpates Lysimachus. On the other hand, the vaguely implicit pedophilia is a little damning for Lysimachus. He is a problem character, as are most of the characters in the play, for these improper sexual desires. No couple has everything just right at the start, and perhaps one of the underlying suggestions in the play is that all desire that ends up appropriate has moments of the inappropriate, and those moments must be mediated through the economy of the sea, the risks and punishments for too much risk-taking or too inappropriate a desire. Moore describes Lysimachus as "shallow, if not opportunistic"[19] but he could more be thought of as one on a continuum of inappropriate desires and as one in keeping with the other characters in the play. His pressuring Marina is his low point, but not his fixed identity.

Lysimachus plays with risks in his own way. It is risky enough for him to patronize a bawdy house that he has to appear in costume, even though the denizens know quite well who he is. They know, of course, because he has been there before, has enacted and re-enacted this scene, much as Antiochus has acted and re-enacted his play-within-a play, as it were. Risk and the allure of the repetition of the risk are once again central to a character in the play. The risk, for Lysimachus as a ruler, is that the people he rules may end up corrupted by a corrupt ruler. Lysimachus, then, is yet another weak political leader. Further, he risks an assignation with a woman who either infects him with disease or with real attraction. Falling for an actual prostitute, rather than for a virtuous woman only accidentally looking like a prostitute, is a risk that Lysimachus ends up on the "losing end" of. He does fall in love, despite a likely preference to avoid love. And he finds that love is the opposite of sex, rather than the analogue. It is the denial, and the purity of the denial, that attracts him the most. Going to a place of sex and finding not-sex is attractive is its own kind of incredulous experience.

Marina and Lysimachus, at the bawdy house, go back and forth, speaking different languages until Marina says,

If you were born to honour, show it now;
If put upon you, make the judgement good
That thought you worthy of it (4.5.96-98).
. . . .
For me
That am a maid, though most ungentle Fortune
Have place me in this sty, where since I came
Diseases have been sold dearer than physic —
O, that the gods
Would set me free from this unhallowed place,
Though they did change me to the meanest bird
That flies I'th' purer air! (4.4.99-106)

Lysimachus replies,

I did not think
Thou couldst have spoke so well, ne'er dreamt thou
    couldst.
Had I brought hither a corrupted mind
Thy speech had altered it. Hold, here's gold for thee.
Persever in that clear way thou goest
And the gods strengthen thee. (4.5.106-111)

Marina replies,

The good gods preserve you (4.5.112).

And as Lysimachus leaves, he hands over even more gold, and he curses anyone who would rob her of her goodness (4.5.120).

This interchange is noteworthy first because we see first-hand how Marina convinces her "suitors" that they are wrong to think her immoral; second, that gold changes hand but in a very different economy from that which the brothel represents more typically; and third, that preservation might be more related to fostering than Dionyza thinks. Indeed, fostering may well carry with it a debt that requires preservation, and while the governor of Mytilene sees the relationship between the two after a brief conversation with Marina, Dionzya has failed to see the relationship between fostering and preservation despite her having fostered Marina, having had many conversations over the years with Marina, and having a hand in the governance of Tarsus. Dionyza misses the mark on every count, while Lysimachus comes to a conversion point.

The handing over of gold as payment for a debt incurred by the provision of conversion is a kind of exchange Marina can accept. Handing over gold for sex, on the other hand, is unacceptable. It is not the gold itself that is the problem, but rather the matter lies with the conditions under which gold is used. Where Socrates would have the guardians never handle gold, Shakespeare's play allows gold when it is put to proper use in a proper economy.

Lysimachus, a once happy customer, exits the brothel with the words, "Avaunt, thou damned doorkeeper! / Your house, but for this virgin that doth prop it, / Would sink and overwhelm you. Away!" (4.5.123-125). The metaphor of sinking suggests the sea, and thus lends credence to the idea that Marina is the sea. She is not allowing the sinking, but rather is holding the house afloat. Her divinity, along with her virginity, are all that are keeping the bawdy house above water. Thus far, the support is moral. No blast from below, or above, will land on the house while she is in residence. Not even a damned doorkeeper is sufficiently damned to bring ruination while Marina resides within.

It is Bolt's turn to attempt rape, and Marina, again, deflects the desire, and then plays employment counselor after a fashion. She recommends that Bolt,

"Do anything thou dost. Empty / Old receptacles or common shores of filth, / Serve by indenture to the common hangman, / Any of these ways are yet better than this" (4.5.177-180). Emptying old receptacles is better than filling a virgin receptacle, serving a hangman is better than serving a bawd. And any low task is better than raping a virgin. Marina gives Bolt a chance to rethink his life. She needs both to confront him with the gravity of his misdeed and give him a way out of his life. His economic and moral positions must be brought into proper balance. Thus far, he has sacrificed the moral for the economic. Were she merely to confront him and make him feel a kind of self-directed incredulity, she might well end up creating in him the same kind of reaction the soul feels in Book X of *The Republic*. Incredulity, blaming the gods, and a kind of impotent, paralyzed sense that what is done cannot be undone. Bolt's life and decisions can be undone. He has not raped physically, though he has certainly conceived of the idea. And he has worked in the bawdy house for some time. He is not, though, past the point of redemption, and Marina, the economy of the sea, gives him a chance to give back, to exchange a life for a life.

She lets Bolt know that she has talents unrelated to prostitution. She says,

Here, here's gold for thee.
If that thy master would make gain by me,
Proclaim that I can sing, weave, sew and dance,
With other virtues which I'll keep from boast,
And I will undertake all theses to teach.
I doubt not but this populous city will
Yield many scholars. (4.5.184-190)

She wishes to be placed "among honest women" (4.5.197). Not only, then, does Marina give employment advice to Bolt, she also has advice for herself, and she has the gold from Lysimachus to buy her way into a better job. Bolt, wanting a better relationship with the gods, even as Pander does, is willing to try to help Marina gain some form of release.

Because Marina is an economy, she does not merely "steal" herself from the bawdy house. She has, after all, been purchased, at both expense and risk, from the pirates, and as a thing purchased, she has taken on something of a debt to the bawd. She has, as it were, been fostered, and has even managed to preserve herself in her pure state despite the attempts of her fosterers to do the opposite. Because Lysimachus has handed her actual gold, she can purchase herself, after a fashion, and she does not have to trade her flesh for gold. Still, she will serve, and pay, the bawd. But rather than serve the flesh with her flesh, she will serve the spirit with her artistry. She will teach singing and weaving and sewing and dancing—precisely the kinds of entertainments that her grandfather used to entertain her father as her parents wooed during the tourney.

The levels of risk-taking and risk management here are multiple. Buying Marina comes with the risk that she might not actually perform as expected. This risk can be mitigated through rape, but it turns out that the men who threaten to rape her are not essentially rapists and so they cannot bring themselves to commit this act. Indeed, the attendants, Pander and Bolt, would rather change jobs than stay on in defiance of decency.

Deciding that Marina is the prostitute one wishes to consort with comes with yet another risk, that of losing one's immoral desires. The gentlemen and Lysimachus, and perhaps others off stage all end up losing this desire. What mitigates the risk they undertake is that this loss is actually a good one rather than a devastating one. They spend a little money, they are lectured about what morality really is, they learn, and they move forward to a more moral life. Marina, like Socrates in the cave, brings truth to those who most need it. Marina's relationship to gold is similar to that of Socrates in the *Apology* as both have others offering payments to help them out of difficulties while still obeying the basic demands of the justice system. Marina makes use of the money while Socrates rejects it within the economy of the *Republic*.

And, of course, the Bawd has the additional risk of losing all of her customers and her whole business because Marina is converting everyone to a life without illicit desire. That turning a town toward morality comes with risk is both surprising and indicative of the entrenched nature of human desire turned toward immoral goals. This risk of loss of the economic underpinnings of a society because of a turn toward morality is noted by Socrates in the *Republic*, and he deals with this issue by getting rid of everyone over the age of ten. They are too entrenched in their ways, too immoral, too attached to money, too fully turned away from the true direction ever to turn around and face the light. Marina deals with this issue differently. She willingly pays the bawdy house to cover their losses over the bet they made by buying her. Indeed, unlike Dionyza, Marina is quite willing to make repayment for the poor risk decisions of others.

Act V begins with Helicanus's arrival at Mytilene, Lysimachus's greeting, and a deeply melancholy Pericles yet again on a ship. This trip, this ship, this Pericles, are a world away from the much younger, much more swaggering and adventurous Pericles we have found on ships, on shores, in jousts, wooing women and drinking wine. This Pericles hardly interacts with the world, hardly seems aware that there is a world. He has been beaten down by risk and loss, by incredulity. Helicanus says, "the main grief springs from the loss / Of a beloved daughter and wife" (5.1.24). Of course, the loss of his family is merely the main grief, not all of the grief. He has also wooed where there is incest, has had to flee for his life, has been through shipwrecks, jousts, rescues, favor trading, hopes, improper burials, and loss he was not able to witness. Without a proper grave, there is no site for mourning, and so mourning is incomplete. Without witnessing death, death takes on a life of its own, as it were, and so Marina's death is left to his imagination. What could it mean to have the sea (Marina) die at night, as Dionyza suggests she and Cleon maintain. The whole trajectory of Pericles's life, so far, has been in the wrong direction. He has risked much, been rewarded some, and lost all. The lottery of life, the market, the ways of the heart, these have let him down.

Lysimachus greets Pericles, but Helicanus is now the language of Pericles and so Helicanus speaks for him. He says, "It is in vain. He will not speak to you" (5.1.33).

We now have an answer for what Pericles will say when he finds out about the death of Marina. He will say nothing until she is not dead any longer. Marina is called to visit Pericles and she brings with her gifts of music and language. He does not respond to her music or to her presence (5.1.73). But then he begins to respond to her being a maid, and her coming of good parentage.

The speech that engages Pericles notes the great losses Marina has suffered, the great heights from which she has fallen. Perhaps his narcissism is awakened by one very much like him and like his wife and like his daughter. Perhaps it is more resemblance to those he has loved and lost. Perhaps it is merely her virginity that attracts him at first.

He says,

. . . . For thou look'st
Like one I loved indeed. What were thy friends:
Disdst thou not say, when I did push thee back __
Which was when I perceived thee—that thou cam'st
From good descending? (5.1.115-119)

Pericles recognizes something in Marina's face and tale that sparks something in him. Her "good descending" would be his own position, and her facial resemblance to his lost wife would be the memory of his beloved. It is, then, something of a combination of his sense of himself and his memories of his wife that spark his return to the world, his conquering not of the sea or love, but of his own melancholy.

Pericles learns that her name is Marina, that she is a king's daughter. With incredulity, he asks, "But are you flesh and blood? / Have you a working pulse and are no fairy? / Motion as well? Speak on. Where were you born? / And wherefore called Marina?" (5.1.143-146).

If, as he is beginning to suspect, this really is Marina, his Marina, in front of him, then she is undead. The risk here is the risk of hope against probability. Pericles did not witness Marina's death, but it happened in language from people he has trusted and therefore it has to have happened. If Marina is in front of him, using language, she has somehow undone death, undone the world, undone what has been done and has restored Pericles and herself to a prior state. Only an adventurer, a risk taker, would be willing to believe this tale, these words, this Marina.

Very quickly, Marina adds in enough detail to make it clear that she is Marina. She relates her story,

The king my father did in Tarsus leave me,
Till cruel Cleon, with his wicked wife,
Did seek to murder me and wooed a villain
To attempt it, who having drawn to do't,
A crew of pirates came and rescued me,
Brought me to Mytilene. (5.1.161-166)

This detailed account is enough to raise the dead Pericles back to life, to tie him to the world. It was supposed to be Marina who was dead, but Pericles died in her place. Marina managed throughout her "death" to stay very much alive. Pericles has been drawn out of himself by Marina's music, words, virginity, face, and finally by a precise set of details, as if the world has slowly been coming into focus for him, with Marina as the single focal point. Marina has given him back his life but has not had to risk her virginity at all. This conversion is far less fraught than those that occurred in the brothel, but the complete moral goodness of Marina is still part of the conversion experience.

Pericles calls Helicanus over and, in another kind of incredulity, one that is both joyous and still mystified, he says,

Helicanus, strike me, honoured sir,
Give me a gash, put me to present pain,
Lest this great sea of joyous rushing upon me
O'erbear the shores of my mortality
And drown me with their sweetness. (5.1.180-184)

Pericles begs for punishments, strikes, gashes and pain that will overwhelm his overwhelmed senses. The joy is too much and must be tempered with pain. The sea has given him much, Marina has given him much, and with much giving, there is a risk of drowning in the gifts. If it is the sea that gives you gifts, the risk of drowning is that much greater. It would be a sweet drowning, but a drowning nonetheless.

Joy, then, can be as much a source of incredulity as can be the hellish consequences of hell-inspired decisions. The soul in Book X of the *Republic* is as overwhelmed as is Pericles. Pericles has spent a metaphorical thousand years down and to the left, and is about to ascend to try all over again to make the right decisions, to play the risks more appropriately. He has learned much and may, perhaps, remember much. To the extent that his narcissism has played a role in his awakening, we can wonder about the learning process, but to the extent that Marina has a hold over him, and that her command of the economy of the sea is complete, we can take a risk and assume that Pericles will now come out well.

Pericles and Marina are reunited as father and daughter once each uses names. Marina has already named herself, but Pericles needs yet more information and wants to know her mother's name, too. Marina demands to hear his name first and he obliges. Once the names are public, and Marina knows "Pericles" and Pericles knows "the daughter of Thaïsa" Pericles is nearly completely ready to throw off his melancholy and rejoin the world. He asks for new clothing, declares Marina a princess, and is now prepared to meet Lysimachus properly, as a king meets a governor.

Pericles is serenaded by the music of the spheres, music that no one else hears, but that seems to indicate that Pericles is now finished with his suffering. Pericles then needs rest, descends into a sleep in which Diana appears and tells him to appear at her temple in Ephesus. He puts Diana's orders ahead of his desire to take revenge upon Cleon in Tarsus, a risk with a tremendous payoff for him.

At the temple of Diana, Pericles gives a brief rundown of the action of the play, his life story, and is reunited with Thaïsa, who has been housed there for all these years of separation. Thaïsa faints. When she comes to, Pericles declares,

The voice of dead Thaïsa! (5.3.34)

For Pericles, Thaïsa has been dead and improperly buried and not fully mourned. That her voice comes to him must seem more like the music of the spheres or the appearance of Diana than the actual voice of his actual wife. It is an impossible moment, one experienced through incredulity, but one that will be resolved in joy and reunion rather than continued shock or rage or melancholy or resignation.

Pericles calls out, in his joy, "This, this! No more, you gods!" (5.3.40). This line could be delivered as much by a victim of torture as by a celebrant. The line between the two moments is a fine one, indeed. Pericles elaborates on his call for "enough,"

Your present kindness
Makes my past miseries sports. You shall do well

That on the touching of her lips I may
Melt and no more be seen. O, come, be buried
A second time within these arms. (5.3.40-44)

The gods have nearly, or perhaps fully, destroyed Pericles only to remake him, and his forgiveness, amazement, incredulity and acceptance of the fates are all brought together in these lines. He would gladly have one more moment with his beloved, a moment that would undo all time back to the moment before she "died" in childbirth and was "buried" at sea. And after that moment, he could die, he could have her properly buried in his arms, they could both die. All of his suffering is as nothing, or is sport. It all fades in the moment.

Pericles ends the main action of the play with a number of declarations.
Pure Dian,
I bless thee for thy vision and will offer
Night-oblations to thee. Dear Thaïsa,
This prince, the fair betrothed of your daughter,
At Pentapolis shall marry her.
And now this ornament
Makes me look dismal will I clip to form,
And what this fourteen years no razor touched
To grace thy marriage day I'll beautify. (5.3.69-77)

And further, Pericles and Thaïsa will reign in Pentapolis while Lysimachus and Marina reign in Tyrus.

Gower lets us know that,
For wicked Cleon and his wife, when fame
Had spread his cursed deede to th'honoured name
Of Pericles, to rage the city turn,
That him and his they in his palace burn. (Epilogue, 11-14)

The resolutions here are significant for understanding what Pericles has become, finally, in what Marjorie Garber calls a "maturation myth."[20] He allows Diana and the gods to take care of righting injustice and more humbly agrees to honor Diana and rule appropriately in Pentapolis, where Thaïsa's father has reigned and has died. His daughter and son-in-law take over Tyre from him. He shaves his beard to reveal his face to the world; that is, he removes an "ornament" in order to reveal the interior that has been hidden. The physical version of what the beard covers is, of course, his face. The more rarefied version is the baring of his soul. As the heavens have shown him their music, so he can now show people his face.

Antiochus and his daughter, sinners both, are done in by a bolt of lightning from the heavens. Cleon and his wife, wicked both, are done in by their people. Pericles and Thaïsa, and Lysimachus and Marina, on the contrary, will rule after much suffering because their sins are lesser, their punishments have worked, and all four have learned modesty.

If we read the tale of these characters back into the *Republic*, we find that Pericles may well fit into the structure of the Myth of Er. He, like the soul that has to pick a life, has lived in a well-ordered city, with a good father. Pericles has not, perhaps, made only good decisions. He has taken on risk and adventure as are appropriate for a young noble man. He has desired where he should not have, he has helped others and been met with betrayal, he has angered the sea but has also been given help by the same sea. He has cycled through an economy of punishment and redemption for his sins, and has come out in better shape than the souls in the *Republic*, for those souls would seem to be in an endless repetition of sin and punishment and redemption, a series in which learning is not permanent, and every other generation or so, one eats one's children, and in the other generations, one picks a simpler life. Pericles seems to have learned to trust the gods, whereas that first soul blames the gods. Pericles shows moments of joyous incredulity rather than angered incredulity, and moments of melancholic resignation rather than rage.

To the extent that Pericles accepts what the gods mete out, he is in better shape morally than Antiochus and his daughter, and Cleon and his wife. These characters seem to play games in repetition and language that deny what the gods have created. They take risks that require the world to be what it is not, and as world-deniers, or god-deniers, they must repay for the complete loss of everything they have taken risks for.

Antiochus's repetitions of sin and killing those who identify his sinning are in a cycle of denying that he has sinned. He acts as if this game changes the reality of the horror of his crimes. But killing those who solve his riddle does not actually return his daughter's virginity and his innocence. It only seems that way to a sick and twisted king whose misrule must be dealt with.

Cleon and Dionyza, too, act as if changing language changes the world. That one could find words to describe Marina's death, that one could simply say that fostering is not preservation, that death happens, is terrible enough. That Marina is not actually dead, but is made to seem dead to Pericles is all the worse. That Leonine is part of the lie-telling and the attempt to alter the world through language and belief means of course that his death, too, must happen. And further, that Cleon and Dionyza enact this world-changing through the denial of the permanent debt that all of Tarsus owes Pericles for his rescue of them when they were starving and contemplating eating their own children and one another is all the worse. Pericles saved Cleon and Dionyza's daughter from being a main course, and as payback, Cleon and

Dionyza end up "eating" Marina. The risks of defying the gods by attempting to change the world through language do not grant a boon in the end. Indeed, such an attempt leads to a complete loss.

The risks of the life of an adventurer, when met with some amount of acceptance of the consequences of those risks, end up in an economy of reward and punishment, suffering and redemption, such that there may be some worth to them. Pericles has to learn how to be a good king, a modest man, satisfied with staying home in the evenings. That is, he has to age significantly. The economy of the sea, the discipline of the gods, the goodness of his daughter all grant him what he needs most.

NOTES

1. "Pericles easily discovers the incest implied," Jeanie Grant Moore, "Riddled Romance: Kingship and Kinship in *Pericles*," in *Rocky Mountain Review of Language and Literature* 17 (1) (2003): 35.
2. Gossett, "Introduction," to William Shakespeare, *Pericles* (London: Arden Shakespeare, Third Series, Thomson Learning, 2004), 107, 1–163.
3. Gossett, "Introduction," in *Pericles*, 115.
4. Gossett, "Introduction," in *Pericles*, 115.
5. Lynda E. Boose, "The Father and the Bride in Shakespeare," in *PMLA* 97 (3) (May 1982): 339.
6. W.B. Thorne, "Pericles and the 'Incest-Fertility' Opposition," in *ELH* 27 (4) (December 1960): 47.
7. Thorne, "Pericles and the 'Incest-Fertility' Opposition," 49.
8. Moore, "Riddled Romance," 42.
9. Harold Bloom, *Shakespeare: The Invention of the Human* (New York: Riverhead Books, Penguin, Putnam, 1998), 605.
10. Moore, "Riddled Romance," 40.
11. Gossett, "Introduction," in *Pericles*, 147.
12. Gossett, "Introduction," in *Pericles*, 149.
13. Moore, "Riddled Romance," 38.
14. Gossett, *Pericles*, note 31, p. 252.
15. Moore, "Riddled Romance," 40.
16. Gossett, "Introduction," in *Pericles*, 139–140.
17. Moore, "Riddled Romance," 40.
18. Annette Flower, "Disguise and Identity in *Pericles, Prince of Tyre*," in *Shakespeare Quarterly* 26 (1) (Winter 1975): 31.
19. Moore, "Riddled Romance," 42.
20. Marjorie Garber, *Shakespeare After All* (New York: Anchor Books, 2004), 761.

Part III

BIRTH AND INFINITE DEBT

THE CHOICE OF MEANING

Prologue
The Republic *and the Philosopher's Birth and Debt*

In part I, the concern is the assumption of either a comic or a tragic outlook such that the possibility of the other position is ignored, leading to either comic or tragic incredulity. The soul who chooses first in Book X of the *Republic* has lived a comic life and fails to take account of tragic possibility and thus finds himself fated to eat his own children. Othello ignores Iago's comic or buffoonish side and ends up enacting tragedy when he could have followed the rules of comedy instead. And in *The Comedy of Errors*, we see multiple enactments of comic assumptions that miss out on the tragic underpinnings before we finally find a comic resolution. The resolution, though, is a tragedy of sorts for the Dromios, even if everything works out for the other characters and for the general economy. Losing sight of either tragic or comic possibility causes terrible harm, in both private and public spheres, and across the political and economic scenes.

Part II of this book focuses on the concerns regarding a balance between polity and economy. Money relations in the *Republic* are problematic as Cephalus tries to figure out what a good inheritance is, and as Socrates decides simply to ban even the touching of gold for the guardians. Any concern with being paid or being rewarded or gaining that is monetary rather than soul and justice focused causes innumerable problems for both individual souls and for the polity as a whole. The goal in the *Republic*, then, is to keep money and polity in their proper places. In *The Merchant of Venice*, we see a similar concern about the boundaries of the two spheres as Shylock misuses the court system and the polity, and misuses money relations and the economy, to deal with revenge issues. We see, as well, that Antonio misuses a variety of relationships to deal with his sense of melancholy and his desire for some kind of excitement. The misuse of money, and the turn to the polity, both incur great risk and the risk leads to paybacks that ripple through the entire political economy of Venice. And finally, in *Pericles*, we see the ways that money and flesh, desire and rule, risk and loss, and the repetition compulsion, all ripple through both political and economic structures. The goal, then, in each of these texts, is to find a balance and a set of boundaries such that the political and the economic can function properly, can guide us and be guided by us, and can help underpin proper human relations, proper marriages, and proper rule.

The final part of this book will focus on the paired terms "birth" and "debt" with an eye toward seeing that the two terms are, in some crucial ways, interchangeable. Where comedy and tragedy must both be watched for, and where polity and economy must both be bounded and balanced, birth and debt must be seen as nearly the same thing, in that each entails the other.

To develop the notion that birth and debt are deeply connected, we will look at the obligations that philosophers have, by virtue of being what they are, to go back down into the cave and there to attempt the turning of souls.[1] Using that notion of obligation by virtue of being (of having been born, that is), we will look then at obligation as it is developed in Shakespeare's *Timon of Athens*, a play that focuses on generosity, gift giving, payback, and philanthropy and misanthropy, and at *Measure for Measure*, which focuses on duty, the problems with Aristotelian incontinence, the gift of mercy, the obligation to marry properly, and the obligation to rule with wisdom and with the idea of justice and soul turning as the general purpose of life. *Timon* and *Measure* both can be read as having structures analogous to the cave in the *Republic*, and this likeness will be explored in this section. In each text, there is deep obligation by virtue of having been born. In the *Republic,* we see this obligation in the need for the rational part of the soul to control the other parts, for the rational part of the city to rule, and for all desire to be muted by a kind of debt to the other parts. In *Timon,* we see the obligations for proper generosity and mercy, and the soul and society wrecking that selfish generosity engenders. And in *Measure for Measure*, we see the ways that lack of self-control bring about harm, whether the lack of self-control is intellectual, spiritual, or physical. Every kind of incontinence is a problem and each character owes proper continence. That there is death by virtue of birth is a truism, but that there is, as well, debt, then, is the focus of this section.

There are a couple of obvious places where debt is a major issue in the *Republic*, and these will be discussed in due fashion. The first focus will be on the somewhat less obvious moments as these will set up the themes for the consideration of intergenerational issues and for the Allegory of the Cave.

In the *Republic*, there is a sustained argument through analogy that there is a profoundly important parallel between the soul and the state. Both have three parts, rational, spirited and appetitive in the soul and gold, silver and bronze for the metals, which correspond to the three classes, the rulers, the auxiliaries and the workers. Further, the kinds of constitution delineated in Books VIII and IX, in their downfall, are tied quite directly to the kinds of people who live in them. There are the three kinds of soul/constitution pairings that are "pure types," in which a part of the soul rules in singular fashion, and then there are "in between states" which are transitional between parts of the soul. In these transitional states, the parts of the soul or the parts of the state, pull in opposing directions. The lower part always seems to win during the decline, almost as if there is some kind of momentum downward, and the fight to rise up (out of the cave, as it were) contradicts some kind of law of political gravity. Socrates does not say that there are equilibria or that there is chaos or that sometimes things go better for a few generations. The downfall is all, for this part of the story. There is no drama, and perhaps not even tragedy anymore as the inevitable happens and is caused by what is there already, with no hope of doing anything differently.

Given that there is this deep tie between the structure of the state and the structure of the soul, between the downfalls of each, and between the two as desire battles reason, it is quite unsurprising that the following interchange between Socrates and Glaucon concludes Book IX:

> And again in respect to honors, he will look to the same thing. He will voluntarily partake of and taste those he may believe will make him better, but those which might loosen his established disposition he will flee both in public and in private.
>
> Then since he is concerned about that he will refuse to take part in political affairs, he said.
>
> Yes, by the Dog, I replied. At least, he will take part in his own city, very much so, though perhaps not in the land of his origin, unless some divine fortune occurs.
>
> I understand, he said. You mean in the city established in reasoning which we are founding and have now described, though I think it does not exist anywhere on earth.
>
> But perhaps it is laid up as a standard or pattern in heaven, I replied, for him who wishes to see and, seeing, to found a colony of it within himself. It makes no difference whether it exists somewhere, or ever will: he acts for this city alone, and for no other. (592a/324)

The most fundamental debt is detailed in this passage. We owe refusal of honors and refusal to partake in imitation political affairs, and we owe deeply to the city that is "laid up as a standard or pattern in heaven," or, clearly, the Form of the City. Existence of that city does not matter, according to Socrates, but the debt is vast, and it is owed regardless of any other consideration. For the ideal city, even if it is a "colony within himself" he, any citizen of this ideal city, owes everything.[2]

To grasp the meaning of any other notion of proper debt and proper life within the *Republic*, we must come to terms with what it means to owe to that which does not exist, or which exists only as a colony in oneself, and what it means to owe that which gives no honors unless those honors increase the amount of indebtedness, for it is only within this notion of debt to a non-existent city, or to a non-necessarily existing city, that we can understand what reward does, what debt is, and what it means to live, to have been born.[3]

It is equally worth noting that this city, to which we owe all, and which does not exist, has been completely separated from "the land of his origin" "unless some divine fortune occurs." What is curious about this line, and what is, equally, crucial for the structure of the *Republic* is the separation of birth place from debt. The Myth of the Metals develops the theme of the tie between birthplace and debt. Socrates says,

> I will say, then—and yet, I do not know how I dare say it or what words to use: I will try first to persuade the rulers themselves and the soldiers, and then the rest of the city too, that what they thought they experienced—namely, that we reared and educated them—all happened as it were in a dream, when they themselves were in truth beneath the earth, being formed and nurtured within it, while their weapons and the rest of their equipment were being fashioned as well. When they were once fully completed, Earth, who is their mother, brought them forth, and now they must take counsel for the defense of their country as for a mother and nurse, if anyone comes against it, and consider the rest of their fellow citizens as brother born of Earth. (414d-414e)

The hope here is first, to create in language a reality that does not quite exist in reality, much the way world-spinning characters in both *Merchant* and *Pericles* try to do. Glaucon, with his finger on the pulse of common thought, replies, "No wonder you kept your fiction quiet so long" (415e). Clearly, at the most pragmatic level, there is much that is odd here, and Glaucon instantly sees the tale as at odds with anything anyone will believe about his or her origins.

More interestingly, though, is the whole idea of trying to create some kind of deeply felt obligation to place, to land, that underlies this myth. If we come from the land rather than from our mothers, we owe the land rather than owing our mothers. If all fellow citizens are brothers, then, assuming a non-pathological sibling sensibility, we owe our fellow citizens, and not merely our gene-sharers. We will be called upon to fight as payment for birth, and we will repay as called upon.

There is another level here that works alongside the land as origin versus the mother as origin, and the different kinds of debt one incurs in these two very different regimes. We might ordinarily think that there is an external, and therefore real, world, and an internal sense, or memory and set of meanings, attached to the real and external world. We trust our internal sense of the external world, but we know full well that any internal world we conjure is the stuff of fantasy and so is not to be trusted. The external world acts as a reality check on internal fantasy, and on the stories we tell about the external world. In many Shakespeare plays, it is clear that the external world always trumps internal fantasy and storytelling.

These terms are reversed, in a special way, by Socrates. We have, for Socrates, an internal and therefore real world and an internal sense or memory of that world, and it is the external world that we should not trust. But "external" and "internal" here are specialized terms. The colony within oneself is clearly an internal world, and it is precisely not tied to the external world, but, because Socrates is unconcerned with whether or not this colony within actually exists, and rather is concerned with a mode of thinking "as if," what ends up happening here is that the internal world, the colony within, acts as a reality check on the external world, the world of appearances.

Where Emilia and Dionzya create worlds in language in the hope that those worlds will come to substitute for the external world, but both do this world-spinning in bad faith, Socrates would have us perform a very different kind of world-spinning such that what we conjure is more real than what our senses dictate. Iago, the master of world-spinning, conjures in the worst faith of all.

What we have to think through here, then, is what differentiates Socrates' version of world-spinning from what Emilia, Dionyza, and Iago all do. What grounds the conjured world such that there is a check on fantasy, and such that fealty to this other world is in keeping with a good soul and a well-ordered state. Further, we need to grapple with the sources of obligation and the things to which we are obligated under the bad faith regime within Shakespeare's questionable or bad characters and what creates obligation within the Socratic regime. What, then, do we owe, when do we owe it, and to whom do we write out the check, as it were?

That final passage in Book IX suggests that we act only for this internal colony—that our chief and only debt is to a good city, a city that might not even exist. Given that our main debt, our only debt, is to this merely possible city, we need to grapple with what it could mean to owe a possibility rather than a necessity or an already-existing structure. Possibility, here, can be seen as a regime of risk. Thus, debt becomes a function of the merely possible rather than the actual. Risk management has to take account of the extra risk involved in creating a system of obligation that only might be a system of obligation. The obligation we take on, then, acts at the level of mere possibility, and yet it binds fully because it is still an obligation.

There are some clear Kantian themes here. For Kant, the kingdom of ends is by definition "merely possible" so that the achievement of such a state cannot act as a motivation for that state.[4] In similar fashion, reward is problematized within the Socratic framework such that we not only should not hope for reward, but in even more strong language, we should realize that reward can be our undoing. Reward that directs us wrongly, reward that empowers the lower parts of the soul, will steer us toward world-spinning that destroys.

What can it mean, then, to owe an internal colony, with no hope of reward? One owes, it seems, that which does not exist and one gets nothing in return. The risk of not paying this debt is that one pays the wrong state, and the risk of accepting a reward as payment for paying off the debt is that one's soul is made worse. The debt, I will argue in what follows, is infinite and unpayable, and yet must be paid. The reward is as non-existent as the internal colony. We owe infinitely, we gain nothing, and yet we must pay. The many paradoxes here will be spelled out as we look at the philosopher's descent into the cave, the guardians' relationship to money, and the debt of inheritance that comes back multiple times throughout the *Republic*. And in light of the suggestion here that this internal colony, this polity that is "his own," exists merely in language, we can rethink the whole of the *Republic* as Socrates' own internal colony, one without a confusion of comedy and tragedy, a misbalance of polity and economy, and one most especially in which debt is properly understood as being one in kind with birth.

Where Emilia and Dionyza would create worlds in language in order to justify bringing the immoral fantastic into being, Socrates would justify creating a world in language to bring the being into the moral fantastic. Socrates, then, is something of the obverse of Emilia and Dionyza, and is, as has been noted, akin to Marina.

Books VI and VII of the *Republic* contain notable stories, or world-spinnings: the ship, the sun, the line, and finally, the cave.[5] There is an inexorable development from ship, through the abstractions of the sun and line, and then back to a social scene in the cave.[6]

On the ship, we are gathered haphazardly and we attempt competitive rule through both physical strength (overpowering the ship's captain) and persuasion (using bad arguments). The crew is in conflict over who should rule, the captain is incompetent, there are attempts to drug one another, the use of violence is the norm, and none save one knows how to navigate by using what is beyond the ship (the stars and the light) (See 488b-d). On such a ship as this one, the oligarchic rule of the owner gives way to democratic attempts at persuasion that then fall rapidly into tyrannical murder as the desire to steer the ship and control the other sailors far outstrips any kind of knowledge of how to do any of this ship-stuff properly. World-spinning for the sake of desire, for power and control leads to disaster both for the ship and for Dionyza and Emilia. Neither the sailors nor these women has the art of navigation, piloting, or rule drawn correctly. None seems to feel any sense of debt to anything save personal or internal desires and public show. It is worth noting here that the ship stands in not merely for the state but also for the soul. The appetitive and spirited soul wrestle with or try to persuade by turns, the "real navigator," or reason while reason is focused on the stars above, or the Forms beyond. The ship of state, then, is also the ship of soul, and navigation of a ship on the water is equally navigation of the soul tossed and turned by desire and spirit.

Further, that the sailors claim that navigation cannot be taught, but merely practiced, means that the sailors would deny any kind of debt to a teacher. Without a teacher, without an art or a skill, without reason, rule becomes a mix of persuasion of the worst sort (world-spinning) and force (drugging, murder, banishment). The denial of both teachers and a teachable subject frees the sailors from the need to learn any kind of discipline, whether of one's soul or a field of knowledge or skill.

Given how much information the sailors are missing about what it really means to navigate or pilot or rule or live, it is no surprise that they fail to learn and to incur a debt that comes from being on the ship, kept safe and sound by proper navigation. Proper navigation, or proper rule, would make obvious the craft and the debt to the craftsmen. But on this ship, as in Tarsus and Venice and Cyprus, rule is improper, debt is inscrutable, and people fail to feel that they owe the world truth, that they should not spin tales to absolve themselves of real responsibility.

The genuine pilot referred to above sees the world differently from the way the sailors see it. The pilot can see beyond immediate desire, beyond the craving for power and drunken revelry. Indeed, the ship, a metaphor for rule, clearly, is also a metaphor for an actual navigator. To see the ship properly, the navigator looks at the stars in space, the seasons in time, the invisible winds. To see, even for a navigator, is to "see" the invisible. To persuade Dionyza and Emilia, Cleon and Iago, that well beyond immediate desire and a sense of resentment there is an unseen world that must guide the use of the seen world, and that this unseen world has no duty to desire, though desire owes the unseen world a profound debt would seem to be an impossible task. Equally impossible would it be to persuade the sailors to put away their drugs and drinks, their muscles and their desires and sit still and listen to lectures about the starry heavens above.

Socrates asks of the sailors, "[D]on't you believe that sailors on ships managed this way will call the true pilot really a stargazer and an idle babbler, and useless to them?" (488e).

The real stargazer, the spaced out dreamer, the philosopher who looks far away to see what is up close, who abstracts from the ship and sees the forces it depends on for safe travel, the one with knowledge of the world, is precisely the one dismissed by the crowd in its immediacy. The debt that would properly be owed cannot be paid. The real stargazer owes it to the crowd to practice his craft, the crowd owes the world to listen to the stargazer, but neither party to this version of the debt can repay. If the stargazer sees the debt, he still cannot repay it as he will be killed unless he can pretend to be what he is not. That is, the stargazer can only repay if he can spin a world that persuades the crowd to listen rather than to kill him. The crowd, of course, cannot understand a stargazer who talks about invisible forces and space and time, because they have no context for understanding how the positions of stars and other things beyond can affect something as concrete and localized as a ship.

If the stargazer is even to attempt repayment of the debt, then, he must lie to the crowd for the crowd's benefit. World-spinning here is part of repayment rather than part of the desiring soul's craving for power. Marina, in this context, can be seen as a world-spinner whose tales of morality are correctives for the lack of sight of those around her. She pilots the bawdy house away from its morally stained purpose. She overcomes her uselessness in clever fashion, though, and thus can maintain both her status as a moral guide and her labor of debt repayment. Marina is, then, something of an answer to the challenge Socrates gives us in the ship analogy. There is a way for the real stargazer to use language creatively to spin a world that arcs toward truth and gives the opportunity to the stargazer both to repay a debt and to show the crowd that there is an art to navigation.

The stargazer is, then, the one who looks up. In his looking, he, of course, sees the stars by which to navigate the ship. One cannot navigate a ship by a path in the water, or by anything that is actually on the ship. The guides are distant, and not actually ship-related.

In the next analogy Socrates uses to try to explain what we should be doing as opposed to what we actually do, there is an extended discussion of the role of illumination. On the way to this discussion, the notion of debt comes up in an awkward fashion. Glaucon wants to know what the Good is, and Socrates replies with a deferral.

> [Glaucon replies] Please speak, he said. You will pay your debt another time for the explanation you owe of the father.

> [Socrates replies] I might wish, I said, that I were able to pay the debt and allow you to receive the principal, rather than, as now, only the interest. But at any rate accept the interest and offspring of the Good itself. Take care, however, that I

do not in some why mislead you against my will, and render a false account of the offspring.[7] (506d-507)

Already, before we have even gotten to the analogy of the sun, we are placed in some kind of debt. We owe the "father," or the Good, a direct and immediate understanding or confrontation. We are not yet ready to pay such a debt as the father is yet incomprehensible. The debt is there, unspoken, and perhaps ever unpayable, and yet we must attempt to come to terms with this father, the Good, at least analogically. Just as the real stargazer looks well beyond the ship to come to understand the ship and its path, so the real philosopher and the real student must look beyond the immediate surroundings to come to understand the Good well enough to pay the debt. In this case, the debt, the interest, and the offspring are all somehow taken up with knowledge. To pay the father back, one must know the father. Knowing the father will grant the offspring and the interest and indeed the principal. The debt, then, can be repaid if the knowledge can be grasped. But the question will remain regarding whether or not any of the analogies offered in Book VII is sufficient for debt repayment.

In the analogy of the sun, Socrates sets up a relationship between the eye as the organ of sight, the object as a thing seen, and light, in this case sunlight, as the medium through which seeing is possible. He notes that "the Sun is not vision, but, as cause of vision, is seen by vision itself" (508b).

The sun causes or is the medium through which vision is possible, and analogically,

> So also then conceive what belongs to the soul: when it is fixed upon what truth and reality illuminate it conceives and knows it, and proves to possess thought. But when it is fixed upon what is mixed with darkness, upon what comes to be and passes away, it judges and becomes dull and changes opinions back and forth, and seems not to possess thought.
>
> . . .
>
> This then, which provides truth to things known and gives to the knower the power of knowing, you must say is the Idea of the Good. As cause of knowledge and of truth, you must understand it as being known. But beautiful as knowledge and truth both are, you will rightly believe it is other and still more beautiful than they. Even as there it is right to regard light and vision as Sun-like, but wrong to believe them the Sun, so also here it is right to regard knowledge and truth as Good-like, but wrong to believe either of the Good. Instead, the possession of the Good is still more to be valued. (508d-e)

The sun provides illumination that is closer to a concrete experience than the "illumination" that the Good provides. If light is beautiful, and if what we see is beautiful, what the Good "illuminates" is far more beautiful. If light lets us see objects, and the Good lets us "see" knowledge and truth, still objects are not light, and knowledge and truth are not the Good.

It is unclear precisely how the analogy is meant to work given that we already revere knowledge and truth far more than we revere anything we see. And yet, we have from Book I the sense that though knowledge and truth sound like really wonderful pursuits, they are laborious pursuits and it might be more fun to circumlocute, to talk about money and inheritance, to talk about sex, to get drunk, to reminisce, to shoot the breeze, and so on.

There is still this debt that Socrates is pointing toward even in the analogy of the Sun. The discussion continues,

> You mean a matchless beauty, he said, if it provides knowledge and truth, but is itself beyond them in beauty. For you surely don't mean it is pleasure.
>
> Don't blaspheme, I replied. But examine the image of it still further in this way:
>
> ....
>
> I suppose you will say that the Sun provides not only the power of being seen to things seen, but also of becoming and growth and nurture, though it is not itself becoming.
>
> ....
>
> And say also for things known, then, not only that intelligibility is present by agency of the Good, but reality and being is also present to them by it, though the Good is not being, but even beyond being, surpassing it in respect to dignity and power. (509a-b)

Glaucon's interjection of the word "pleasure" here is a breach of what is owed to the beauty of the Good. Even the negative that goes with the mention is unacceptable to Socrates, and seems to cause a moment of incredulity. There is a proper way to talk about the Good, and pleasure is clearly not the right affect to bring to bear on the lofty sensibility Socrates is gesturing toward. Pleasure is too taken with the animal part of the soul and is not at all what should motivate action. Further, pleasure suggests a debt to the body rather than a debt to the rational soul, a gesture to the concrete rather than to the abstract, a gesture to some object in the world rather than to something beyond.

Noting that the sun does more than merely illuminate is the next step in the development of this analogy. The sun provides energy and growth, nurture and therefore parenting, possibility and therefore futurity. We owe all that we are and all that we might be to the sun, and we need to repay this debt by respecting the sun on its own terms. As the sun grants us so much, so the Good "grants" us yet more. Whatever it is, it is "beyond being," with greater dignity and greater power than what it makes apparent to us. Underlying this gesture toward the ineffable is an important distinction between the medium of experience and the experience itself outside of its medium.

What we have access to, here, most concretely, is still vision and an object we see, and something of an understanding that the sun makes it possible to see that object, but is separate from both the object and the eye that does the seeing. That is, we are right back at the start of the analogy, in the more concrete experience of seeing. We still need to make some kind of journey from this concrete sense of what it is to see, to "see," to be and to become, to be possible, to be nurtured, to be beautiful beyond beauty. We need to come to terms, equally, with what is wrong with Emilia and Dionyza's world-spinning and what is right with the way Marina uses language, for Marina gestures toward the Socratic, while Emilia and Dionyza fail to do so.

The line analogy develops this journey from the concrete to the abstract, from the less true to the more true. Just as the real stargazer knows the ship best by looking up to the stars, and just as we know the things we see because of the light of the sun, so we journey along the line from what seems to be known to what is really known. (See 509d-510c)

At the bottom of the line are shadows and reflections, things that are "close-grained and smooth." These are the copies of objects that lose detail in the process of copying. They are smooth because they are missing the imperfections of surfaces and the gaps or lacunae or aporias that take up the spaces between the constituents of things. A mirror image is as smooth as the mirror, not as uneven as a face or as a reflected bedframe. A watery image is as smooth as the water, not as jagged as a tree branch.

We can extend this notion of images here to the kinds of smoothed out memories we have of events, of the passing of time, of our lives. The images of life, or the memories, typically lack the bumps and bruises that actual life contains. Thus, as Cephalus is reflecting from his age at his life, he is smoothing out his contradictions. And, further, we can start to see that any narrative account of a life will go through this same kind of smoothing process and leave us with a less than accurate sense of the life being narrated. If narration causes this much loss of information, and it certainly seems to, then the Book X choosing of a new life is all the more fraught for anyone who lacks philosophical training.

The animals and plants themselves take up the next space on the line. They are more concrete than the images of them, less ill-defined, and certainly not at all smooth. Rough skin, rough hides, full lives in time, raw emotions and actions in the world, all would go into this category. Here also would be people, as they are animals-in-the-world, rough in skin and rough in thought.

Iago, Emilia, and Dionyza have an odd existence in that they are not real people, and so belong at some level in the lowest category on the line—images. They are poetic creations, and as such, have a kind of timeless smoothness about them. But they are, at the same time, something like real, in that they have wrinkles and roughness, they try to create smooth worlds out of the roughness of their complex desires. As poetic objects, then, they have a mixed status on the line, somewhere between images and objects in the world.

At the top of the line, we find a distinction between the part that is dependent upon images in order to make arguments, and the part that needs nothing beyond itself in order to know. Dependence on images, or independence from images, is what is at stake in the move from merely being able to draw conclusions from arguments to the more full knowledge that comes from gaining access to first principles. Underlying this move up the line from shadows of object to first principles is a kind of economy of debt and obligation that comes from the mere fact of existence.

Shadows and watery reflections depend for their existence on the objects that cast the imitations and on the media that carry the imitations over. For their very existence, then, there is a debt taken on, and the debt is paid, badly perhaps, by the act of containing an image. The image is imperfect, in that it is smoothed out, though perhaps we would like to think of it as perfected by the smoothing out of imperfections. (No doubt, memories and soft lighting, and perhaps a little petroleum jelly on the camera lens, make us all more beautiful than we were.)

But the smoothing out of images, like the cleaning up of data outliers, is a partial truth, and therefore does not fully repay the debt that is owed. In fact, the telling of tales, the falsification of images, the spinning of worlds, ends up causing enormous problems as it gives us a false sense of what is and misguides our actions. The result of the bad guidance that images give us is either our own death at the hands of a tyrant or the devouring of our children at our own hands.

Further up the line, there is dependence on images even as we have moved into the intelligible realm. The lower section of the intelligible still needs images in order to make arguments, and is still looking, as it were, downward instead of upward. The upward climb along the line has a downward pull, and that downward pull resides in an economy in which debts to the lower must be repaid. Just as Marina, up higher than anyone else in the bawdy house, still needs to repay her debt, still needs to look down, so the lower part of the intelligible still needs images of a sort.

It is only when we reach the top of the line, where we are moving to first principles through the use of purely abstract concepts that we finally move away from a real tie to the world. Even though at this point, images have fallen away and knowledge is purely conceptual, there is still a kind of debt to be repaid, and there is still a kind of economy within the line. To reach the top requires a climb, and without the bottom sections, there is nothing to climb on. Hence the top needs the structure of the bottom, the climber needs the mountain. Further, the structures of relationships between parts and wholes, or shadows and objects, or conclusions and first principles, only make sense as structures in a whole discourse. They may well eventually be independent of the prior steps, but structural thinking comes developmentally rather than all at once in immediacy. To become acquainted with the most abstract, the least dependent, then, requires a journey through the dialectic from the shadow to the light. Anyone who makes it all the way up owes what is below for the train fare.

The line analogy is rendered without people who make the journey up, and so the sense of debt is obscure, even if it is constitutive. It is in the cave analogy that the notion of debt becomes explicit once again. (See 514a-b) The people in the cave are physically bound, sensorially bound, denied any information save what comes to them passively. They cannot look up in order to, say, gaze at the stars and navigate, they cannot look to one another and make eye contact and develop deep bonds to one another. They are in a kind of imitation space with imitation light and imitation bodies and imitation images. They are at the bottom of the line, unexposed to the sun, to conversation that might correct their views, to any kind of comparison that would lead them to turn.[8] Their vision is limited to the shadows cast by the puppets; their hearing is limited to the echoes of sounds seemingly coming from the shadows. "Such prisoners, then . . . would not acknowledge as true anything except shadows of artificial objects" (515c).

The images that the cave dwellers think are most true are actually well-removed from reality. They are fakes by being shadows, they are all the more fake by being cast by fake objects, and still more fake by being cast by flickering firelight that plays on the fake objects. Further, sounds deceive, and the lack of bodily motion and human conversation create still more degrees of separation from anything approaching truth. The multiple degrees of removal from what is real keep the cave dwellers from recognizing their positions in the world, from narrating events with an eye toward truth, from developing relationships toward truth and toward one another that might carry real debt. The cave dwellers, then, do not recognize their dependence on anything outside of themselves as causes of their experiences. Socrates says, "Such prisoners, then . . . would not acknowledge as true anything except shadows of artificial objects" (515c).

Without experience outside their system, without dialogue, without comparisons, "summoners," to use Socrates' word to describe relative values, people cannot see their own flaws and strive toward amelioration. Without a system of indebtedness to one another, such as comes from recognition of the value of the perspectives of others, no one has the kind of personal incentive to change. It is precisely through the mediation of others and of alternative perspectives that people can begin to feel the debt they have taken on as they have begun to change.

Socrates next asks us to consider "what release and healing from the bonds of unwisdom would consist in" (515c). This language is striking as the sense is clear that not only is there profound ignorance among those stuck in this cave, but further, there is great harm from which the prisoners must heal. Bonds of the sort that keep people in unwisdom do great harm. Bonds that develop between people as a part of healing, though, are different in kind.[9] Such bonds, what this text is terming infinite debt, are a condition of existence rather than a source of wounding from which we must heal.

Socrates gives us a path out of the cave, a path dependent on release, one whose trajectory is upward towards the sun and one that begins the healing process that must occur in after the damage that imprisonment has done. (See 515c-d) There is a transition from the physical pain of the bonds—a stiff neck and squinting eyes and a backache—to the psychic pain of being pushed away from beliefs one has held as true toward a different set of beliefs based on new evidence.

Having to change beliefs based on new evidence is often painful in the extreme because of the familiarity of the old, the sense of the rightness of one's habits and even a kind of feeling of debt, a false debt, one feels toward one's beliefs. Clearly, Cepahlus falls into this pattern of preferring familiarity. He is not alone in this discomfort with change. This sense of owing oneself fealty to one's (incorrect) beliefs is painful to overcome. It is not so much the other people to whom one feels debt in the cave, as communication and relationships are false, but rather the sense of debt one feels at one's success in the artificial economy of the cave. Socrates briefly describes this economy, suggesting contests and prizes for the winners.

The former cave dwellers who have escaped are not interested in this economy, but those still imprisoned are convinced that they have a handle on what matters, that they have discerned important patterns, that they are ahead of the curve, as it were. They strive for reward in their economy of guess-and-win, and the reward is worth the labor they put into pattern recognition. Those who have been unchained, have turned, faced the light, been "forcibly dragged . . . up the rugged steep ascent" out of the cave into first, shadows, and then images in water, and then objects, and then starlight and then moonlight and then sunlight (515c-516b).These people have started at the bottom of the line and have been dragged, in pain, up the line until they can contemplate the sun itself. Socrates then asks us to think about how such a person might feel about his life, how one released might feel pity for those in the cave.

Pity is an important emotion here. That one who has escaped can remember "where he came from" suggests that there is already, at the moment of escape, a kind of debt. Pity moves us to amelioration, fellow-feeling moves us to help those who have suffered, and self-identification moves us to work with those who are where we have been. One's origins are not to be escaped from, despite the need to escape from them. That is, one can leave, but one must return. The debt is an original debt that stems simply from having been born into a condition in which others, too, are born.

This debt holds despite what Socrates says people in the cave, in the thick of competition, would think of a returning former inmate. Such a one would be a source of comedy, a target of scorn and disbelief. A more ominously, such a returning one would be a target of violence. The bringers of misunderstood truth are considered threats.

Those who have never left the cave cannot at all understand what it means to have left. They cannot see what a returnee has seen, they lack the vocabulary, the conceptual categories, the imagination, the perspective on images and objects that would allow them to understand anything that the escapee has experienced. Without experience, then, there is no conception of experience. We are, that is, stuck. We are stuck where we are unless someone rips off our chains and drags us away so that we can see our situation in perspective, with difference and distinction. We need to understand both the medium through which we experience the world and the world itself as we experience it. None of this experience is possible without a guide of some sort, unless it happen by luck or accident.

Regarding the accuracy of the tale, Socrates responds in his customary fashion that we cannot really know what is true, only God can. But, "In the visible place it gives birth to Light and to the Sun, the Lord of Light; in the intelligible place it is itself Lord, and provides intelligence and truth. It must also be inferred that whoever intends to act wisely in public or private must see it" (517b-c). The theory of the Forms, the supremacy of the Form of the Good, the appearance/reality distinction itself—these are known only by God, and are merely inferred by humans. But the inference that things are thus is a worthwhile one if for no other reason than that we are better off thinking these things to be true rather than risking staying in the cave competing over our ability to predict which shadow comes next. If we act as if we are on such a journey, and if we act as if we might reach the end, and if we act as if there is a proper kind of debt, we can avoid the kind of world-spinning horror that

Dionzya renders. We can, instead, accept Marina's view that the good is both possible and necessary. To bear in mind that one might possibly be in a cave, as it were, is to keep in mind comic and tragic possibility, the possibility of being wrong, and the possibility of being released and owning one's liberators. Indeed, keeping in mind the workings of modal thinking is crucial for maintaining the kind of flexibility needed to avoid joining the Book X feast.

The language Socrates uses here, "lord" (*kurios*), "light," (*phos*), and "intelligible" (*to gnoston* and *to noesis*) is, perhaps, the language he might bring down to the cave in order to convince us that the turning and upward journey are worth the pain.[10] Cave dwellers are not in the position of always already having experienced multiple perspectives, escape, or direct light, and so it is only through analogy and imprecision, world-spinning for good purpose, that Socrates can communicate. At some level, perhaps, Socrates fails to repay his debt, and yet, necessarily he must try.[11]

Socrates then begins to widen the explanation of the debt that leads to the obligation to go back down into the cave,

> But isn't it also likely, I replied, and even necessary from what has been said, that a city cannot ever sufficiently be governed by those who are uneducated and without experience of truth, nor again by those allowed to pass their whole time in education Not the one, because they have no single target in life at which to aim in every action, public and private; not the other, because they'll be unwilling to act, believing they've been transported to the Isles of the Blessed while still alive. (519b-c)

One who has no education, no turning of the soul, does not know the good and therefore cannot aim the city toward the good. One who has only education is too comfortable, too good, to be willing to work and suffer.[12] Without a debt to the good, the city can aim at anything, and anything can seem like the good for a time. Because city and soul are united, misaiming a city is simultaneously misaiming the souls in that city. Ruination of all is the result. Just as misrule in *Pericles* leads to the destruction of those in the cities Pericles visits, so misrule for Socrates leads to general ruin.

The philosophers who refuse to govern with knowledge of the truth are not allowed to stay within the soul-turning realm, for they will mistake their life for their death. To have birth, debt, and death miscategorized is to risk the worst—the destruction of one's soul for having abided a destroyed city. To be unable to make that final decision in Book X, the final decision that is equally a first decision, is to ensure the worst. Birth, then, for a philosopher, is debt.

Continuing, Socrates says,

> Then it is our own task as founders . . . to compel the best natures to attain to the knowledge which we formerly described as most important: to see the Good

and rise upward in that ascent. And when they have ascended and sufficiently seen, not to allow them what is now allowed.

. . . .

To abide there . . . and refuse to go back down again among the prisoners and share their labors and honors, whether of lesser or more serious worth. (519c-d)

Philosophers must make the upward trek, despite the pain. They must make the downward trek again, despite the pain. They cannot be allowed to shirk this duty, to fail to repay the debt. They must share work, they must share value, and they must do so despite a strong preference for a very different sort of living death. Philosophers must live as humans, with all the potentials for failure, for death, for suffering. It is only through this attempt to repay the debt incurred by the ascent that philosophers can have a chance of preserving their souls.

Finally, Socrates says,

[W]e will not do an injustice to the philosophers who arise among us; we will speak justly to them in requiring them to care for and guard the rest. For we shall say that people of their sort born in other cities reasonably do not share their labors; for they grew up on their own in spite of the constitution in each city, and it is right that as self-sustaining and indebted for nurture to no one, they should not be quick to make payment for being nurtured. But as for you, we will say, we bred you for yourselves and for the rest of the city, as kings and leaders in the hive. You are better and more perfectly educated than the rest, and more able to have a share of both ways of life. You must go down then, each in his turn, to dwell with the others and become accustomed to see in the darkness. For once used to it, you will see immeasurable better than those there, and you will know each of the images for what it is, and of what it is an image, through having seen the truth of things beautiful and just and good. And in this way you will govern our city wide awake instead of in a dream, as most cities are now governed, where people fight over shadows and quarrel about office, supposing it a great good. The truth is surely this: that city is necessarily best and most free of faction in which those least eager to rule shall rule, and the city governed oppositely gains the opposite. (520a-d)

One's constitution is simultaneously one's fosterer and one's preserver, and one owes it deeply, even as it owes those it sustains, though Dionyza sees it otherwise. The city is the soul, the reluctance of the soul to govern is improper. The debt is incurred merely by being under a particular constitution, and so the philosophers cannot escape the very cave they have escaped.

Still, the reluctance of the philosophers is so great that Socrates has to spin something of a world to convince them of the obviousness of the debt. They must go back down, he says, as payment for nurture, as they were bred for this purpose, as they were better educated than others. He plays, then, on guilt, purpose, and honor in order to convince them that they must go back down into the darkness, readjust their eyes, and govern despite a deep desire not to.[13]

The nature of desire, then, is central to the problem of rule. The bad rulers in *Pericles* wish very much to keep their rule, and it is only when Pericles has suffered and lost everything, has devalued rule, that he can rule properly. It is only when Lysimachus values Marina more than he values his own desire for satisfaction that he can be recognized as a proper husband for Marina and as a proper ruler. Overcoming internal desire and ruling despite a preference for not ruling are the conditions for proper rule. It is, then, the very reluctance to rule that makes the king. Equally, the real stargazer, the one who would rather not navigate the ship, the one who sees that the ship is not the ship, as it were, is the best navigator.

In the discussion that follows, we will trace through the connections between birth and debt in two more plays by Shakespeare, *Timon of Athens*, which focuses on generosity and debt, and *Measure for Measure*, which focuses on proper governance, moral duty, debt, incontinence, death and birth, among other issues.

From *Timon*, we will develop a notion of the proper uses of generosity, the problems with debt that masquerades as generosity, and the misuse of the gift. Over the course of the play, Timon goes from being generous to a fault to using that generosity to destroy, even as the political system is implicated in the same cycle of corrupt giving and taking. And from *Measure for Measure*, we will draw on Isabella's responses to debt, showing that her incontinence is problematic. Characters in both plays display moments of incredulity as they encounter the complicated relationships between birth (existence) and debt. It is as if each city has a city-level moment of shock as the citizens discover that they owe far more than they had ever realized and that what they had thought they could concern themselves with turns out to have been improper.

The texts, then, deal simultaneously with individual and political incredulity, with the difficulties in trying to figure out what is owed from the fact of being in the world. If birth indeed entails debt, if existence is obligation, then the individuals and the political system must respond to one another in ways that allow this obscure and perhaps infinite debt to be settled to the extent that such a debt can be settled. Each of the characters in these plays struggles with precisely what the nature of debt is, and with how to settle accounts.

NOTES

1. In *Natality and Finitude* Ann O'Byrne develops the notion of "natality," or the quality of having been born and being in the world. She uses the Greek tradition and a number of more recent philosophers including Hannah Arendt to look at issues not far from some of the concerns in this book. Being born into the world, being that which is finite, being that which must work, having a limited future, but a future nonetheless (death is later) all come in for profound examination in her book. See Anne O'Byrne, *Natality and Finitude* (Bloomington, IN: Indiana University Press, 2010).

2. Sallis comments, "This city is a city *within man*, the city within Glaucon. So, in educating Glaucon, Socrates has indeed founded a city . . . in the sense that in and through his speech he has founded a city *within* Glaucon." If this reading holds up, then there is a kind of success in Socrates' work in the text. Much, then, rests on whether or not Glaucon has taken all of this to heart, or to soul. Sallis, 454.

3. This notion of responsibility is taken up by Jacques Derrida in his book *The Gift of Death*. He discusses the relationship between Jan Patocka, a Czech activist and philosopher who died in police custody, Socrates, and Jesus. Death, responsibility, mystery, and religion are linked together in the text. If, say, the cave or the *anabasis* (rise) from the cave, or the choice of a new life (which is implied by the rise from the cave) requires both mystery and release, it has the sense of the orgiastic, as Derrida terms it. That is, the mysteriously bound subject in the cave, the mysteriously bound soul in the afterlife, is released during some kind of spectacle or rite. The rite is one of unbinding and re-binding, freeing and capturing. The moment of freedom is a kind of orgiastic release that turns immediately into a new kind of stricture, a responsibility, an ethical demand to act based on the experience of release. The moment of the re-binding is the moment of taking on the responsibility to act, to be, in a certain way. A released subject in the cave must rise, must turn, must rise more, must suffer, must experience light. And upon experiencing this light, must sacrifice the light for the dark again. A soul, bound in the afterlife, is released from the afterlife so that it might choose a new life in which to bind itself. The new life, the new fate, is chosen with odd ceremony, with release from what the soul is into what it will and must be. The necessity, the fate, is as well a kind of responsibility. Given that the fate is necessity, the soul's choice is necessary, and so the responsibility is there at the moment of choosing as well as for the kind of choice made. The freed soul is bound, even in its freedom. The workings of responsibility and freedom, for Derrida's discussion in this text, are wrapped in mystery. See Jacques Derrida, *The Gift of Death*. Translated by David Wills (Chicago, IL: The University of Chicago Press, 1981).

4. See Kant on the notion of the possible kingdom of ends as one of the formulations of the Categorical Imperative, *Grounding for the Metaphysics of Morals*, third edition. Translated by James W. Ellington (Indianapolis, IN: Hackett Publishing Company, 1993), Second Section.

5. In a gesture similar to my notion of "world-spinning," Fagan writes that "although we may want to read Plato as though all he writes is the philosophical argumentation, that is precisely what he does not do. The dialogue enacts the ideas of the argumentation, adding to it through what is not always explicitly stated. Plato writes

a world—his world—writes philosophy as an element in that world, and demands that we read his culture as well as his philosophy." For Fagan, though, the world creation is something akin to a literary and referential system in which poetic creation is a part, reflection of the world is a part, and philosophy itself is a part. In my work, world-spinning has more of a sense of the falsification of a world. This falsification can be used to good end, as it is in the *Republic*, or to wicked ends as it is used by Iago and Emilia. See Patricia Fagan, *Plato and Tradition: The Poetic and Cultural Context of Philosophy* (Evanston, IL: Northwestern University Press, 2013), xiv.

Fagan further develops this notion through the distinction between myth and *muthoi*. Myths recount important cultural values through the use of traditional stories, while *muthoi* are stories Socrates seems to fabricate. The cave, then, is an example of what Fagan considers to fall under *muthoi*, while references to traditional poetry fall under what she considers myth. What is at stake here is first, the status of the poets in the *Republic*—they are not exiled, but rather preserved in many ways, and a sense that there is some kind of world that stakes a claim, even in the innovation that the city Socrates describes seems to call forth. World-spinning, in story and poetry, has some grounding that grants it a kind of legitimacy that sets it apart from the comedic absurd. See Fagan, 81.

6. One pass through the ship-sun-line-cave is through a story of debt, and this is the one in the body of the text. There is another pass through that though tangential to a story of debt within the text of the *Republic*, is related to a notion of the text's debt to the poetic tradition it is a part of. Fagan develops a reading of music, the Sirens from the *Odyssey*, and the texts Socrates discusses in Book III. We can extend the reading of the Sirens in the *Odyssey* to a reading of the ship analogy and the cave analogy. The binding, the desire to pause in experience where one is and to get lost in that experience, the need to have some unbound who are responsible for rescuing those who are bound, the falsity or digression from purpose—these are all elements in the ship in the *Odyssey*, the ship of state in the *Republic*, and the cave. The sun and the line give us mediating figures to help us with a purpose for rescue. See Fagan, *Plato and Tradition*, 50.

7. *Tokos* means both interest and offspring, so there is a pun embedded here. See translator's note, Plato, the *Republic*, R.E. Allen, trans., 219 (Book VI, note number 17).

8. Adriana Cavarero takes the cave analogy in a literally different direction. She develops the notion of uprightness, or verticality, in her chapter "Plato Erectus Sed," giving us a way to see uprightness as a body position that is relevant to the way we inhabit the world. See Adriana Caverero, *Inclinations: A Critique of Rectitude* (Stanford, CA: Stanford University Press, 2016).

9. Derrida's work on the *pharmakon* and the therapeutic value of philosophy are worth thinking through here. Therapy also comes up in Schmid.

10. I am grateful to Jonathan Mannering of the Classics Department at Loyola University for help with the Greek translations and transliterations.

11. Note that as Nightingale discusses, the *theoria*, the journey to see or be enlightened or to attend a religious ceremony will lead to experiences of visions. The visions are not easily translated into language that others can understand. Just as prophecies

are frequently misunderstood in Greek tragedy, so, too, are visions misunderstood. This dynamic plays out both in the *Republic*, as Socrates attempts to get others to "see" the intelligible, and in the *Apology* as Socrates tries to get the men of Athens to "see" Socrates for what he is and not for what his reputation says he is.

12. Note that what is too comfortable here is not what Glaucon originally wanted with couches and pastries, but rather is philosophical comfort—knowing the truth, seeing the light.

13. Jacques Derrida, *The Gift of Death*, discusses the issue of self-sacrifice, the giving of death, in both Christian and Platonic contexts. Within the Platonic context, we can see that the philosopher (always Socrates) gives his death, owes his death. And yet, as Derrida notes, one cannot actually die in the place of another because every living person has his own death. What is displaced, then, by the sacrifice, by the gift of death to another, is akin to some kind of mystery. The philosopher risks all by going back down to the cave where his very knowledge is both a gift and a death. He has knowledge to give, he has life to lose, his knowledge should be, must be, given, and yet it will be rejected. We see the dynamic from the beginning of the conversation in Book I, and it continues in the cave, and it comes up again in the Myth of Er. The souls are warned by one who knows, and that first soul rejects the care of the soul, the responsibility to the soul, and to the offspring of the soul. The payment of interest in money matters more than the payment of philosophy to the offspring. See Derrida, *The Gift of Death*, 33.

Section 2

The Gift of Debt in *Timon of Athens*

Shakespeare's character Timon from the play *Timon of Athens* embodies the tensions we find in the *Republic* regarding birth and debt, generosity and expectation of return, giving and economy. Timon seems to see himself as infinitely generous and supplied with an infinitely regenerating supply of money that he can give from infinitely. The characters around him are less sanguine about Timon's motives for giving, and indeed Timon's critics in the play have an important perspective on Timon's actions and motivations.

What seems to be a sense that one ought always to give regardless of one's resources turns out to be a faulty understanding of the debt inherent in existence. Timon, rather than being a godlike generous figure turns out to be a corrupting figure and by the end of the play generosity ends up being a destructive force rather than an appropriate reaction to the world. The play, then, explores variations on giving, mercy, expectation, rage, revenge, and destruction. In the opening lines of the *Groundwork*, Kant suggests that the only completely good thing is a good will and that any action absent a good will can be wicked.[1] Timon's generosity is a clear illustration of the point Kant is making in these opening lines. Timon's will is anything but good, and the wickedness spirals out of control by the end of the play.

The errors inherent in Timon's character and actions, then, are first misunderstanding what generosity means; second, lacking a good will; third, thinking that though he seems to give freely, though he is actually "property-ing" those to whom he gives. Free giving turns out to be unfree binding, and this sense of debt that Timon thinks others should feel because he feels debt towards others is perhaps the most profound error.

The Alcibiades subplot, in which Alcibiades's comrade is refused mercy, Alcibiades is banished, and then turns against Athens and overthrows the government, shows another set of issues pertaining to debt and gift, death and life. This subplot, along with the complete reversal of Timon's character, work together to illustrate improper and proper notions of debt.

With his money, Timon purchases art, freedom, and love, justice and the state, enjoyment, and friendship. He thinks that these purchases are real, that these can be purchased, and that he has the wherewithal to make the purchases. He discovers otherwise and in his rage he purchases war, destruction, prostitution, ruination, disease, and the fall of the Athenian government. Timon feels that he owes help in the first part of the play, is owed help in the middle section, and he eventually comes to believe that what he really owes is the destruction of all that he has created, including himself. A perverted theological reading is possible here. A god creates, corrupts, destroys, commits suicide. Timon may well see himself as a godlike figure, but in this, too, he is mistaken.

The play opens with a conversation among a poet, a painter, a jeweler and a merchant regarding their creative output and the possibility of Timon's purchasing these items. None of these men would be allowed into the smallest of the cities discussed in the *Republic*, and only the merchant would be allowed in the more expanded version. Each of these men brings a kind of corruption to Athens of the sort Socrates is concerned with. There a willing world-spinning that comes from a need to distort the world in order to please Timon. Though the Poet and the Painter may have some sense of the truth, they have a more intense desire to produce marketable works, and in the Athens of the play, Timon is the market. The transactions among these characters demonstrate the ways that misunderstanding debt can destroy cities.

The poet asks the painter "how goes the world?" and the painter replies "It wears, sir, as it grows" (1.1.2-3). This opening suggests that time is felt more as melancholy degradation than as joyful creation. Birth leads to debt and death, growth precisely is decay. The painter is not alone in his sense of melancholy, though. The poet comments, "When we for recompense have praised the vile, / It stains the glory in that happy verse / Which aptly sings the good" (1.1.16-18). What is striking here is the sense that the poet sees his creative output as a mercenary praising of the worst in men. Creation, for the Poet, is the destruction inherent in flattery. It seems that both men, then, have some sense that what they are doing, selling their wares to Timon, they are doing in corrupt fashion. There is a tension in the play between Timon as a good and generous man and Timon as one whose generosity is corruptive, profligate, wanton, and completely inappropriate. Generosity, in this play, ends up being a vice rather than a virtue, even as birth is death rather than proper debt. And this transformation, by itself, is a source of incredulity for the characters involved.

Further on, the poet continues this thought, saying,

You see how all conditions, how all minds,
As well of glib and slippery creatures as
Of grave and austere quality, tender down
Their service to Lord Timon? His large fortune,
Upon his good and gracious nature hanging,
Subdues and properties to his love and tendance
All sorts of hearts . . .(1.1.54-60)

Timon "subdues and properties" others as they are in need of his money. His generosity demands a kind of "glass-faced flattery" from all the hangers-on. Giving, then, is a kind of taking in that those to whom Timon gives become his property. Further, the giving corrupts both sides as flattery is a doubling of corruption. The giver and recipient of flattery both lose out on the expression of truth and both become caught up in a false economy of gift and debt.

In stark contrast to Timon's wanton and corrupting generosity is Marina's refusal to give anything at all unless the gift is appropriate or is not at all a gift but rather a proper repayment of a debt. Marina pays the brothel as a return on debt, but she refuses to give her chastity, or to sell her chastity, to anyone outside of a proper marriage. She does not participate in the immoral sexual economy of the brothel, nor does she allow flattery to corrupt her sense of self. Where Marina refuses the role of whore, or of giver of sexual favor, Timon embraces the role. He gives far more than is appropriate and he ends up turning the Poet, the Painter, the Merchant, and even the misanthropic Apemantus into players in this corrupt economy.

While Apemantus gives lip service to misanthropy, Timon enacts that very misanthropic impulse through improper, and therefore corruptive, giving. The fundamental misunderstandings Timon has of gift and debt are both a product of and a cause of a generally corrupt government under which Timon lives. The corruption circulates in an economy best thought of as a vicious circle that only seems virtuous at the beginning as each of Timon's feats of generosity outdoes the previous one.

The first act of generosity that takes place during the action of the play is the bailing out of Ventidius whom we first hear of from Timon. Timon exclaims, "Noble Ventidius, well! / I am not of that feather to shake off / My friend when he most needs me. I do know him / A gentleman that well deserves a help . . ." (1.1.102-105). Ventidius is "noble" and yet lacks the ability to pay off his creditors. Timon, who sees himself as one who feels debt from knowing Ventidius, who feels that friendship comes with a bond to pay off such debt, willingly pays the debt in order to buy his friend's freedom.

Timon closes out the scene with the Messenger by saying something that also has a kind of double reading to it, "Commend me to him, I will send his ransom / And, being enfranchised, bid him come to me; / 'Tis not enough to help the feeble up, / But to support him after. Fare you well" (1.1.108-111). Timon, here, clearly wants something of a repayment for the ransom—he wants to see Ventidius in person. Is this line an example of the property-ing of all to whom Timon gives? Or is it that he really wants to "support him after?" If Timon's goal is to turn Ventidius into another hanger-on, to see in person the gratitude and flattery he is spending is money on, then it would seem that the corruptive influence and the bad faith of improper giving are present from the beginning. It would seem, further, that the Poet understands Timon better than Timon understands himself. On the other hand, perhaps Timon only wants to "help the feeble up" and then support the feeble from then on. We cannot yet determine the worth of Timon's generosity and we cannot yet separate out proper from improper senses of debt. The debt is paid in order to purchase the freedom of a man imprisoned for debt, and that the repayment of the debt incurs yet another debt, this time to Timon.

The next incident of Timon's generosity is aimed at love. The daughter of an Old Athenian Gentleman wishes to marry one of Timon's servants, but the servant, Lucilius, lacks the money required by the Old Athenian as a precondition of marriage. Timon agrees to stake Lucilius so that he can buy into the partnership with the woman he loves. Timon thus buys love to go with the freedom he has just purchased for Ventidius.

The Old Athenian's complaint regarding Lucilius is that he has raised his daughter at "my dearest cost" (1.1.127) and that Lucilius just does not have enough money to be a reasonable return on the father's investment. From her breeding and birth, the daughter has incurred a debt to her father, her father has invested his "dearest cost" and demands a kind of repayment for this debt. He has no other kin to whom he can give the money as punishment for her refusal to pay back the investment, and he asks Timon a favor as a help for one who would presumably deserve the help. He wants Timon to refuse the giving of the daughter to the servant. In the father's plea, there are numerous levels of debt and repayment that need to be teased out, as each moment of Timon's generosity presents a variation on the theme of debt and gift, life and debt.

The father, as is proper for a father, invests in his daughter. He assumes, though, that the investment will pay off in some economic sense. His notion of gift of life seems to be more a notion of investment with return than outright gift with no expectation of return. One could imagine his taking his daughter to afterschool lessons of one sort or another under the assumption that every dance class, every soccer lesson, and every scouting meeting will bring her that much closer to marrying a millionaire. The daughter, it would seem, has a different view of the debt she owes for her life. She wishes to marry for love, and would seem to think that love is enough of a repayment for all the childhood schlepping about.

It is worth pausing to think through Timon's purchases thus far, for each has this double reading that has been noted here. Being in a society in which freedom and love, two powerfully significant features of humanity, are for sale is clearly a kind of corruptive position. That Ventidius could incur significant money debt, that the Old Athenian Gentleman feels that his daughter's life and love are subjects of a particular structure of debt means that things that are outside the economic sphere are brought into the structure of debt and return in an improper way.

Timon's generosity, then, is a response to a corrupt system in which what should be granted freely, freedom and love, are implicated in a system of money, debt, payment and repayment. On the other hand, Timon's participation in the money system of debt, and his profligate spending within this system, both makes the system possible and keeps it going. That is, he gives it life, fosters it, and preserves it. At least until he destroys it.

Apemantus's lines, and those of Alcibiades in the next scene, are replete with both cannibalism and sexual consumption. Apemantus says, "I eat not lords," but that ladies do "eat lords" (1.1.207, 209). And Alcibiades says, "Sir, you have saved my longing, and I feed / Most hungrily on your sight" (1.1.258-259). Timon replies, "Ere we depart we'll share a bounteous time / In different pleasures. Pray you, let us in" (1.1.260-261). In these lines we see the other side of Timon as one who not only gives but wishes to receive sexual favors, and we see that Apemantus sees the relationships between Timon and the others as a kind of devouring.

That Timon has a wanton sexual side, that his banquets and his seeming friendships are laden with an underlying cannibalism gives a fair amount of support to the idea that Timon is not merely a figure of infinite generosity, but is, rather, corrupt in his seeming generosity. If Timon gives to property others, and if others eat Timon even as he eats them, then debt and gift are features not of the granting of life and creation but rather the granting of death and destruction.

Clifford Davidson, in "'Timon of Athens': The Iconography of False Friendship" emphasizes more Timon's good side. Though he notes the theme of cannibalism, he suggests that it is more that Timon is being eaten than that he, as well, eats, and though he notes that Timon is wrong to rely on false friends, he does not see Timon as creating the need for the falsity in the first place. Timon comes off pretty well in this essay. Davidson describes the first set of Timon's acts of generosity as "tremendous,"[2] and emphasizes Timon's sense of the bond of friendship.[3] He downplays the sexual undercurrent by noting the dearth of women in the play[4] but does not seem to pick up on the homoeroticism that is clear from the lines above. The wanton giving of money, wanton devouring of one another, and wanton sex are all tied together in the play, and it is important to see that Timon's generosity has a corrupting side to it.

Davidson cites Renaissance understandings of generosity and writes that some amount of "carelessness"[5] was considered an acceptable form of generosity. Davidson's discussion may make us wonder about asymmetries between a putto's pouring out heaps from a cornucopia and Timon's lavishing his hangers-on with more than he has to give, and in such a way as to demand from his seeming-friends a kind of performance. Further, Timon has enough of a sexual presence, and there are enough undercurrents of consumption in the play, that one is led in a different direction from seeing Timon as rightfully having some space for a "certain carelessness." He is not merely careless, he is corruptive.

Davidson suggests, further, that, "Nevertheless, despite his interest in Timon's prodigality as imprudent economy, Shakespeare really insists upon focusing on the matter which he considers more basic—the subject of friendship."[6] It is not, though, a matter of mere accountancy as against excessive generosity that is at the heart of Timon's corrupt nature. Rather, it is inappropriate generosity as against appropriate generosity that needs to be highlighted. There are proper ways to lavish gifts upon others, and there are proper kinds of gifts to be given in proper kinds of relationships. Giving sexual favors outside of marriage is indeed quite generous, but we know from Marina's stay in the brothel that it is also completely inappropriate. Receiving the products of cannibalistic feasts, metaphorical or not, is inappropriate, and therefore, handing out such feasts is corruptive. And finally, monetizing that which should not be thought of in monetary fashion—liberty, love, creation—these things are meant to be handed out with much liberality and not converted into three or five talents.

In the next scene, Ventidius makes his appearance in order to thank Timon for bailing him out, and in order to note that his father has died and left him a fortune. He notes that "It hath pleased the gods to remember / My father's age and call him to long peace" (1.2.2-3). He offers to repay Timon, and Timon responds,

O, by no means,
Honest Ventidius, you mistake my love:
I gave it freely ever, and there's none
Can truly say he gives if he receives.
If our betters play at that game, we must not dare
To imitate them; faults that are rich are fair. (1.2.8-13)

Timon's sentiment here is central to seeing his errors. First, we note that Ventidius's father's death is the source of Ventidius's good fortune, but not his freedom. The gods gave Ventidius's father life and then took repayment by calling him back. Ventidius is happy to pay for his own freedom, in arrears, and is happy to double the payback.

The first suggestion here is that the gods give and do not mind taking. Second, parental death can be quite a good thing for offspring, especially if the death is constructed as the gods' suddenly remembering an old account that has come due. No need for guilt, but there is lots of gilt. Third, Ventidius is bound by Timon's generosity and would seem to prefer to be unbound. The obligations that generosity puts on others, even if those obligations are not conceived of by the giver but only by the recipient can be uncomfortable to bear. Being given things may actually be unpleasant. Timon seems to prefer to avoid being given anything as payback. He conceives of his generosity as a one-way non-transaction, and yet this one-way generosity ends up creating obligation. It is this obligation that Ventidius would like to avoid.

Timon refuses the repayment, and says that the gift would be destroyed through repayment. This Derridean theme of the impossibility of the gift as running through this play is developed by Ken Jackson in "'One Wish' or the Possibility of the Impossible: Derrida, the Gift, and God in 'Timon of Athens'."[7] Clearly, Timon feels that being repaid would mean that he has never actually given anything at all, and if anyone is going to "play at that game" it will be the gods who give life and then take it back when they call their accountants. The gods may well play mere accountancy, then, but humans are better off never thinking transactionally.

While it may feel comfortable for Timon to avoid thinking transactionally, he puts others in the position of needing him, of being called to appear before him, of making and doing for him, of depending on him for liberty and love and fostering and preserving. The dependencies Timon creates are a kind of devouring, and they blur the line between debts that are properly monetized and debts that should never be monetized.

At some level, Timon seems to understand something of the point. He says to Ventidius,

Nay my lords,
Ceremony was but devised at first
To set a gloss on faint deeds, hollow welcomes,
Recanting goodness, sorry ere 'tis shown.
But where there is true friendship there needs none.
Pray sit, more welcome are ye to my fortunes
Than my fortunes to me (1.2.14-20).

That one ought not to recant goodness, that within friendship there is no need for ceremony, that friends ought to wish the best for friends and not for self—all of these sound fine under the right circumstances. But because Timon seems to monetize his relationships, because his fortunes are about to change, or really, because they have long been changed but he has been unaware of the dire nature of his financial circumstances, he really ought not to wish his own ruin on others. And yet, he does. Curses in Shakespeare's plays are generally enacted in the world, and here a kind of blessing is to be enacted in the manner of a curse. Timon's ruin will become clear, and he has wished that ruin on others in this passage.

The banquet scene that follows furthers both the spectacle of Timon's generosity and the theme of cannibalism. Eating Timon's food is metaphorically related to eating Timon, for his food is part of his over-giving, and is related as well to the theme of sexual giving. Proper sex, proper diet, proper giving and receiving are all perverted in the play, and all of these perversions must be worked out. Apemantus links these themes together when he says,

O you gods, what a number of
men eats Timon and he sees 'em not! It grieves me to
see so many dip their meat in one man's blood, and all
the madness is, he cheers them up too.
I wonder men dare trust themselves with men,
Methinks they should invite them without knives –
Good for their meat and safer for their lives (1.2.39-45).

It is Apemantus's judgment that Timon is unaware of his being eaten, and further, that the process of eating Timon includes the odd image of dipping meat in blood and being cheered on in the process. Dawson and Minton note the likeness here to communion, and they note that the communion here is utterly perverted.[8] The dipping of one's own meat into the blood of a mother-like figure of complete self-sacrificial generosity might also suggest a kind of violation of the rules for keeping kosher. Regardless of the source of the passage, there is clearly a concern about inappropriate appropriation, improper mixing of meat and blood, and a kind of celebration of the very inappropriate nature of the mixing. Apemantus may still harbor some sense that Timon is truly self-sacrificing, truly unaware of his own being eaten, truly unaware of the dipping of meat in blood, but Timon's enjoyment in over-giving and his desire to "let my meat make thee [Apemantus] silent" suggests otherwise (1.2.37). Timon enjoys the devouring in its many forms, cannibalistic and sexual, inappropriate all.

Timon and Alcibiades continue the theme of eating, bleeding, and meat, but in a more bantering tone. Apemantus then comments that he would wish for Alcibiades to kill all the flatterers at the dinner, and then Apemantus would gladly eat them. He says, "Would all those flatterers were thine enemies / then, that then thou mightst kill 'em, and bid me to / 'em" (1.2.80-82). Apemantus, already declared one who prefers roots to meat, would eat Timon's enemies to save Timon from being himself eaten by those enemies. If Timon himself is the one who has created the enemies who would then eat him, and if he has regularly fed and nourished those who are eating him, it is quite possible that Apemantus is not quite cynical enough in his reading of those around him. He professes cynicism and misanthropy, but he has a soft spot for Timon. This softness is perhaps mistakenly granted.

The Poet's line that Timon "subdues and properties" others is worth looking to in the context of this speech. In Timon's notion of friendship here, his giving to others turns the wealth of others into Timon's own property. He "commands" the fortunes of his "brothers" by giving them money. He thus perverts the sibling and friendship relations by monetizing them, handing out gold, and then claiming a stake in their wealth. And the seeming beauty of this seeming extortion brings tears to his eyes, tears he can only hold back by drinking. Giving the way Timon does, with the definitions and contractual stipulations that Timon insists on, is not quite the figure of generosity.

The banquet comes complete with a masque that Apemantus calls a "sweep of vanity" danced by "madwomen" (1.2.131, 132). He continues,

Who dies that bears not one spurn to their graves
Of their friends' gift?
I should fear those that dance before me now
Would one day stamp upon me. 'T has been done,
Men shut their doors against a setting sun (1.2.140-144).

Apemantus's concern augurs Timon's future even as it mistakes the spurn, the graves, and the gifts. For Timon, will use his gifts to spurn those he has thought of as friends, and even as Timon goes to the grave spurned by his friends, he gives gifts that will send others to their graves, spurned by the giver. Just as those dancing to entertain may stamp on the ones they have entertained, so too can gift giving fall into its opposite—harm giving. Opposites switch places as a matter of routine in this play, largely because the characters fail to understand debt.

Lords Lucius and Lucullus give gifts to Timon, "four milk-white horses, trapped in silver" and "two brace of greyhounds" (1.2.184-5, 1.2.192). Timon immediately undoes the gift giving by promising to hunt with the givers so that, in fact, their gift is theirs to use. A gift to Timon is never a gift to Timon because it would put him in the position of recipient and therefore of indebtedness, a position he rejects completely for himself. His fantasy is to be the giver not the recipient.

Flavius, in an aside, warns the audience of the fantastical nature of all the gift giving Timon engages in, especially at this banquet. Flavius says,

> What will this come to?
> He commands us to provide and give great gifts,
> And all out of an empty coffer; Nor will he know his purse or yield me this:
> To show him what a beggar his heart is,
> Being of no power to make his wishes good.
> His promises fly so beyond his state
> That what he speaks is all in debt, -- he owes
> For every word. He is so kind that he now
> Pays interest for't; his land's put to their books (1.2.194-203).

Here we begin to see Timon in a somewhat different light. Still, there is some reverence for his generosity, but there is a more realistic sense of Timon as a fantasist, as someone who is, in important ways, the opposite of what he is. No giver is Timon, but rather a debtor whose very words are the start of debt.

It is clear from this passage that there are conflated meanings of debt that need to be teased out. Timon feels a bond with friends, with Athenians, with his coterie of hangers-on and that bond is expressed by giving money and expensive gifts, and by allowing himself to be devoured in a barely metaphorical sense. He sees the obligation of the social as a monetary obligation, and he feels the need for fantastical sums of money so that he can meet this obligation. That others may not have fantastical wealth allows Timon the fantasy of being the one true giver. He keeps within him a sense that his giving does create a bond with the recipients, but it is a deferred bond that he refuses, thus far, to call on. Gifts to him are given back and repayment is rejected.

If social debt is merely monetary, it cannot function in a one-way fashion. The money needs to circulate but Timon refuses the circulation. He does not keep for any time and he does not accept repayment that would allow for more flow of capital. Without circulation, capital accumulates in one place and debt in another. Without a true social bond, the circulation never gets going, and the disparities of wealth turn people to despair. Timon misses the social side of the obligation we bear for one another as he sees only the monetarization of relationships.

Timon, in between acts of generosity at the banquet, says,

> I take all and your several visitations
> So kind to heart, 'tis not enough to give;
> Methinks I could deal kingdoms to my friends,
> And ne'er be weary. Alcibiades,
> Thou art a soldier, therefore seldom rich –

It comes in charity to thee, for all thy living
Is 'mongst the dead and all the lands thou hast
Lie in a pitched field (1.2.223-230).

These lines mark crucial types of social debt that Timon misses. The soldier pays a dear debt to the city, and the living must be aware of the dead. These are non-monetary debts, and yet Timon's response to them is to wish to deal kingdoms to all and to give money to Alcibiades so as to compensate him for his rough life. The lands Alcibiades "has" are battle fields, the lands Timon wishes to give are kingdoms. Of course, kingdoms typically come through pitched battles, but Timon seems to miss this fact, in the same way he misses the fact that his fortune has to have come from somewhere and has to have some kind of renewal as it is not infinite and not self-generating.

Apemantus comments again on Timon's foolish giving,
Thou giv'st so long, Timon
I fear me thou wilt give away thyself in paper shortly (1.2.248-249).

And, indeed, Timon has given himself away fairly completely at this point. He has given wantonly, extravagantly, and without any understanding of what he really owes. Apemantus ascribes the giving to Timon's love of flattery, but there is much more going on in Timon's head than a mere love of flattery. Timon's whole psychic structure depends upon a fantasy of infinite giving with no actual receipt, but an implicit debt of others to him. Timon does indeed property everyone to whom he gives. But his propertying comes at the level of fantasy. The Senators who come in Act 2 to collect are a different sort of propertiers.

The first Senator gives a speech that outlines Timon's notion of an economic system:

And late five thousand; to Varro and to Isidore
He owes nine thousand, besides my former sum,
Which makes it five and twenty. Still in motion
Of raging waste? It cannot hold, it will not.
If I want god, steal but a beggar's dog
And give it to Timon, why, the dog coins gold (2.1.1-6).

Timon owes a lot of money. The sum he gives to Ventidius is trivial compared to the sums above, and yet Ventidius took a considerable sum. The amount promised to Lucilius for his marriage is also considerable, matching as it does, talent for talent whatever the Old Athenian Gentleman has. Timon has been giving without having, akin at some level to Antiochus's recreating virginity that does not exist. The wanton nature of the giving in both cases is fantastical, impossible, and destructive.

The speech above shows the fantastical side of infinite generosity. Give, ask for nothing in return, and somehow assume infinite giving rather than circulation. If the horse (in the following lines) would foal us all, if the dogs would coin more gold, if giving would multiply giving (without, say, generating infinite inflation or some other economic problem) we might well be okay with infinite giving. But, as the Senator says, "It cannot hold." Infinite giving without circulation does not work. Identity without boundaries does not work. It is not enough for Timon to property those around him as a way of ensuring his own place in the center of an economy. He cannot give, using what he has given as a surety against which the giving is guaranteed. Timon's open gate sounds deeply good, until it becomes clear that the open gate encloses all who walk in, locks them to a propertying they might not wish for.

Timon's creditors come to him to press him for their money, and his response to his servant Flavius further shows Timon's inability to understand debt. Timon's initial reaction is to blame his servant for not fully laying out the state of his estate. That Timon's incredulity at the state of his estate is expressed through the chastising of a servant shows something of the limits of his generosity. He is not generous of spirit, only of money. We find, next, that indeed Flavius has attempted multiple times to warn Timon that money and debt do not work the way Timon thinks they do. Timon could not bear hearing such a thing. His epistemic closure is another signal regarding his character. A man generous of spirit would willingly give an ear, but Timon only willingly gives when he can property the recipient. Generosity, this is not.

Timon then notes that perhaps he had been warned, but only when he was unable to understand the warning for some "indisposition." Therefore, once again, the situation is the clear fault of the servant, not of Timon. Timon cannot accept responsibility for his actions, cannot owe or receive in a moral sense. There is a nice parallel here between Timon and Thrasymachus, who tells Socrates that one is only what one is when one is performing one's function properly. Thus, a warning is a warning only if it warns, and Timon can only be warned if he is in a state of readiness to receive a warning. If Timon is never ready, he can never be warned.

Flavius gives us more detail of Timon's tantrums. Timon throws the accounts, "checks," or chastises or rebukes or perhaps even hits Flavius "not seldom" over the state of the accounts, and prompts Flavius to break down in tears. The scene plays out repeatedly, and in ugly fashion. Flavius resorts to selling land (2.2.146) and there is no more land to sell. Timon has run out of time. There is no way to pay the debts. Timon's response to the details, "Prithee, no more" (2.2.163). Even now, Timon does not want to hear that there is a limit, or that his notion of generosity is the wrong one. He suggests that Flavius has no idea just how wealthy Timon really is. Timon says that "you," "Mistake my fortunes: I am wealthy in my friends" (2.2.183-184). Timon's more considered response, after telling Flavius to stop talking, is to deny any kind of limit he might have. He has, after all, a lot of friends and his friends have money, and their money is his money, largely because he has given them their money. "Given," that is. To be wealthy in friends may not really mean to be wealthy in the property of friends.

The defense Timon gives of himself, that he is perhaps unwise, but certainly not villainous in his giving, is as misconstrued an impression of himself as he can have. His very giving has corrupted people, has corrupted art, and has encouraged the monetization of liberty and love. His comfort with using "men and men's fortunes" suggests, again, the propertying of friendship itself. All human relationships are monetized for Timon. And as he finds that monetized relationships are not at all the same as friendships, he will throw what could be characterized as the ultimate literary tantrum.

In stark contrast to Timon and his behavior is Flavius and his response. Flavius attempts numerous times to speak truth to power, as it were, and to render proper accounts and accounting. He bears the slings and arrows of an outraged employer, and he does all of this with quiet dignity. He manages land sales and leases, he props up Timon as he can, all the while trying to warn Timon that there is something rotten in the state of his accounts. Flavius, then, is closer to Marina and Socrates than he is to Timon. There is not an absence of a financial relationship, as Flavius is as much an employee of Timon as Marina is of the brothel. But in each case, the characters negotiate these financial relationships with proper notions of debt and repayment.

To the extent that there is far more to debt than mere monetary relations, both Marina and Flavius press others for more moral behavior. Marina takes seriously the duty to turn bodies towards soul, and Flavius takes seriously the task of rendering proper accountancy and trying to instruct Timon regarding duty. Flavius fails, Marina succeeds. Both play the role of philosopher, both have Socratic elements, and both have a sense of debt as something that exceeds monetary relations.

Timon, thinking he is "wealthy in friends," sends three servants to ask help of three friends. He also asks Flavius to approach the senators regarding assistance. Flavius responds to this request that the senators act in unison to deny aid to one who has helped them in the past. They express their regrets in a pro forma fashion, and dismiss the request as something that simply cannot be met. Timon is denied three times, and more. The imagery here is deliberate, both in its Christian suggestion and its being not quite Biblically accurate.

What is striking here, or would be striking if one considered the request within the realm of possibility, is the lack of consideration, deep apology, actual attempt to try to help. Indeed, what is missing is any kind of gesture of sincerity or friendship. What stands out is the unity of refusal, and even more, the unity of refusal to consider the request in any real way. The senators do not really feel any kind of debt at all, and yet Timon has felt very deeply that his generosity has earned him property in their person, in their regard, and in their property. Timon's gifts, meant at some level as investments, have, thus far, been a bust. It is only Flavius who has been of assistance, and yet, Timon has limited regard for Flavius.

The power of Timon's incredulity grows from this moment on, but is still muted here. He is already taken aback by his sudden awareness of the change in fortune, but now he is starting to see part of what he has been unaware of, but what Flavius and Apemantus both have known all along. Timon says,

You gods, reward them!
Prithee, man, look cheerly. These old fellows
Have their ingratitude in them hereditary.
Their blood is caked, 'tis cold, it seldom flows,
'Tis lack of kindly warmth they are not kind;
And nature as it grows again toward earth
Is fashioned for the journey, dull and heavy (2.2.213-219).

There is an interesting tension here between a call to the gods to reward the senators for their unkindness, and a sense that they are merely human, have inherited their unkindness and have become dull and heavy as a price for their age on earth. Their blood does not flow, they are incapable of cheerful sanguinity, they are cold, old, and not what Timon would have hoped for. He still finds something to excuse them, however. It is a natural state for them to be as they are, and so, though he is shocked, he cannot yet fully condemn them.

Timon's next gesture is to ask Flavius to go to Ventidius, for Ventidius has of late inherited money, as we already know. Timon still has hope, as he says to Flavius, "Ne'er speak, or think, / That Timon's fortunes 'mong his friends can sink" (2.2.230-231). Forbidding speaking, forbidding thinking of the unspeakable and unthinkable is in large measure the cause of Timon's downfall. He refuses to hear Flavius's warnings, he refuses to think through what his giving does, and he refuses to know the proper nature of debt, and the boundaries beyond which monetization should never venture. Timon's fortunes will sink, though perhaps not among his friends, for he has no friends.

The creditors' wealth and display are entangled with one another in curious ways. One creditor wears a jewel that another creditor is owed for, but Timon plays the intermediary role here, and so the debt is not creditor-to-creditor, but runs through Timon. He gives to one what he has taken from another, or, rather, what he has borrowed from another. That he could give what he does not directly own, but rather what he has propertied suggests a kind of generosity with other people's money rather than a generosity of his own. Of course, he has given away what once was his, but only within this curious sense that everything is always his, regardless of whom he has given it to. What Timon gives, he does not give, what other have, they do not have. Timon feels a kind of security of social love in all of this, but the hangers-on and the creditors feel a great deal of insecurity in the same relationships.

One could imagine enlarging this entanglement of debts and gifts so that some kind of exchange of gifts, were the creditors willing to make such an exchange, could put everyone back at equilibrium with no debts. For this kind of exchange to happen, the gifts would need to be nullified, something Timon rejects when Ventidius offers repayment. And yet, now Timon very much needs to annul all gifts and all debts in some kind of exchange jubilee. The jewel that one creditor wears should simply be given to another creditor, and as gift, it should be givable. The creditors, though, have no interest in evening out the debts while leaving Timon's role as intermediary out of the process of exchange of debt and gift.

A fully recognized propertying of all the creditors is precisely the kind of economic system that would allow the regifting process to take care of the debts. But regifting is an act of ingratitude, an annihilation of the gift, and so it will not come about. The gift will be destroyed by Timon, and perhaps has been destroyed by Timon already in that he has needed some kind of regifting to allow his perverted economy to continue. The underlying economic issue here may well be the status of money as stock or as flow. Timon seems to have a preference for money as flow. That is, money moves from one place to another in a dynamic and unstable system. But sometimes the flow stops, sometimes money is stock, a fixed thing, and at that moment, at the moment that the flow stops, debt becomes impossible to manage and the system of flow collapses as creditors try to account for a stock of money. When the Senators need money for war, they suddenly cannot depend on flow, they need to convert all flow into stock. They call in the chips, and Timon has no stock left for the conversion. Economic collapse is the necessary result of the Senators' call for accounts. Where money had been something like a fantasy, where it had been able to be everywhere at once, it suddenly needed to be real, in a real place, and counted.

While clearly Timon's "friends" are false, only willing to flatter when they get something out of the flattery, Timon, too, is false as he is willing to be kind to his friends only when he is confident in his propertying of them. Once this side of the relationship breaks down, once Timon realizes that his friends are not friends, that their property is not his property, his seeming godlike love for all humanity collapses into a hate that cannot but be powered by a kind of falsity in his prior love for these same people.

Flavius, a true friend, and perhaps even a real gift, though unrecognized as such and unable to give Timon any more money than he has given through his careful stewardship of Timon's diminishing fortune, says to the other servants,

Ay,
If money were as certain as your waiting,
'Twere sure enough.
Why then preferred you not your sums and bills
When your false masters ate of my lord's meat?
Then they could smile and fawn upon his debts,
And take down th'interest into their gluttonous maws.
You do yourselves but wrong to stir me up,
Let me pass quietly.
Believe't, my lord and I have made an end,
I have no more to reckon, he to spend (3.4.44-54).

Flavius, here, shows great loyalty to Timon to the very end. He condemns the other servants for serving masters who ate Timon's meat, who ate Timon, all the while loaning him money, charging him interest, and enjoying the spectacle of Timon's misunderstanding of gift and debt. They have enjoyed using and consuming Timon to the end of Timon. Consumption of this sort verges on the apocalyptic, giving without end in order to bring about the end.

Even as the creditors have granted credit, and even as Timon has borrowed in order to give all the more, and even as this economy has ground down to its end, Timon will find a new source of giving that will bring about a much larger end. Microeconomic and macroeconomic forces will be reconciled by the end of the play.

The stage direction notes that Timon should enter "in a rage" in Scene 4. He cries out, in language reminiscent of that of stock and flow,

What, are my doors opposed against my passage?
Have I been ever free, and must my house
Be my retentive enemy, my jail?
The place which I have feasted, does it now,
Like all mankind, show an iron heart? (3.4.77-81).

He has thought of himself as unbonded, freely flowing, and he has become stock, unable to move, needing to be accounted for. To make matters worse, all the creditors pile their bills on Timon. His friends are now his enemies, his home is his prison, his freedom is gone and cannot be purchased, his home and hearth are now showing an iron heart. He had everything, he has nothing.

He cannot understand what has happened to change everything. The incredulity intensifies, and his fundamental error in confusing debt with life, money with human obligation, obscene generosity with the generosity of spirit that is proper between people leaves Timon with nothing but rage at those whom he set up for this very scene. Peripety piles upon discovery, with enough hysteresis to suggest that the turn of events will not completely convert Timon, that he will rebound most of the way to what he was before the shock. The notion that what Timon becomes is what Timon has always been is central for a reading of him and his generosity.

Just as the soul in Book X of the *Republic* gets it all wrong and rages in response to what he has wrought, so too does Timon. He had been seemingly rewarded many times over for his seemingly good deeds, but he had not studied the proper role of generosity and the proper boundaries of the economic. His lack of study costs him dearly.

The scene closes with Timon's desire to hold one more banquet, this one a perverted last supper in which the main dish is tepid water and is served almost as a kind of perverted baptism as Timon splashes the bowls of water on those seated at the table. For this one, he declares, "Go, I charge thee, invite them all, let in the tide / Of knaves once more: my cook and I'll provide" (3.5.11-12). His friends are now knaves, letting them in is now letting in a tide with no porter to guard the door and make sure that only the good come. The tide prefigures the dinner that will be served at the banquet.

The Alcibiades subplot is a variation on the theme of giving, debt, justice, mercy, and what can be purchased. Alcibiades meets with a group of Senators to settle a soldier's fate. This small but important scene deals with another kind of obligation, that of a soldier to the state and the state to the soldier. Should there be mercy after the gift, because of the gift, or is the law fixed? Does a gift obligate the recipient, even when the recipient is the state and the gift is a term as a soldier? These questions are much at issue as the play tries to deal with debts of various sorts.

Alcibiades is defending a fellow soldier who got into a drunken fight and killed yet another soldier. The punishment for this killing is death. The ironies are many here. First, of course, a soldier is precisely trained to kill, to lose a certain level of humanity in order to do so, and many soldiers turn to drink in order to deal with the general brutality and the difficulties in the life of a soldier. The soldier who committed murder has, "…done fair service / And slain in fight many of your enemies. / How full of valour did he bear himself / In the last conflict and made plenteous wounds!" (3.6.63-66). The service done can be thought of as a gift. The soldier offered his valor, wounded others as he was tasked to do, and did so precisely because he is a soldier and this is the service that soldiers properly give. The temperament that a soldier develops in order to be good at soldiership can lead to precisely the kind of drunken fighting that Alcibiades's soldier engaged in. What do the Senators owe a soldier who has given so much? What kind of gift is a soldier's gift to the state?

Alcibiades understands the gift as something that can be repaid through mercy in certain circumstances, but the first Senator says bluntly, echoing concerns that Angelo has, "…'tis necessary he should die. / Nothing emboldens sin so much as mercy" (3.6.2-3). The first Senator's words here show both the concerns that the state has with regard to performance of contracts, with the limits of reciprocity for the proper gift of citizenship (valorous service to the state), and with any notion of mercy. If mercy is what states can properly give, and mercy is seen as causing sin rather than forgiving sin, then states cannot structurally give what it is that they properly give. That is, states are tasked with being merciful, and yet this Senator finds mercy to be worse than crime. The soldier is sentenced to death, and Alcibiades is banished for angering the Senators (3.6.97).

The defense of the First Senator's position is that no one can expect a gift of mercy from the state, for such an expectation invites citizens to sin and then ask for redemption or mercy. It is a concern we will see again with Angelo in *Measure for Measure.* Just as the church can promise absolution, so too can the state. There is certainly room for corruption in an economic system of sin and forgiveness. Soldiers give their passion to the state, commit crimes of passion against fellow soldiers; soldiers give their honor to the state and commit crimes to the honor of fellow soldiers. And all is forgiven by the state. The First Senator is concerned with the problem of governance and Alcibiades is concerned with the problem of mercy.

To mediate the conflict, we need to look again at the notions of gift and debt, or birth and debt, so that we can see that the debt cannot possibly be paid, and yet we assume impossibly that the debt must be paid. Within this contradiction is a cognitively dissonant solution to the problem, a solution that changes the location of the incredulous response from rebellion against the city to the oddity of believing in a debt that both cannot be paid and that must be paid.

If the state never grants the notion that it must be merciful, and yet is merciful, if the soldier never grants the notion that he is giving his life and honor to the state, then the gift of mercy is not subject to what contemporary social thinkers call "moral hazard." That is, mercy cannot increase the number of crimes of passion if the assumption of mercy cannot be made.

The moral hazard issue is two-sided, though, and that is what Alcibiades picks up on. If the state does not have to risk anything by granting mercy, then it has an incentive to wage war, eat up its own citizens at will, and continue on its corrupt path. It is precisely the tension between needing to use up the gifts of honor and life, to repay with mercy when the passion for war becomes an attack on fellow citizens, and the hazard of increasing the number of crimes of passion that can function as a check on the corruption of the state.

There is a need, then, to occupy the odd conceptual position of managing moral hazard on both sides of the issue by denying the very debt that is always being paid, and paying the very debt that is always being denied. Better to be incredulous at the conceptual level than to release citizens from any hope of mercy such that citizens do not feel indebted to the state. Without the notion of debt to the state, any citizen is ripe for rebellion.

Alcibiades, in his turn, has a moment of incredulity. He says,

> Now the
> Gods keep you old enough, that you may live
> Only in bone, that none may look on you!
> I'm worse than mad: I have kept back their foes
> While they have told their money and let out
> Their coin upon large interest—I myself
> Rich only in large hurts. All those, for this?
> Is this the balsam that the usuring senate
> Pours into captains' wounds? Banishment.
> It comes not ill: I hate not to be banished (3.6.102-111).

Alcibiades starts with a curse, that the Senators will live a skeletal life of deprivation in keeping with what they have taken from their soldiers. That they should be preserved and yet without fostering, alive without being kept is a turn on Dionyza's line that fostering is not preserving. Here, preserving is not being fostered.

After the curse, Alcibiades turns to his own case and notes that he has given much to the state to allow the state to have an economy while not demanding to be part of that economy. Alcibiades has preserved the state, has hardly been fostered by it, and has certainly not been invited to profit from his gifts. He has not demanded any kind of return on his gifts to the state, and has allowed the state to profit. It is the valor of Alcibiades that has allowed the Senators to lend to Timon and to profit on the money while receiving gifts from Timon. And finally, after the curse and the rage and self-defense comes Alcibiades's acceptance of the situation and his learning suddenly to enjoy it. If, after giving all he has given, his reward is banishment, then he will be happy to be at odds with the state. He promises to "strike at Athens."

We now have two kinds of gift giving, two kinds of requests for reciprocity in the wake of gift giving, and two kinds of refusal to give back after having received. In Timon's case, the giving is entangled in the monetization of social bonds such that he feels that he owes others even as they owe him. He fails to see that what social bonds really entail is something other than, or beyond, money.

On the part of the senators, there is a more disturbing kind of misunderstanding about giving. The soldiers give their honor, their bravery, and their lives for the city. They ask for very little in return, save something like honor, recognition, and a stipend to live on. They risk everything for almost nothing, and indeed, often for nothing, as anonymous soldiers outnumber the ones who are awarded or named. The Senators, in the scene with Alcibiades, could indeed give mercy for an honor killing, a crime of passion related to the soldier's honor. But the First Senator refuses this gift, noting as is pointed out above, that mercy, rather than being the proper gift of the state, is actually the one gift that corrupts.

A city that thinks that a gift of mercy corrupts is not likely to encourage a jubilee, clearly. Nor is it likely to model proper giving for its citizens. Indeed, a city that does not know, and therefore does not model, proper gift giving cannot encourage its citizens to give properly, and such a city is the one Timon inhabits, and such senators are the ones who receive from Timon. Timon cannot give properly because the entire political system misunderstands the nature of the gift, of debt, and of what is proper to return to others.

Because the city gives Alcibiades the unwanted death of his soldier, an order of banishment, and a refusal even to allow petition for redress, for it is Alcibiades's voicing of a complaint that leads to the order of banishment, Alcibiades returns the favor through rebellion. A government needs to allow its citizens to voice concerns and citizens need to know that the government can respond with mercy. An unmerciful government cannot, then, continue to have a relationship with its denizens that one would consider a citizenship relation. Just as Timon's friends are false, so the citizens of Athens are false because their government is false in its refusal to allow petition for redress and its refusal to grant mercy.

The debts here, then, are completely misunderstood. Timon monetizes friendship and properties his friends. He perverts art, love, justice, and commerce, and refuses to listen to truth and to true friends. Timon's friends loan him money that he then uses to give to other friends such that the debts are entangled, the friends are entangled, and Timon is the single nodal point through which all of the money must pass, but cannot pass. They should not give, he should not give, not when the gifts are used as they are used. The soldiers give their lives and honor for the right of citizenship, but are not given the right of citizenship as proper return for the gift of life.

As Timon's collapse continues and his incredulity increases, he holds a final banquet for his supposed friends. This banquet continues the theme of feeding and of eating the food of another, but the energy changes abruptly, for Timon "feeds" his "friends" tepid water rather than a lush array of foods on beautiful dishes, accompanied by dancers and singers. The only entertainment at this final supper is Timon's curses.

May you a better feast never behold,
You knot of mouth-friends! Smoke and lukewarm water
Is your perfection. This is Timon's last,
Who stuck and spangled with your flatteries,
Washes it off and sprinkles in your faces
Your reeking villainy.
Live loathed and long,
Most smiling, smooth, detested parasites,
Courteous destroyers, affable wolves, meek bears –
You fools of fortune, trencher-friends, time's flies,
Cap-and-knee slaves, vapours and minute-jacks!
Of man and best the infinite malady
Crust you quite o'er! (3.7.87-98).

From his earlier giving of money and jewelry, freedom and love, compliments and jokes, to this curse in which Timon wishes long misery on the worst of the worst is a journey that is both long and short. The long side is the seeming distance between his excessive love early on and his excessive hate here. The two seem to be far apart, bridged only by a huge betrayal and made possible only through a near impossibility. Timon, so good, can only be made this bad if something nearly impossible, or perhaps actually impossible, has happened. That Timon must confront the thing he most cannot confront, the seeming impossibility that his accounts due are empty, may be the transformative event.

On the other hand, if one reads Timon as misconstruing generosity, debt, gift, life, and the proper use of money and the proper way to befriend others, then the journey between excessive gift giving and excessive destructive wish is not far at all. As generous, Timon has been destructive, and as enraged he will be equally destructive. The gifts he gives in the first part of the play are mirrored by gift giving in the second part of the play, and in each case, the giving is destructive. The only difference between the giving is Timon's intentions, but his intentions cannot govern how a gift is used once it is given. His propertying of others makes him think he can control the gifts once he has given them, but in fact he cannot keep control of what he has given. A gift, once given, leaves the giver.

Timon, in a fit of rage, curses all of Athens,
Let me look back upon thee. O thou wall
That girdles in those wolves, dive in the earth

And fence not Athens! Matrons, turn incontinent;
Obedience, fail in children; slaves and fools,
Pluck the grave wrinkled senate from the bench
And minister in their steads. To general filths
Convert o'th' instant, green virginity,
Do't in your parents' eyes. Bankrupts, hold fast;
Rather than render back, out with your knives
And cut your trusters' throats! Bound servants, steal:
Large-handed robbers your grave masters are
And pill by law. Maid, to thy master's bed,
Thy mistress is o'th' brothel. Son of sixteen,
Pluck the lined crutch from thy old limping sire,
With it beat out his brains. Piety and fear,
Religion to the gods, peace justice, truth,
Domestic awe, night-rest and neighbourhood,
Instruction, manners, mysteries and trades,
Degrees, observances, customs and laws,
Decline to your confounding contraries –
And let confusion live! (4.1.1-21).

In every curse there is a sense of repayment that violates what we normally think we owe one another for our lives, our livelihoods, out knowledge. The wall that holds us safely should betray us, women and children should disobey, slaves and fools should rule while the senate loses power, what is dirty should take over from what is clean, debtors should kill creditors, servants should steal, maids should violate their masters' marriages as their masters' wives have been sent to the brothel already, sons should kill their aging fathers, and all social conventions should break down completely. Timon does not leave anything behind in his cursing. In short, the whole world should be turned upside down, and those who owe should destroy those to whom they owe. Even our debt to the gods for our very lives and fates should "decline to your confounding contraries." We should be able to know nothing, do nothing, count on nothing save confusion.

Social function depends on a proper notion of debt, especially the debt that comes from our having been born. We owe our fosterers and our preservers much, and we need to understand how this debt comes about and how it is to be repaid. If we do as Timon does and monetize the debt, we pervert its meaning. If we turn to anger, as Timon does, we end up denying any kind of debt at all, and we wish for the kind of destruction that Plato warns a tyrant is willing to engage in. A tyrant, for Plato, is one who willingly engages in any kind of food or deed in order to benefit himself. Timon, in this curse, calls for tyrannical destruction of all human relations.

In the aftermath of the waterlogged banquet and the drowning of the fantasy of infinite food, gift without debt, monetized friendship, and the propertying of all, the servants gather to witness the ruin. Flavius says, simply, "All broken implements of a ruined house" (4.2.16).

The implements, and the house, are broken. The people who work there are ruined as well. They have nothing left, no way to make a living, no way to live. Out of this nothing, Flavius makes an offering.

Good fellows all,
The latest of my wealth I'll share amongst you.
Wherever we shall meet, for Timon's sake
Let's yet be fellows. Let's shake our heads and say,
As 'twere a knell unto our master's fortunes,
'We have seen better days;. Let each take some,
Nay, put out all your hands—not one word more,
Thus part we rich in sorrow, parting poor (4.2.22-29).

Out of the broken house and the broken implements and the broken economy, out of nothing, that is, Flavius produces something. He gives his fellow servants some of what he has, "for Timon's sake" and for theirs. He gives everyone "some." Gift giving, indeed, is the act, but it is a gift giving so alien from what Timon does that it deserves its own word. Timon gives when he has nothing to give, but he has no awareness ever that he has nothing to give. And even if he knew at some level the dire nature of his financial situation, the mere fact that he properties everything he gives and everyone to whom he gives means that he can never really feel the nothing that he has. He gives not out of true generosity, then, but out of an economy of plenty. Such a gift is an easy one.

Flavius, on the other hand, is the accountant. He knows what he has, what he is, and what money does. And still he gives. Not lavishly, but to the "latest" of his wealth. He gives money, but does not monetize the relationships. Rather, the gift is in honor of a man's honor, it is merciful, it does not force the servants to bear the full risk of their having worked for their master. In short, this simple gift undoes both the overgiving of Timon and the undergiving of the First Senator. And in giving of himself, Flavius even outdoes Alcibiades, who after all, does not really give of himself for his soldier, but merely asks the state to give. Flavius carries a sincerity and goodness of heart that is akin to Marina and Socrates, and is far more the model of gift giving than is Timon, or Alcibides, or the soldier or the First Senator.

Flavius has his own kind of incredulity as he cannot quite take in the problems Timon has. His failure is one of understanding that Timon's seeming generosity is misdirected, and that his own, more proper generosity, is precisely the model to be used. Flavius says,

> O, the fierce wretchedness that glory brings us!
> Who would not wish to be from wealth exempt,
> Since riches point to misery and contempt?
> Who would be so mocked with glory, or to live
> But in a dream of friendship –
> To have his pomp and all what state compounds
> But only painted, like his varnished friends?
> Poor honest lord, brought low by his own heart,
> Undone by goodness! Strange unusual blood
> When man's worst sin is he does too much good.
> Who then dares to be half so kind again?
> ....
> I'll ever serve his mind with my best will:
> Whilst I have gold, I'll be his steward still (4.2.30-51).

Here we can see the troubled thoughts running through Flavius's mind. That wealth can be harmful rather than all good disturbs the accountant in him. He is accustomed to stewarding wealth and to thinking that wealth is good, and that wealth is monetized. The idea that perhaps it might be better to have less wealth and thus to be less managed by the need to manage the wealth is surprising to him. That what he thinks is real is actually painted or varnished is precisely the revelation that the philosopher has once he has emerged from his bonds in the cave. Indeed, it is only after exiting the seeming bonds of the cave and the seeming obligations that real bonds and real obligations can be properly conceptualized, for Socrates. Flavius is exiting his own cave here, with his own kind of incredulity. To the extent that he has dined on or off Timon, he now finds himself willing to serve as he can.

That riches are wretchedness, that fortune is affliction, that friends are monsters, that a steward with gold could serve a master without gold—these are the kinds of reversals of terms that incredulity captures. There are mistakes in thinking behind every one of these reversals, and the pain of getting them straightened out is the pain of emerging from the cave, emerging from conceptual confusions, and coming to know the truth.

Flavius manages the upward journey with pain, but without insanity and death. Timon, though, is not at all positioned to handle his incredulous journey so well. Indeed, Timon falls into madness, destructiveness, evil, and finally death. Though he has no children to eat when he sees his fate, he does have a whole city the destruction of which he is more than happy to pay for.

These very different responses to the incredulity of coming into conflict with one's own conceptual errors is at the heart of the very different characters that Timon and Flavius have. Timon's improper generosity stands in stark contrast to Flavius's attempts at accountancy. Though Flavius is not without error, even as Marina is not completely without error, both Marina and Flavius have the ability to see the errors and to attempt better.

Timon, in his abject poverty, discovers a new trove of gold, most likely left buried by a band of pirates. Timon will give this gold to a parade of comers, just as he has given to these people in the past. This time, though, the express purpose of giving will be to destroy rather than to sustain. He will still property those to whom he gives, but it will be with an ill will rather than with even a shred of goodness. The discovery of the gold is noted thus,

What is here?
Gold? Yellow, glittering, precious gold?
No, gods, I am no idle votarist –
Roots, you clear heavens! Thus much of this will make
Black white, foul fair, wrong right,
Base noble, old young, coward valiant.
Ha, you gods, why this? What this, you gods? Why, this
Will lug your priests and servants from your sides,
Pluck stout men's pillows from below their heads.
This yellow slave
Will knit and break religions, bless th'accursed,
Make the hoar leprosy adored, place thieves
And give them title, knee and approbation
With senators on the bench (4.3.26-38).

The arrival of opposites at one another's door is clear here, and is the source of Timon's incredulity. That what is precious is base, that what is foul is fair, that what Timon thinks should be good turns out to be bad enrages him. He has lived in a cave-like dwelling in which opposites of the truth are taken to be the truth. He cannot manage the conceptual revolution and stay sane. Instead, he asks for, pays for, gives for, the destruction of the world he feels owed him something it did not pay back in kind. His destructive force is akin to that of Alcibiades, and indeed he gives Alcibiades some of his newfound gold in order to help defray the cost of the revolution against the senators.

In the topsy-turvy world Timon is discovering, he even gives advice to the gods. He warns them that by giving him this gold, they are asking for problems. The gold will corrupt the priests who serve the gods, will create and destroy religions, will help the worst among us and hurt the best, and will overturn the political order to boot.

Not even the gods, it would seem, understand the structure of the gift here. But just as the soul in Book X of the *Republic* misunderstands the nature of the decision he is about to make, and just as he blames the gods for what he himself has done, so Timon locates the blame for the conceptual breakdown not in himself, but in the gods who foolishly give when they should not. Timon thus still has problems with the boundaries of the gift and the debt that gift incurs. Giving wisely may be as important as receiving wisely, and since what is given has been received, these two are inexorably tied together.

The parade of characters who come to Timon for assistance in the first part of the play come back again in another parade, this time seeking Timon not in a house fit for a lord, but rather in a cave fit for an animal. Alcibiades comes with two prostitutes, showing the perversion of both love and justice that we witness at the beginning of the play. Timon asks Alcibiades to destroy Athens, the perversion of good soldiership, and he asks the prostitutes to spread disease, the perversion of love.

Eventually, Flavius comes to Timon, and his opening comments show his love. He cries out,

O you gods!
Is yon despised and ruinous man my lord,
Full of decay and failing? O monument
And wonder of good deeds evilly bestowed
What an alteration of honour has desperate want made.
What viler thing upon the earth than friends
Who can bring noblest minds to basest ends?
How rarely does it meet with this time's guise,
When man was wished to love his enemies.
Grant I may ever love and rather woo
Those that would mischief me than those that do (4.3.453-463).

Flavius is incredulous at the change in Timon from one so honorable to one who is a ruin of a man, one suffering "desperate want." The turnabout in a man whom Flavius admires, loves, and has served is overwhelming to him. He blames the change on friends who betray, who bring the highest down to the lowest, and he declares a preference for those who might want to harm him but fail over those who actually do harm. The desire to harm can be identified and managed, the ones who actually do harm can disguise themselves and their intentions.

Flavius's language here is just ambiguous enough to point to Timon, even if it is directed more at Timon's supposed friends. Timon's seeming good deeds may do harm, Timon's noble intent may bring down those on high, and Timon may be a disguised doer of harm rather than an open and honest man.

Flavius does not at all apply the language to Timon, though, and because he does not see Timon's flaws at this level, he suffers pain from the turnaround in Timon's state.

Flavius and Timon negotiate their mutual relationship, with Timon at first preferring that Flavius, "Away!" (4.3.467). As they go back and forth, with Flavius reiterating his status as a servant, a steward, and loyal to the end, Timon softens until he can say,

One honest man. Mistake me not: but one,
No more I pray, and he's a steward.
How fain would I have hated all mankind,
And thou redeem'st thyself. But all save thee
I fell with curses.
Methinks thou art more honest now than wise,
For by oppressing and betraying me
Thou mightst have sooner got another service... (4.3.492-499).

Timon has found one man who is not a thief, one thing in the universe that does not steal. But this very quality, for Timon, is proof of honesty rather than wisdom. A wise man would betray and steal to protect his self-interest, whereas an honest man is fated to suffer.

Timon has the categories almost correct here. Flavius is indeed honest, as a steward, as a friend, and Timon failed to recognize this fact during the tenure of Flavius's service. Indeed, all of the checking and chastising and failing to listen to Flavius is one of causes of Timon's downfall. That a servant could be more a friend than friends are, that friends could fail to serve, these are hard lessons for Timon, but he seems to have accepted them at this point. At the same time, Flavius really does fail to see Timon's flaws and Timon's own partial responsibility for his own downfall. That Timon failed to see Flavius's honesty, that Timon failed to understand the nature of the gift, that Timon monetized when he should not have, these are major issues Flavius missed completely. And yet, Flavius has kept his compassion, loyalty, and willing service throughout. There is a special kind of wisdom in maintaining compassion in the face of the errors Timon has made.

As old habits die hard, Timon offers some of his newfound gold to Flavius, but only under the condition that Flavius,

Go, live rich and happy,
But thus conditioned: thou shalt build from men.
Hate all, curse all, show charity to none,
But let the famished flesh slide from the bone
Ere thou relieve the beggar. Give to dogs

What thou deniest to men. Let prisons swallo 'em,
Debts wither 'em to nothing; be men like blasted woods,
And may diseases lick up their false bloods!
And so farewell and thrive (4.3.520-528).

We already know that Flavius has divided his remaining money with the other servants of the house, that Flavius does not curse all humanity, that even though he is angry with the false friends of Timon, he is not a likely bet to work to destroy them, starve them, or to enjoy their diseases. Timon, hysteresis at his side, is right back to propertying his gifts, to decreeing how the money is to be used, to working to change the characters of others to suit his own ends. Timon does not give gifts, he invests for returns specific to his purposes.

The final piece in Timon's life is an interchange between Timon, near his death, the only honest man, Flavius, and the corrupt political system Timon has paid to have destroyed, in the person of two Senators. Flavius tells the Senators that Timon is not likely to be receptive to their pleadings, but the First Senator replies, "It is our part and promise to the'Athenians / To speak with Timon" (5.1.5-6). There is, here, a suggestion of duty to fulfill promise as an action that must be carried out, and an embedding of that very promise to act in the impotent language of speaking rather than doing. That is, just as the artists have linked promise to a kind of inaction in fulfilling the promise, promise to a kind of theater that is, so the Senators carry out the same kind of promise without action as fulfillment. They feel the weight of duty to their people, but that weight is a light one, and their duty is fulfilled by speaking with Timon. They have had the duty to be merciful, and in the face of that duty have silenced speech and acted by giving a death sentence and giving banishment. Their actions, misguided fulfillments of a misguided interpretation of duty, have led them to the current situation in which they can keep their promises in language only, and not in action. Their loss of power over the preservation of the live they had thought they were fostering is surprising, to say the least.

Timon cries out, "Speak and be hanged!" (5.2.16), a gesture to Alcibiades's attempts to speak to power and power's response that the soldier will be executed nonetheless and that Alcibiades is to be banished. To speak is to be punished if the speech is not what the hearer wants to hear. Of course, Timon himself is guilty of chastising Flavius for speaking the truth.

Timon, in the end, has refused and refuted the mercy/money equivalence, the love/money equivalence, the liberty/money equivalence. But what he has substituted in its place is death. And death is most certainly not mercy, love, or liberty of the sort people actually want. Timon, in his hatred of all, in his conceptual confusion, in his inability to give the way gifts should be given, has now offered to give death to every Athenian. And he has done so in a way that would thwart Alcibiades's attempts at overthrow of the regime. In doing so, Timon has offered to undermine the purposes of the man he has paid to carry out his instructions of destruction. To the very end, Timon properties and takes over, even to the point of denying the first round of propertying and doing a meta-level version in its place.

Timon dies slowly, in the manner of, perhaps, Desdemona, who has to keep talking even after she has died the first time. He has a number of lines as he fades, and then he has a posthumous appearance played by his epitaph. His last spoken lines are as curse-ful as one would expect, with, perhaps, a tad bit of self-pity:

Come not to me again, but say to Athens
Timon hath made his everlasting mansion
Upon the beached verge of the salt flood,
Who once a day with his embossed froth
The turbulent surge shall cover; thither come,
And let my gravestone be your oracle.
Lips, let sour words go by, and language end:
What is amiss, plague and infection mend;
Graves only be men's works and death their gain,
Sun, hide thy beams, Timon hath done his reign (5.2.99-108).

Clearly, we will not have Timon to kick around anymore, but we can visit his place of death and relive it over and over each day at high tide.[9] That is, we can do so if we do not all die from plagues and infections, for they are our everlasting curse, compliments of Timon. Our reward for life is death, our work is only grave digging, and Timon's death foretells our own.

There is some truth in some of Timon's speech. We will die, the tide will come and go, we will dig graves, language for one will end, lips will stop. On the other hand, a little mercy and a lot less emphasis on the monetization of human relationships can go a long way towards making our ends less bitter. A better understanding of the nature of the gift, of the relationship between being given life and owing for that gift, a better sense of when it is appropriate (adjective) to appropriate (verb), would go a long way to allowing us a much less bitter end.

Timon does not save the Senators or the Athenian regime. He dies, and the Senators have to rely on their own wit, the hope of mercy, and Alcibiades's mood for the day. Alcibiades starts out pretty much as one would expect after the execution order and his banishment. He hopes the Senators will feel short of breath from "fear and horrid flight" (5.5.11-12). As they confront each other at the walls of the city before Alcibiades enters, the First Senator tries one tactic to argue for mercy,

Noble and young,
When thy first griefs were but a mere conceit,
Ere thou hadst power or we had cause of fear,
We sent to thee to give thy rages balm,
To wipeout our ingratitude with loves
Above their quantity (5.5.13-18).

And the second Senator adds that they also tried to be nice to Timon. It is hard to believe that the offer of forgiveness came long before the Senators had cause to fear Alcibiades's power, for no one spoke up for Alcibiades when he asked for mercy. Indeed, mercy itself was condemned. And we know from the text that the Senators were most afraid of Alcibiades by the time they went to Timon for help. So there is likely a certain amount of misremembering here.

The First Senator has one very good argument, based on a kind of practical wisdom of political rule and based on a kind of wisdom of morality. "All have not offended" (5.5.35). And therefore, "kill not all together" (5.5.44). The lines distantly echo Abraham's negotiations over the fate of Sodom and Gomorrah, and more directly, they are crucial for understanding political obligation, the goals of revolution, and Timon's very serious flaws. If all have not offended, then all should not bear the responsibility of the offense. That Timon would curse all of Athens shows that he has significantly less sense than the Senators do (and less honor than Abraham does), and yet, that the Senators would willingly refuse mercy and then beg for that very mercy suggests that they are not completely sincere themselves.

There is, in this scene an important issue of the debt to hosts even from those who wish to overthrow regimes. The Senators feel that Alcibiades owes Athens a certain amount of concern, a certain level of justice and fairness, despite the fact of war. Those who most bear the faults deserve punishment as the laws of Athens see fit, but those who do not deserve punishment ought to be kept safe. The Senators are part of the political system and they see political justice as central. They hope for the very mercy they have denied others, however, and they hope for an uncorrupt Alcibiades, even if they have been corrupt rulers. They contain multitudes.

Alcibiades willingly agrees to the conditions the Senators lay out. He says,

Those enemies of Timon's and mine own
Whom you yourselves shall set out for reproof
Fall, and no more; and, to atone your fears
With my more noble meaning, not a man
Shall pass his quarter or offend the stream
Of regular justice in your city's bounds,

But shall be remedied to your public laws
At heaviest answer (5.5.56-63).

The balance between mercy and law's condemnation is being drawn here. Enemies properly named and convicted by the proper local law have earned, do owe, their lives to the city. But they owe through public law, and they owe through regular justice, and they owe only if they are true enemies. It may be harder to tease out who deserves what fate than Alcibiades thought when he spoke up for mercy for his soldier, and when he, enraged, declared war on Athens. Debt is difficult to sort out, and this difficulty makes us sometimes turn to money to solve our problems, even when money does not quite work.

Timon interrupts the action to speak from his epitaph, "Here lie I, Timon, who alive all living men did hate, / Pass by and curse thy fill, but pass and stay not here thy gait" (5.5.70-71).

It is not clear that all living men hated Timon. Indeed, Flavius, Apemantus, and Alcibiades seem to have been closer to true friends than not. And indeed, the chances are that no one will curse Timon while walking past Timon's watery grave. And it is likely that Timon's death, instead, will make men sit by his grave and contemplate the nature of gift and friendship, guilt and complicity. Timon would prefer to be cursed and passed, but perhaps he would prefer this fate largely because he would still be propertying the behavior of those who remember him. Asking to be cursed is not far from asking the living to feel guilty over one's death. Indeed, Timon may well feel that guilt is what is owed given the circumstances of his death.

Alcibiades's response to Timon's epitaph is,
These well express in thee thy latter spirits.
Though thou abhorred'st in us our human griefs,
Scorned'st our brains' flow and those our droplets which
From niggard nature fall, yet rich conceit
Taught thee to make vast Neptune weep for aye
On thy low grave, on faults forgiven. Dead
Is noble Timon, of whose memory
Hereafter more. Bring me into your city,
And I will use the olive with my sword,
Make war breed peace, make peace stint war, make each
Prescribe to other, as each other's leech (5.5.72-82).

In these lines, we see Alcibiades come of age as a political ruler for whom mercy must triumph. We see him come to understand that Timon's affect in the second half of the play is not at all something that can be part of a political system. The melancholy coupled with choler, the incredulity coupled with a desire for revenge, the generosity coupled with a bad will, must all give way. Indeed, Timon must be put to rest before Alcibiades can enter the city. Mercy, faults forgiven, the sword's lying with the olive, these must come to the fore. War must yield its passion to peace, and peace must use its wiles, its love of bondage, to hold war back. They must eat each other, as leeches suck. Cannibalism, transmuted to the mutual leeching of war and peace, must become the ruling sensibility. By refusing to carry on with Timon's purposes, Alcibiades puts to rest Timon's propertying. The proper rule of law takes over, and mercy and justice can have their place under a new regime with old laws.

NOTES

1. Kant opens the *Grounding* with, "There is no possibility of thinking of anything at all in the world, or even out of it, which can be regarded as good without qualification, except a *good will*." Immanuel Kant, *Grounding for the Metaphysics of Morals*, 7. Immanuel Kant, *Grounding for the Metaphysics of Morals*, Third Edition. Translated by James W. Ellington (Indianapolis, IN: Hackett Publishing Company, 1993).

2. Clifford Davidson, *"Timon of Athens*: The Iconography of False Friendship," in *Huntington Library Quarterly* 43 (3) (Summer 1980): 185; 180–200.

3. Davidson, *"Timon of Athens*," 185.

4. Davidson, *"Timon of Athens*," 186.

5. Davidson, *"Timon of Athens*," 186–187.

6. Davidson, *"Timon of Athens*," 192.

7. See Ken Jackson, "'One Wish' or the Possibility of the Impossible: Derrida, the Gift, and God in 'Timon of Athens'," in *Shakespeare Quarterly* 52 (1) (Spring 2001): 34–66.

8. Anthony B. Dawson and Gretchen Minton, editors, *Timon of Athens* (London: Cengage Learning, Arden Shakespeare Third Series, 2008), see note for act 1, scene 2, lines 39–41 page 186.

9. There is, perhaps, some echo here of the Biblical flood in Genesis and perhaps an echo of the repetitions in both *Pericles* and *Merchant*. If Timon is more to be thought of as a wicked character who only thinks of himself as God-like but is mistaken, then the daily washing of his grave by the rising of the sea would seem fitting. And to the extent that repetition fits with a kind of psychic state that shows up in a number of Shakespeare's plays, this reading, too, would make some sense. Timon dies daily and is washed daily, and is washed away daily.

Section 3

Isabella's Incontinent Incredulity in Her Silence in *Measure for Measure*

Measure for Measure, within the critical literature, is a problem play and a problematic play.[1] In this section, the problems with the way Isabella and the Duke are drawn will be recast to show that the underlying "problem" in the play is that of debt and the misunderstanding of debt. Skura suggests that "The play is about finding—or restoring—lawful order."[2] The claim can be enlarged to include the notion that the order that needs to be restored is broader than just the lawful. There is, as John Wasson notes, a theme of Aristotelian incontinence running through the play.[3] Incontinence, for Aristotle, comes from a failure of knowledge in syllogistic reasoning.[4] One can see the major premise, one can even see part of the minor premise, but one fails to apply the minor premise properly to one's situation. Incontinence, then, is an excess that comes from a lack of self-understanding. Each of the characters has moments of this lack of restraint, and so each fails to pay some debt that is owed to the larger political and moral system. If there is a single term that can characterize the debt, it is that we owe the moral order enough self-understanding that we can apply the major premise properly to our actions so that we act in ways in keeping with the moral order. Restoration, then, is restoration of proper restraint across all dimensions, and not merely the lawful order.

All is topsy-turvy in Vienna. Characters are profoundly in debt to one another, to proper concepts, to the proper conduct of life. The law has been fixed, but has not been followed because it is not properly understood. The notion of debt has been misunderstood by nearly every character (the Provost is the one exception to this, and he is the moral center of the play). Restoring the law, restoring morality, stopping the baby from beating the nurse—these can only be accomplished when proper conceptual understanding of debt is in place.

Incontinence and indebtedness are central themes throughout the play, but this section will focus chiefly on Isabella's incontinence and her debts to her brother, to herself, to the city, to Mariana, and to the Duke. Further, Isabella carries debts to language and silence, to self-understanding and to what could be termed "the proper"—a broadly conceived notion of what, in the *Republic*, is minding one's own business.

As a brief summary of the plot, the Duke, Vincentio, leaves Venice temporarily and puts Angelo in charge of the city. The Duke justifies this move privately by saying that Venice is out of control morally and needs to be reined in and since he has been unable to do so, he will leave it to the stern Angelo to put things aright. There is some suggestion in the text that perhaps the entire plot of the play has been designed by the Duke in order to expose Angelo and force him to marry Mariana, but it may be that there are other motivations for the Duke's absence, including his sense that he has lost control of his own city. Publicly, he simply announces that he must leave and Angelo is in charge. Angelo starts arresting people for morals violations, and one of the ones arrested is Claudio, who has impregnated his fiancée. Claudio's sister, Isabella, intervenes with impassioned speeches. Angelo falls for her, makes an improper proposition, and is eventually caught. There are subplots regarding a house of prostitution, Isabella's status in a convent, a bedtrick, a pirate's head, and the behaviors of some other characters. Eventually, after a number of false deaths, the play resolves as a comedy with marriages and impossible forgiveness for all.

What stands out, in terms of the issue of incontinence that runs through the play, is the varieties of incontinence on display. There are the basic ones we would expect, incontinence of desire for food, drink, sex, and power. But then there are some surprising variations that include incontinence with regard to the use of words, the desire for restraint, and a fantasy of heroic action. Further, there is incontinence with regard to time, and the final moment of incontinence, and incredulity, is an intense and odd silence, a silence that is incontinent despite its being restrained rather than exuberant.

In each enacting of incontinence, there is a misunderstanding of debt. We owe a proper understanding of basic physical behavior—there is proper sex, proper eating and drinking, proper marriage, and proper use of power. And there is, further, a debt to a proper understanding of time, birth, death, and language. The characters struggle with both the more concrete versions of incontinence and the more abstract versions. They owe, they do not necessarily understand what they owe or to whom they owe. Their lack of understanding of the debts leads, as it will, to a number of moments of incredulity throughout the action. If there is a problem in this problem play, it is that the characters need to come to understand proper debt and proper payment. If there is something that remains problematic in the play at the end, it is Isabella's odd silence in the face of what is to be properly paid.

The characters are, as the critics note, not drawn quite to life, but in defense of this play, the characters stand in for a variety of debts and these debts, misunderstood as they are throughout, are profoundly difficult to account for and to come to terms with. Each character struggles with the more abstract versions of debt, and many struggle with even the easiest. For all their stiffness and oddity, for all the awful demands the plot puts on these characters, they do seem to illustrate real issues about debt, duty, struggle, and self-understanding and self-restraint.

In his discourse with the Friar, the Duke confesses that he has been overly permissive, has, "bound up the threatening twigs of birch, / Only to stick it in their children's sight / For terror, not to use" (1.2.23-24). The Duke's permissiveness and his refusal to curb the desires of his people have together enabled the fall of Vienna, the fall of Claudio from "too much liberty" (1.2.117), and perhaps even the fall of Angelo. If the Duke can be said to be incontinent, he is incontinent in his use of restraint. He is too restrained to use restraint properly, and his too light a hand has caused a general collapse in the moral order of the city he owes proper rule. That Isabella can ask for more restraint at the convent suggests a lack of general restraint in the city and that other characters cannot restrain anything at all provides all the more proof that Vienna has been badly run and badly controlled by the Duke. Improper rule leads to the collapse of order. Finding a way to re-order, to restore propriety, is a central problem for political rule, especially for rule in fallen states, as we see in the *Republic*, where fallen states do not seem to recover well.

The play, then, rests upon the need to balance internal and external controls over behavior, the need to develop the proper notions of debt toward self and other, and the need for judgments of equity to supersede judgments of the equal which John Dickinson discusses in detail, showing that Aristotelian themes run throughout the play.[5] What is proper for each character and each role in the play is the proper end to a properly conducted search. Each character, save the Provost, is out of balance and in debt because of the lack of balance. This lack of balance and the indebtedness that comes from it drives both the conflicts and the action in the play.

The need to control desire, to be more than a mere desiring body, but to be not too much more than a body with desires (that is, to make no claim to the divine), is central to the proper demands of the city and of just rule. One ought not to be angelic, disembodied, "above" desire, nor merely desiring and "below" decency. Angelo, who is described as snow cold, clearly needs to be the right temperature, neither too hot (toward Isabella), nor too cold (toward Mariana). He needs to be less concerned with his own desires, but not frozen from all desire. He needs to avoid living up to his name, for he is no angel at all. Angelo must come to terms with desire in proper measure. He must, as well, come to understand the nature of promises, of justice, of the proper time for death and for mercy.[6] He understands none of these by nature, and it is unclear how much his understanding grows during the course of the play. He is forced into life, into marriage, into proper behavior at the end of the play, but he gives no speech in which he shows understanding of any of this. He will pay a debt, but he may never actually internalize the meaning of his debt.

Desire and time figure together in the relationship between Claudio and Julietta. They are too speedy in their desire and the consequences of this haste include an ill-timed child, and an early meeting with the figure of the Angelo of Death, as it were. The cheating of time, the refusal to pay time, is repaid through their suffering. Julietta agrees to bear the stain of her untimely desire, and Claudio faces his untimely "death" with limited grace.

Time figures as well for Angelo. He, himself, tries to cheat time and death by hurrying Claudio's death as a second breach of promise (after the marriage promise to Mariana), and he has to pay for the mistiming of death. Claudio dies so that Claudio might live, and Claudio dies so that Angelo might live. Angelo faces his own death, even asks for it as just punishment for his seeming murder of Claudio. What Angelo owes, then, is a proper relationship toward time, death, marriage, virginity, and Mariana. Each of these must be satisfied for Angelo to rise to his name and become what he is most properly.

In this context of debt and time, it is worth noting that the Provost, and even the notorious pirate Ragozine slows time and the workings of death. This delay is a return to the proper from Angelo's attempts to hasten death. Further, the bedtrick is a hastening of a previously egregiously delayed intimacy between Angelo and Mariana such that Angelo's mistimed character all the more matches that of Claudio. Death and sex, hurried beyond their proper measure, or delayed for far too long, are both violations of what is owed temporally. If the title of the play has a notion of justice underlying it ("measure" as a legal act) it also has a temporal or musical notion. Measures are timed, in harmony and balance. If they are thrown off, the whole work of music is off, and it takes a conductor or a composer to find the error and repair it. The repair work will affect all other measures. The metaphor of musical harmony plays a central role in the *Republic* as it gets at what is properly owed by each instrument or voice, and at which time the debt must be paid or played.

If the citizens of Vienna owe the city progeny, properly conceived in the right measure and at the correct time, then they owe as well a great deal of self-control when it comes to sexual desire. The pregnant women throughout the play clearly owe their progeny a moral Vienna even as they owe Vienna their progeny. There are, as well, a number of misbehaving men who owe themselves and their city better behavior. If "the baby beats the nurse, and quite athwart / Goes all decorum," (1.3.30-31) the goal of the play is to undo the inversions, restructure the debts, and make sure that all is paid, and paid properly.

Pompey owes Vienna for his being a notorious bawd, and he is sentenced to pay his debt through the delivery of death sentences (which presumably will never happen in the newly cleaned up Vienna). Pompey also owes Vienna an understanding that though we are all bodies with desires, we are not merely bodies with desires. We are equally citizens, moral agents, social beings, and beings who must exert self-control for a greater good. The avoidance of disease, protection from emotional harm, and the keeping of promises are all incumbent upon us. Pompey reduces us all to physical desire, and he is sentenced to the job of putting an end to such desire. In this reduction, he is both akin to and opposed to Angelo. For Angelo, physical desire has been absented, but it lurks under the coldness of his exterior. The return of the repressed dominates Angelo's character, even as the lack of repression dominates Pompey's character. Pompey, though, seems to have more compassion in his physicality than Angelo does in his denial of the physical. Each has a role to play in the dealing of death, and for each, the dealing of death will be deferred infinitely. Angelo will be responsible for no deaths, despite his best efforts, and one assumes that the Duke will be as sparing with death sentences as Angelo is generous with them. Without death sentences, Pompey carries no death (unless sexually transmitted infections count as a kind of death sentence.)

The Provost owes his first loyalty to the Duke and the laws of Vienna, and is the character most unproblematic. Escalus owes a better self-understanding and a better understanding of what the law demands and what mercy requires. Where the jailer shows a proper understanding of duty and has, in Socratic language, the courage of his convictions, Escalus loses sight of duty and is drawn in to Angelo's world because he lacks the knowledge he needs and does not listen even to correct opinion, at least when Angelo is around.

The Duke, himself, owes Vienna far better rule than he has delivered as the play opens. He has lost control of the moral order and has allowed decay largely because he has been uninterested in rule. He owes justice to Mariana and he owes a rekindling of his passion for rule. The course of the play is at some level a seduction in which the Duke's attraction to justice for Mariana, to punishing Angelo, to hiding and revealing, and finally to Isabella are all there to allow the Duke to fall in love with proper political rule and with the righting of a moral order he has betrayed. The Duke, then, parallels Angelo's falling out of love, though for the Duke, it is Vienna he stops loving, and for Angelo, it is Mariana-without-a-dowry who is lost to love.

Vienna, then, is teaming with breaches of proper order concerning desire, duty, time, death, love, and seduction of the proper sort, and the play is a working out of all the bad effects of misunderstanding what is properly owed in every sphere. As such, it is a problem city presented in a problem play, and the resolution of the problem of misunderstanding and mis-fulfilling debt can be seen most clearly in the character of Isabella.

Isabella is at once overly stern and duty-bound, overly passionate and misguided. She is unloved in the critical literature but deserves a fair hearing, especially since it is her call to "justice, justice, justice, justice" that the entire play focuses on. The rest of this section will consider Isabella in terms of her duty to language, to her passions, to her brother, to Vienna, to her friendship with Mariana, and to the Duke. Much has been made of her silence at the end of the play, and this, too, will be explained in terms of debt.

Our introduction to Isabella comes, interestingly, from her brother and not from her own words. Claudio is under arrest for lechery, and he asks the morally questionable Lucio to go find Isabella, let her know what is going on, and beg her to intercede. Isabella is about to enter a convent and take vows, and Claudio needs her to speak before she is under convent restrictions. He describes her to Lucio, saying,

For in her youth
There is a prone and speechless dialect
Such as move men; beside, she hath prosperous art
When she will play with reason and discourse,
And well she can persuade. (1.2.173-176)

Claudio sees in Isabella a "prone and speechless dialect" that causes her audience to be moved to passion. Isabella has a way with words that is described here in nearly sexual terms. She can seduce, impassion, move, speak without words, use "reason and discourse" to overcome reason and discourse and push men toward passion. Her passion, expressed in language, overpowers the passions of the men she speaks to and they lose control. She is a seductress and she is "prosperous" in a way that, perhaps, Mistress Overdone could envy.

Seeing Isabella as a kind of seductress who can either misuse her art or can use it for good purpose, for physical seduction or for the seduction to justice, shows how she can be likened to both Mistress Overdone and to those most properly in the convent or most properly married. Isabella's chief debt is to control her verbal seductions, use them properly for justice's sake, and avoid, thereby, improper seduction, but it is not a debt she fully understands at the outset of the play. Neither her desire for greater restraint nor her willing breach of any and all restraint in the face of the unjust condemnation of her brother bodes well for Isabella's understanding of moral propriety. Further, neither her impassioned speech nor sudden silence is quite expected. Each response—too much desire for restraint, too easy a break from the convent, too much passion in speech, and even too much silence—suggests that

Isabella's inner sense does not match the world, and each shows her need for some kind of guidance.

In the brief scene at the convent where Isabella meets Francisca, a nun, Isabella shows some self-awareness that is at the same time a moment of self-blindness. Isabella asks for a "more strict restraint" than what she thinks she will have at the convent (1.4.4). This "strict restraint" echoes both a realization that she lacks self-control and an odd frisson with regard to restraint. Isabella's passionate voice needs to be controlled, but for there to be proper control, presumably she ought not enjoy the process of being silenced. Her need to come to terms with her passion and to control it without external force is, paradoxically, her most strict duty, and it is the one restraint she finds impossible to follow.

The nun cautions Isabella that once she has taken her vows, she has a choice of showing her face or using her voice, but never both together. The union of voice and face is overwhelming in its ability to seduce, and the rules of the convent are designed to keep the seductive powers of this union from having effect in the world. Half of Isabella must disappear if she takes her vows, and as the play proceeds, it will become clear that her voice is a call to her face, her face and voice together are powerfully seductive, and her silence at the end, her unvoiced face, will mark a moment of profound shock.

Lucio's interaction with Isabella is striking, in that it is completely without seduction. Lucio, a verbally and physically unrestrained character for the most part, regards Isabella as "a thing enskied" (1.4.34) and this view of her inoculates him from any kind of seduction her face or voice might enact. As he gives Claudio's backstory, he refers to Isabella as a virgin and as a saint. He predicts that she will be granted her request for mercy for Claudio because when maidens "weep and kneel, / All their petitions are as freely theirs" (1.4.82).

Since Lucio does not fall under the spell of Isabella in this encounter, we still have only Claudio's description of her, and Lucio's description of all maidens, to go by. Her maidenhood protects Isabella from Lucio's typical lechery. That Lucio would allow this to happen suggests a kind of moral status for him that puts him above Angelo, and perhaps above the Duke, both of whom are seduced by Isabella's voice and face. He is properly immune to her. Lucio fails to see, or fails to hear, or sees and hears but refuses the charm. What this suggests is that the convent's restrictions are not the only way to guarantee the purity of women. It may be that men could simply control themselves, and though Lucio often does not control himself, he seems to have the ability to do so at least in the company of Isabella. For all of Lucio's significant flaws, then, he has this as a redeeming characteristic.

Isabella's unwitting seduction scene with Angelo, where her full voice, full face, and full passion are on display, where her "prone and speechless dialect" gets a full viewing is striking on many levels. For a man who wishes to avoid making "a scarecrow of the law" (2.1.1), Angelo certainly does something similar, if opposing. He turns justice into an empty but seductive construct. He is the embodiment of justice, he sets up a hollow hope in Isabella, he seduces her as much as she seduces him. Rather than being an empty form of a man designed to scare away bad behavior, Angelo is an empty promise of sustenance designed to seduce and then destroy. Where Isabella will "bribe" Angelo with prayer, Angelo will bribe Isabella with a false promise of life for her brother.

Isabella's "prone and speechless dialect," along with her "prosperous art" are put to full force against Angelo. He has condemned her brother, without mercy, for immoral conduct with the woman Claudio intends to marry. Julietta is pregnant, the two plan to marry, but they rushed things before they got social and familial permission to marry. They lacked the dowry, but had the desire. Money and sex are crossed for these two, and the result is an intersection with a kind of death as Angelo imposes a death sentence on Claudio for his conduct.

Isabella responds to this treatment of her brother with a profoundly impassioned speech defending justice, mercy, restraint in the imposition of death sentences, and an understanding that were roles reversed, Angelo would want something very different from what he is meting out. Lucio, in a number of asides, cheers Isabella on, suggesting that she has something of the performer in her, and the Provost offers a simple aside, "Pray heaven she win him" (2.2.126). Isabella has a powerful effect on everyone who hears her voice.

The two lines that seem most to affect Angelo are as follows:

But man, proud man,
Dress'd in a little brief authority,
Most ignorant of what he's most assur'd—
His glassy essence—like an angry ape
Plays such fantastic tricks before high heaven
As makes the angels weep; who, with our spleens,
Would all themselves laugh mortal. (2.2.119-124)

And . . .

Because authority, though it err like others,
Hath yet a kind of medicine in itself
That skins the vice o'th'top. Go to your bosom,
Knock there, and ask your heart what it doth know
That's like my brother's fault. If it confess
A natural guiltiness, such as is his,

Let it no sound a thought upon your tongue
Against my brother's life. (2.2.135-142)

These words, together, sum up Angelo's character. He is, indeed, a proud man dressed in a little brief authority and he is more like an angry ape than like a human. He mimics a notion of justice he does not fully understand, he acts with emotion in precisely the places he thinks he is meting out justice. He shows himself bored early in the play when he and Escalus are dealing with the actual workings out of daily justice and small crimes, and he shows himself ignorant when he agrees that he and Escalus should actually talk about what it means to be a just ruler. Angelo has no patience with time, with justice, or even with his own desire.

The lack of patience Angelo exhibits is matched only by his lack of self-awareness until Isabella calls him to look into himself and see if there is anything that might be a "natural guiltiness" like that of Claudio. This calling of Angelo to examine his own soul and see what is there that is also in Claudio is, however, something of a tactical error on Isabella's part. For while Isabella might see guilt and a need for repentance and mercy, Angelo suddenly sees heat, passion, desire, and lust. And he sees it all as it relates to Isabella.

Isabella's voice, joined with her face, Isabella's prone and speechless dialect, joined with her ability to use reason, have led Angelo, already astray, even further astray. If Aristotle would call for us to correct for untoward tendencies and thus end up in the moderate middle, Angelo, under Isabella's call, overcompensates and ends up completely overtaken by his inner lust.

The two part with Angelo's request that Isabella return the next day, and then he offers a soliloquy in which we see the depth of his newly uncovered desire, the absolute shock he feels at the discovery that he is a desiring being, that he is overcome by the heat of his desire. Angelo has been melted, but the melting does not come with an earnest desire to marry and live well.

For all of Isabella's calling for Angelo to find what in him is like what is in Claudio, Angelo cannot see the likeness beyond the sharing of lust. Claudio, though in a hurry for physical satisfaction, is still wedded to Julietta. Angelo, in a hurry for sex, in a hurry for death, in a hurry to cover his own depredation, is not at all able to enjoy the time of proper marriage. He is incredulous at the discovery of an inner lustful nature, and at the direction his lust is pulling him.

He sums up his odd view of his lust,
O cunning enemy, that, to catch a saint,
With saints dost bait thy hook!
. . .
Never could the strumpet

With all her double vigour, art and nature,
Once stir my temper: but this virtuous maid
Subdues me quite. Ever till now
When men were fond, I smil'd, and wonder'd how. (2.2.180-187)

Angelo, here, gestures toward the Duke's use of Isabella as a saint to catch a saint, but Angelo does not at all recognize that he is not a saint. Were he a saint, he could not be caught up in Isabella's words. He would be more like the Provost who is immune to Isabella's charms (he wishes only for the good of Claudio), or even a little like Lucio, who is also immune to Isabella's charms (in a different way from that of the Provost.) He has a sudden understanding of the power of love and lust, and he sees in himself precisely what has overcome all of Vienna. His reaction to passion is not, though, the reaction of a saint or an angel. And he is overcome by shock at what it is that he is.

Angelo, then, is not far from the soul in Book X who picks the life of a tyrant. He does not know what he needs to know in order to live this new life, and he consumes what he should most love. As he finds out his own nature, he reacts with a kind of shock and fascination, and when he finds his own death, he reacts with acceptance rather than denial.

In the second scene with Isabella and Angelo, Angelo is explicit in his desire. He suggests that she "Give up [her] body to such sweet uncleanness" in order to redeem her brother (2.4.54). That Angelo finds uncleanness "sweet" is striking and that he offers this transaction as a kind of justice is equally striking. Angelo has shown himself to know neither the nature of desire nor the nature of justice, and here we see the evidence for both.

Uncleanness is not sweet. Claudio and Julietta are promised to each other before they enjoy their sweetness, and justice requires a moment of mercy. When Angelo propositions Isabella, then, there is neither sweetness nor proper mercy for Claudio. When Angelo demands that she "lay down the treasures of [her body]" to save her brother it becomes all the clearer that he misunderstands the nature of justice, mercy, love, and desire. If, for Angelo, justice is mere transaction in which the powerful benefits, then Angelo is a combination of the worst tendencies of Cephalus and Thrasymachus. He gives in to unnecessary desires and he does so with a kind of business deal.

Isabella has much to say to Angelo in response. She refuses the proposition, declares that it is better that "a brother died at once, / Than that a sister, by redeeming him / should die for ever" (2.4.106-108). Though perhaps surprised and sickened by Angelo's proposition, Isabella is resolved and certain in her response. She is unwilling to sacrifice her moral position for the life of her brother, she is sure in the knowledge that she will be judged well in the long run. And in the final soliloquy of the act she declares that she will go to her brother and he will certainly agree with her that he should die. She says of Claudio,

> Yet hath he twenty heads to tender down
> On twenty bloody blocks, he'd yield them up
> Before his sister should her body stoop
> To such abhorr'd pollution.
> Then, Isabel live chaste, and brother, die:
> More than our brother is our chastity. (2.4.178-184)

Isabella's resolve, her certainty, her ability to resist both incredulity and silent inaction come because she has both moral certainty and a fantasy image of her brother as hero. That he would die twenty times to save her virginity, despite the fact that they are siblings and not heroic lovers, is striking in its naïveté, in its unreality, and in its misunderstanding of the desire to live. Further, the fantasy misconstrues the nature of debt. Claudio likely does not owe twenty lives to Isabella's virginity; Isabella does not owe being raped to preserve Claudio's life; the tyrant who constructs such a transaction is no angel at all.

The jail scene between Isabella and Claudio is tense. He resolves to die, finds he may live if Isabella agrees to the transaction, wishes to live, is told by the Friar/Duke that death is certain. Claudio has, seemingly, no way out, no way to be resolved for death, no way to conceptualize the time he has or the things he must suffer. Isabella, though shocked that her brother, does not actually wish to lay down twenty heads on twenty blocks for twenty choppings off, manages to stay resolved, and manages to have retorts and responses to her brother. He is not what she has thought him to be, but she manages as she has managed all of the challenges thus far. She uses her prone and speechless dialect, she plays with words and reason, and she holds herself together.

Once the Friar/Duke intervenes with Claudio to say that there never really was such a deal, that Claudio simply was to die the next day, Claudio responds with, "Let me ask my sister pardon; I am so out of love with life that I will sue to be rid of it" (3.1.170-171). Though he owes a kind of readiness for death at all times, and he owes a readiness for death because of his untimely sexual relation with his not-quite-yet-wife, he cannot ready himself without world-weariness. He is, then, not far from Cephalus here, for Cephalus cannot give up the physical world while he still has desire. It is only world-weariness and an aging, impotent body that will allow him to be resolved for death. On this point, Isabella's fantasy falls far short of the truth of Claudio's nature. Isabella has hoped for a resolution for death based upon Claudio's noble and proper love of his sister's virginity, but Claudio's resolve, it turns out, is based upon hopelessness and emotional exhaustion, not at all on the cult of virginity or the enskied nature of Isabella.

Briefly, The Friar/Duke intervenes with Isabella, offers the bedtrick as a way both to preserve Isabella's virtue and to save Claudio's life. The deception sits well with Isabella, for it is the content of virtue and not the appearance of virtue that matters to her, and it is all set up by the Friar/Duke who is a fantasy power figure for Isabella. She is not deeply shocked by the proposition, and she willingly assents to meeting with Mariana, and helping her while saving her brother, serving the Friar, getting back at Angelo, and maintaining her virtue. The bedtrick will be a silent act, gesturing toward both Mariana's silence and Isabella's silence.

The final scene, crescendo and resolution, happens in the most public place, in the public square with the return of the Duke as himself. All the characters are assembled, save for those in prison, and all is revealed to all. Isabella is granted a speech for which she has been promised denunciation, but which she promises to complete. Every bit of her prone and speechlessness, every bit of her verbal ability, all of her play with reason come out. Just as her passion and language seduced Angelo early in the play, so, too, will this scene promise to be a seduction.

Isabella publicly denounces Angelo, relying on many shades of the word "strange." It is strange that Angelo is not as he seems, and yet it is true that he is not what he seems. The truth is strange, and strange enough that Isabella's denunciation of Angelo becomes, for a time, a denunciation of herself. The more she insists on the strangeness of the truth, the less rational she seems. Her prone and speechless dialect, her way with reason and language, seem to fail her here. The more she is what she is, the less she seems to be what she is. For Isabella to seem to fail at what she is best at doing would be strange for her, but she has been warned that, "He [the Friar/Duke] tells me that, if peradventure / He speak against me on the adverse side, / I should not think it strange, for 'tis a physic / That's bitter to sweet end" (4.6.4-7). This caution allows Isabella to survive the mocking and arrest. It does not, though, prepare her for the Duke's proposition, though the phrase "sweet end" may be a hint at what the Duke is starting to think about.

At this point in the text, Isabella thinks she knows that Angelo thinks he has had sex with her on the promise of freeing her brother, and that Angelo has, instead, had her brother's execution hurried. Angelo is as great a monster, as much a tyrant, as could be. He is a "virgin violator" in intent if not in deed, and he is a false promiser and a murderer. He is deeply unholy, despite his name and rank, despite the respect he has from the people of Vienna, despite Escalus's deep regard for him.

When Mariana asks Isabella to, "But kneel by me; / Hold up your hands, say nothing: I'll speak all" (5.1.435-436), Isabella responds without verbal hesitation,

> Most bounteous sir:
> Look, if it please you, on this man condemn'd
> As if my brother liv'd. I partly think
> A due sincerity govern'd his deeds
> Till he did look on me. Since it is so,
> Let him not die. My brother had but justice,
> In that he did the thing for which he died:
> For Angelo,
> His act did not o'ertake his bad intent,
> And must be buried as but an intent
> That perish'd by the way. Thoughts are not subjects;
> Intents, but merely thoughts. (5.1.441-452)

Isabella is, once again, able with full voice and face, to speak to justice, to ask forgiveness, to make clear and reasoned distinctions among kinds of justice, kinds of mercy, kinds of misdeeds. There is no strangeness here, and there is no hesitation. She is unshocked by Mariana's appeal to her, she is more than willing to get on her knees and beg forgiveness for her rapist-by-intent who merely and only accidentally did not rape. As Isabella notes, disturbingly and correctly, thoughts are not subjects, fantasy is not action, and what Angelo intended to do is not what Angelo actually did do. Reality, not fantasy, people, not thoughts or wishes or dreams, are subject to the law.

Within two pages of this speech, Claudio is restored to life, Lucio is tamed, Angelo is married off, Barnardine is spared, and, most jarringly, the Friar/Duke, only just revealed as the Duke, declares to Isabella,

> Dear Isabel,
> I have a motion much imports your good;
> Whereto if you'll a willing ear incline,
> What's mine is yours, and what is your is mine.
> So bring us to our palace, where we'll show
> What's yet behind that's meet you all should know. (5.1.531-536)

The Duke has propositioned Isabella, publicly, with full voice, with a crowd of witnesses. The intent is made public, in contrast to the promise of Claudio and Julietta, in contrast to the false and strange promises of Angelo and Mariana, and Angelo and Isabella, and Isabella and the convent, and Lucio and his "punk."

The marriage promise is made properly, after a fashion. And yet, it is strange. And stranger still is the well-noted silence with which Isabella receives the news that she is to be married to the Duke. Her silence is striking on a number of counts. First, she has not yet been silent when confronted by the horror of her brother's death sentence, by news of Julietta's pregnancy, by confronting injustice in Angelo, by Angelo's proposition, by the strangeness of the bedtrick, by Angelo's executing her brother, by the public denunciation of her character and actions, or even by Mariana's request that Isabella get on her knees and beg forgiveness for her rapist-by-intent. Not any of these scenes took away Isabella's voice or face, her way with language, her ability to parse reason and make arguments.

And suddenly, the Duke propositions her and she is silent. Her silence is public, unlike that of Mariana in the bedtrick. Her silence is free and open, unlike that of the drunken Barnardine in prison. Her silence is more strict than what the convent would impose. Understanding what motivates this silencing of Isabella is crucial to understanding what it is we owe, how it is we must pay, and how we handle our errors.

The Duke has been in a slow process of something like becoming attracted to Isabella, or he has been suddenly struck by her. The suggestion of a "sweet end" is ambiguous on the timing of the Duke's realization that he is in love with Isabella. The sweet end could easily be the re-emergence of Claudio, or it could be the marriage proposition, or it could be all of the resolutions together. What seems to crystalize the Duke's attraction to Isabella is her final speech asking for proper justice and mercy for both Mariana (a female friend, and so an easier target for mercy) and for Angelo, her sworn enemy. Asking for justice and mercy for enemies, for those who have attempted to harm us, is, perhaps, the hardest thing we do and the thing we most profoundly owe. That Isabella can carry out the deed, the face, of mercy, and at the same time argue rationally and coherently for the principles of justice behind this face, that she can reveal in voice and face what is most properly human, is her highest gift. It is also the very thing her brother notes gives her the ability to seduce.

From Isabella's perspective, then, there is a moment of horrific repetition. She has, yet again, using her voice and face, her prone and speechless dialect and her way with reason and language, seduced another man and brought about another unwelcome proposition. The incredulity that Isabella speaks through silence shows that she still does not quite understand the power she has that is clear to Claudio.

Of course, a public proposition from the reigning Duke is a far cry from Angelo's private and wicked intentions. And it is different from the other relationships in the play. It is proper, public, open, voiced, and faced. The sharing of property and identity are public, and Isabella's material circumstances will improve from the marriage. And yet, she is shocked into the first silence of her life.

Isabella's impassioned speeches seduce both Angelo and the Duke. They convince both Lucio and the Provost. They make it clear to Claudio that his sister has a special gift of both silent and reasoned seduction. Isabella has a profound understanding of the nature of justice and yet when she seduces Angelo, she does not seduce him to justice; rather, she seduces him into giving in to a heated desire he was previously unaware of.

Because the play ends before Isabella speaks again, and because we do not see into the future of the Duke and Isabella, we do not know entirely what she has brought out in him. He is an imperfect figure of justice in the play for it is his failings as a ruler that have caused the fall of Vienna into immorality. We know, though, that the Provost, perhaps the only fully moral character in the play, is both convinced by Isabella and not at all attracted to her. And we know that Lucio is both unconvinced and unattracted, largely because he sees Isabella as a thing utterly different. It does not occur to him to be attracted, and, equally, it does not occur to him to change his life because of her words.

Where Socrates, too, is both impassioned and reasoned, where Socrates, too, speaks at length about the requirements for living a just life, and where Socrates is willing to sacrifice his own desires repeatedly for the good of justice, Socrates shows "Isabellean" tendencies. Socrates, though, falls short of the Isabellean ideal, even as Isabella falls short of the Socratic ideal. Socrates does not seduce anyone to the path of justice, though Glaucon comes closest. But Glaucon is already justice-curious and thus the willingness he shows to listen to Socrates's impassioned defense of justice, even to egg Socrates on to stronger arguments, is not so much a product of seduction as it is a kind of cooperative foreplay.

Isabella wishes to serve justice, to save her brother, and to convert Angelo. Instead of getting her wishes, though, because of her lack of restraint, she ends up speeding up the execution of her brother (as it were), refusing to act to save him through real self-sacrifice of a sort well beyond what might be called for, and waking, heating, and seducing Angelo. Something clearly goes wrong in Isabella's conduct, but then something also seems to go wrong in Socrates's conduct.

Because Isabella's passion, her prone and speechless dialect, are found by both Angelo and the Duke to be potently seductive, she cannot help but move them. Passion is that which causes action, and Isabella is all passion. She wishes to be removed from the world of action and to live a kind of restrained and prayerful passion, but the kind of passion she has is not the kind that fits into a prayerful life. The moment the world calls her, the moment her fleshly sibling needs her, the moment she has a moment to defend the justice and the flesh of the world, Isabella gives up all restraint. She is unaware of this characteristic of hers, and she is unaware of how her passion moves those around her.

Socrates, also passionate about justice, also able to use words and reason is surprising ways, fails to move those around him. Cephalus returns to habit, Polemarchus remains fairly clueless, and though Thrasymachus, the most impassioned character, gives up, it is not clear that he is at all converted to a Socratic love of the Form of the good. And, of course, by the time the collapse of the city has been fully developed, it becomes clear that Socrates cannot really succeed in turning every soul toward the upward path.

If the love of justice is not a product of seduction, and it is not a product of argumentation, then we are left, for both texts, with a notion of a kind of happenstance, a need for good governance, and likely, frequent moments of incredulity when we think we have done things properly, when we think we have paid our debts, but in fact, we have failed. Socrates's reasoning and Isabella's passions both fail to fix what is wrong with the world. Both figures have high hopes for their work, both figures feel deeply the debt to the world and to souls, but neither quite gets things right, and both have moments of incredulity.

Where there is quiet hope in the *Republic* is with the idea that there are individuals "out there" with philosophic souls who manage, despite it all, to cultivate that knowledge, to maintain the proper balance between the parts of the soul, to mind their own business in proper fashion. Where there is quiet hope in *Measure for Measure* is in the careful attention to justice that the Provost renders. No one else, not the Duke, not Isabella, not Claudio, not Angelo, not even Mariana, quite has things right. The matching of understanding and a feel for justice, intellect, and good behavior is what the Provost displays. Though Elbow and his pregnant wife are married, and so are sexually well-timed, they lack a certain amount of understanding of the nature of language and justice. Elbow is a clumsy with words as Isabella is dexterous. Elbow's being a man of the law equates him with Angelo, Escalus, the Provost, and even the Duke. But it is only the Provost who has all the parts of the law in balance.

Mario Digangi sees Mistress Elbow as a promise that Julietta, Mariana, and Isabella's marriages may well not deliver what marriage is supposed to. The "resolution is fictive, for she [Mistress Elbow] provokes, instead of dispelling, the anxieties that surround and interpret (Juliet's) active sexual desire on the one hand and (Isabella's) virginity on the other."[7] One could read it less as a promise of failure and more as a suggestion that marriage is a necessary but insufficient debt. Each woman owes marriage and childbearing, but more, each woman owes an understanding of language and passion and self-control. Mistress Elbow is as incontinent toward prunes as Isabella is toward words, Julietta is toward Claudio, and Mariana is toward Angelo. Untoward desire in its many forms must be rebalanced with debts repaid.

In another philosophic path through the text, through the improper timing of action as fulfillment of desire, Aristotle's language of incontinence is illuminating. Wasson invokes incontinence in his title and declares flat out in the essay, "The conclusion is inescapable, I think that Shakespeare was intentionally portraying an incontinent man here."[8] Wasson could easily broaden the application of Aristotelian incontinence to characters throughout the play and not merely to Angelo. The mistiming of actions, the misuse of language, the immediacy of pregnancy cravings, prostitution in the face of sexually transmitted infections, the Duke's desire to rule less and even to turn the dirty work over to Angelo, Pompey in totality—nearly every character exemplifies some version of incontinence. And, as Baines hints, even the babies lack sufficient self-control and beat their nurses.[9]

Incontinence, again, is, for Aristotle, a failure of knowledge.[10] One can admit the universal, but one fails to apply the universal to oneself. The failure of knowledge, the failure to tie the universal to the instantiation, is at the heart of the kinds of errors each of the characters commits. And it is at the heart of Isabella's silence at the end of the play. She does not see herself the way she is seen. She is without a mirror. Her self-opacity, her inability to see what her verbal incontinence brings about, is the root of the shock. And indeed, Burkhardt points out the same dynamic for Angelo.[11] Having a character in contradiction or in tension with universal law and discovering that tension is the kind of error that leads to shock. Where Isabella's shock leads her to an incontinent and incredulous silence, Angelo's leads him to wickedness.

The prone and speechless dialect, displayed in variation by heads on chopping blocks, the silent bedtrick, Isabella's ways, the Duke's absence qua Duke and presence qua Friar, Barnardine's general silence, the gift of the notorious pirate among other instances, is an important problem here. That communication can go awry, that dialect can be speechless, is one more way that we can be seduced by passion with no recourse to argue against it or to present alternatives.

If words and reason fail to make a just world because they stir the passions, a prone and speechless dialect is all the more worrisome for it allows for no intervention at all. To the extent that Isabella, along with other characters in the play, lacks the awareness of the effects of prone and speechless dialects, they are all subject to incredulity. To the extent that Socrates and his interlocutors are subject to the limits of reason to control passion, they, too, are subject to incredulity. To the extent that we remain unaware of our debts to justice and the currency we use to pay our debts, we all risk Isabella's shocked silence or the Book X's cry to the heavens.

Angelo's chief challenges to political rule are first that he uses rule for his own lawless desires, precisely the definition of a tyrant in the *Republic*, and second that he sees mercy as a thing that the state cannot grant without risking increased crime through the structure of moral hazard. In this, Angelo echoes the concerns of the Senators in *Timon*. Isabella's ability to defend mercy and then to apply it to both Mariana and her would-be rapist Angelo shows the difficulties inherent in the granting of mercy and the need to do so regardless.

The proper use of mercy is the chief debt the political system owes the people, and the proper use of restraint is the chief debt the people owe the greater good. To get to propriety requires the kind of study of rule and of citizenship that Angelo defers at the beginning of *Measure for Measure* when Escalus asks him about what it means to be a ruler. While the Duke displays an understanding of what is going on in Vienna, and he shows the ability to act in order to right the ship, he has clearly failed in the past to recognize his errors and guide the ship of state. To the extent that he put his own unnecessary desires ahead of the state's needs, he has shown himself to have been a flawed ruler. That he finds a way to correct the direction of the ship of state shows that there is hope.

NOTES

1. Berman notes that, "Coleridge found *Measure for Measure* 'painful...disgusting...horrible'" (Ronald Berman, "Shakespeare and the Law," in *Shakespeare Quarterly* 18 (2) (Spring 1967): 141; 141–150; Skura notes "The problems which have made Shakespeare's *Measure for Measure* a 'problem play' have always been clear: the action is stiff, the characters unpleasant and the ending contrived." (Meredith Skura, "New Interpretations for Interpretation in *Measure for Measure*," in *boundary* 27 (2) (Winter 1979): 39–60; in a response to W. W. Lawrence's defense of the bedtrick, Harding writes that "Unfortunately, the conception which Professor Lawrence has given us of Elizabethan betrothal-relations is inaccurate and misleading" (Davis P. Harding, "Elizabethan Betrothals and '*Measure for Measure*,'" in *The Journal of English and Germanic Philology* 49 (2) (April 1950): 140; 139–158; the litany of criticisms of just about every aspect of this play figure in the beginnings of many critical essays, with Berman's contribution to the genre as a notable highlight.

2. Skura, "New Interpretations for Interpretation," 40.

3. John Wasson, "*Measure for Measure*: A Play of Incontinence," in *ELH* 27 (December 1960).

4. Aristotle, *Nicomachean Ethics*. For Aristotle, incontinence stems from misapplying a syllogism's minor premise. One might grant the universal claim, and one might even see the conclusion at some level, but one fails to see how one is a participant in the syllogism at the level of the minor premise. It might the case that all people should do something, but this particular thing does not fall under this heading, and so I am not bound by the argument's logical conclusion. See Book VII of the *Nicomachean Ethics*. Aristotle, *Nicomachean Ethics*. Translated by David Ross, J.L. Ackrill and J.O. Urmson, revised (Oxford: Oxford University Press, 1980).

5. John W. Dickinson, "Renaissance Equity and 'Measure for Measure'," in *Shakespeare Quarterly* 13 (3) (Summer 1962): 287–297.

6. Here we see another Aristotelian theme in the play. Aristotle suggests that ethics arises from habit and its development into understanding. One can be habituated into doing the right thing, but without a full understanding of the reasons for the

rightness of the action, one operates at the level of mere habit. Mere habit is insufficient. See Book II of Aristotle's *Nicomachean Ethics*.

7. Mario Digangi, "Pleasure and Danger: Measuring Female Sexuality in *Measure for Measure*," in *ELH* 60 (3) (Autumn 1993): 592.

8. Wasson, "*Measure for Measure*: A Play of Incontinence," 272.

9. Barbara J. Baines, "Assaying the Power of Chastity in *Measure for Measure*," in *Studies in English Literature 1500-1900* 30 (2) (1990): 284–285.

10. See Book VII of Aristotle's *Nicomachean Ethics*.

11. Louis Burkhardt, "Spectator Seduction: *Measure for Measure*," in *Texas Studies in Literature and Language* 37 (3) (Fall 1995): 42.

Conclusion

There is something a little risky in writing a conclusion for a work that suggests that conclusions are fraught with risk. The motivation for this book is that we make the most important choice there is, the choice of what kind of life is the proper life, without enough knowledge ever to get it right. To conclude that one is living a comedy can lead to the worst tragedy possible—that of devouring what you love most and what you most live for and what motivates you to decide in the first place—if, that is, you are not actually in a comedy. Since we can never know the dramatic mode of a life while the life is in progress, and since life is ever in progress if a decision regarding how to live must be made, then we are in a bind and we need to find ways to manage.

The suggestion at the end of the *Symposium* that Socrates has some insight into both comic and tragic narratives conjoined in the same writer's soul gives us some glimmer of hope that we, too, can figure out how to write a life, how to decide a life, how to enact a life that is aware of both of these poles. The double-awareness of a double life and the double possibilities may give us room to hedge the risk, or may give us political and economic structures that allow us to mitigate the risks. The Shakespeare plays and the text of the *Republic* discussed here show us some of the perils of failing and some of the possibilities of managing the comic and tragic risks we face.

We are not immune, we cannot be preserved for all time, we will err on one side or the other. In the *Republic*, the certainty of error is presented through the Spindle of Necessity, the fall of the state, the intervention of human desire into human life despite the attempts to push all desire out of the city. Since desire cannot be purged, poetry cannot be purged, and the entire narrative rests on the Homeric texts, clearly we need social structures, soul structures, and narrative structures to help us through the cycles of life and death, comedy and tragedy.[1] That is, we cannot live without the kinds of ambiguity that desire, poetry, and Homeric narrative bring about. The ordering of society and the ordering of the soul and the ordering of narrative, as informed by philosophy, are what seem to be called for in the *Republic*.[2]

The obligation to find a way through, the obligation to build inner and outer structures and to tell stories and find visions is fully binding, if fully impossible. That there might be a truth, that we must live as if there is a truth, that we must consider that tragedy does have an Aristotelian certainty of magnitude, even if none of this is true, is at the heart of the presentation of Socrates in the *Republic*. The indeterminacy, if enacted as determinate, leads to catastrophe. The indeterminacy, if understood as such, gives us a chance to make better decisions about how to live. Thus, we must look for noon at two o'clock, as Derrida writes in *Given Time*, but we must do so with a twist.[3] We must look for noon at two o'clock, while fully knowing that it is indeed not to be found. In other words, we must look for comedy in tragedy, we must look for tragedy in comedy, knowing that we may never find what we are looking for. We must contradict our experience in order to have experience, we must look to the stars to navigate our ships, though stars and ships are never to be found together. We must, still, find them in the same author, even as comedy and tragedy are the last men standing, side-by-side, at the end of a long night.

Hope for the impossible is perhaps the paradoxical way through the kinds of errors we have discussed throughout this book. Being open to tragic and comic possibility and being willing to reinterpret as needed, balancing inner psychic needs against the proper boundaries of the polity and the economy, and coming to understand what we owe in the face of our very existence, being merciful despite the risk—these are the claims the moral order has on us regardless of how well or badly we are served by that order—and therefore they are our chief obligations.

It is clear from these texts that the devouring of our own children, the destruction of an order in which they can live so that we can satisfy a temporary, unnecessary, or lawless desire, is the chief threat that looms over us. If we do not get these terms straightened out, we will join Socrates and a cast of many at the most unfortunate banquet of all. We will dine on bad arguments, we will dine on people we love, and our souls will be marked permanently with the results. We will cry out to the heavens, with our incredulity intact.

NOTES

1. Here, it is worth noting Harvey Yunis' essay "The Protreptic Rhetoric of the *Republic*." Yunis suggests a protreptic reading of the Republic, one that shows the text as propelling us to live differently from how we have been living. From the beginning of the Republic, Socrates is laying out a case for the worthiness of a

project of justice as the guiding project of human life. We should be compelled by argument (Yunis 1) and we should be compelled by story and character. See Harvey Yunis, "The Protreptic Rhetoric of the *Republic*," in *The Cambridge Companion to Plato's Republic*. Edited by G.R.F. Ferrari (Cambridge: Cambridge University Press, 2007), 1–26.

2. In a somewhat different tack, Rachana Kamtekar gets at a similar set of concerns. She discusses the tensions within the personified parts of the soul, the "imprecision" involved, and what results from it (Kamtekar, 89). Kamtekar works to balance the goals of precision against the imprecision lurking in the psychology of the Platonic soul. See Rachana Kamtekar, "Speaking with the Same Voice as Reason," in *Plato and the Divided Self*. Edited by Rachel Barney, Tad Brennan, and Charles Brittain (Cambridge: Cambridge University Press, 2012), 77–101.

3. Jacques Derrida, *Given Time I: Counterfeit Money*. Translated by Peggy Kamuf (Chicago, IL: The University of Chicago Press, 1992), 34.

Works Cited

Adelman, Janet. *Blood Relations: Christian and Jew in 'The Merchant of Venice.'* Chicago, IL: The University of Chicago Press, 2008.
Allen, R.E. "Introduction." In *The Dialogues of Plato*, Vol. 1. Translated by R.E. Allen. New Haven, CT: Yale University Press, 1984.
Annas, Julia. *An Introduction to Plato's Republic*. Oxford: Oxford University Press, 1981.
Aristotle. *Nicomachean Ethics*. Translated by David Ross, J.L. Ackrill and J.O. Urmson, revised. Oxford: Oxford University Press, 1980.
Aristotle. *Poetics*. Translated by Ingraham Bywater. New York: Modern Library, Random House, 1984.
Baines, Barbara J. "Assaying the Power of Chastity in *Measure for Measure*." *Studies in English Literature 1500-1900* 30 (2): 283–301 (1990).
Baracchi, Claudia. "Beyond the Comedy and Tragedy of Authority: The Invisible Father in Plato's *Republic*." *Philosophy and Rhetoric* 34 (2): 151–176 (2001).
Baracchi, Claudia. *Of Myth, Life, and War in Plato's Republic*. Bloomington, IN: Indiana University Press, 2002.
Baracchi, Claudia. "Animals and Angels: The Myth of Life as a Whole in *Republic* 10." In *Plato's Animals: Gadflies, Horses, Swans, and Other Philosophical Beasts*. Edited by Jeremy Bell and Michael Nass, 209–224. Bloomington, IN: Indiana University Press, 2015.
Bates, Jennifer Ann. *Hegel and Shakespeare on Moral Imagination*. New York: State University of New York Press, 2010.
Benardete, Seth. *Socrates' Second Sailing: On Plato's Republic*. Chicago, IL: The University of Chicago Press, 1989.
Berger, Harry Jr. "Acts of Silence, Acts of Speech: How to Do Things with Othello and Desdemona." *Renaissance Drama*, New Series 33: 3–35 (2004).
Berger, Harry Jr. *The Perils of Uglytown: Studies in Structural Misanthropology from Plato to Rembrandt*. New York: Fordham University Press, 2015.
Berman, Ronald. "Shakespeare and the Law." *Shakespeare Quarterly* 18 (2): 141–150 (Spring 1967).

Blanchard, Olivier and Lawrence Summers. "Hysteresis in Unemployment." NBER Working Paper 2035. Cambridge: National Bureau of Economic Research, 1986. http://www.nber.org/papers/w2035.pdf, Accessed 12 January 2017.

Blondell, Ruby. *The Play of Character in Plato's Dialogues*. Cambridge: Cambridge University Press, 2002.

Bloom, Harold. *Shakespeare: The Invention of the Human*. New York: Riverhead Books, Penguin, Putnam, 1998.

Bobonich, Christopher. "Akrasia and Agency in Plato's *Laws* and *Republic*." In *Essays on Plato's Psychology*. Edited by Ellen Wagner, 203–237. Oxford: Lexington Books. 2001.

Boose, Lynda E. "The Father and the Bride in Shakespeare." *PMLA* 97 (3): 325–347. (May 1982).

Brennan, Tad, "The Nature of the Spirited Part of the Soul and Its Object." In *Plato and the Divided Self*. Edited by Rachel Barney, Tad Brennan and Charles Brittain, 102–127. Cambridge: Cambridge University Press, 2012.

Brill, Sarah. *Plato on the Limits of Human Life*. Bloomington, IN: Indiana University Press, 2013.

Burger, Ronna. "The Thumotic Soul." In *Epoche: A Journal for the History of Philosophy* 7 (2): 151–167 (Spring 2003).

Burkhardt, Louis. "Spectator Seduction: Measure for Measure." *Texas Studies in Literature and Language* 37 (3): 236–263 (Fall 1995).

Cavell, Stanley. "Epistemology and Tragedy: A Reading of *Othello*." *Daedalus* 108 (3): 27–43 (Spring 1979).

Caverero, Adriana. *Inclinations: A Critique of Rectitude*. Stanford: Stanford University Press, 2016.

Coates, John. *The Hour Between Dog and Wolf: Risk Taking, Gut Feelings and the Biology of Boom and Bust*. New York: The Penguin Press, 2012.

Daniel, Drew. "Let me Have Judgement, and the Jew His Will': Melancholy Epistemology and Masochistic Fantasy in *The Merchant of Venice*." *Shakespeare Quarterly* 61 (2): 206–234 (Summer 2010).

Dasgupta, Partha. *Economics: A Very Short Introduction*. Oxford: Oxford University Press, 2007.

Davidson, Clifford. "Timon of Athens: The Iconography of False Friendship." *Huntington Library Quarterly* 43 (3): 180–200 (Summer 1980), University of California Press.

Derrida, Jacques. *Politics of Friendship*. Translated by George Collins. New York: Verso, 1977.

Derrida, Jacques. *Dissemination*. Translated by Barbara Johnson. Chicago, IL: The University of Chicago Press, 1981.

Derrida, Jacques. *Given Time I: Counterfeit Money*. Translated by Peggy Kamuf. Chicago, IL: The University of Chicago Press, 1992.

Derrida, Jacques. *The Gift of Death*. Translated by David Wills. Chicago, IL: The University of Chicago Press, 1995.

Descartes, Rene. "Meditations on First Philosophy." In *Discourse on Method and Meditations on First Philosophy*. Translated by Donald A. Cress. Indianapolis, IN: Hackett Press, 1998.

Dickinson, John W. "Renaissance Equity and 'Measure for Measure'." *Shakespeare Quarterly* 13 (3): 287–297 (Summer 1962).
Digangi, Mario. "Pleasure and Danger: Measuring Female Sexuality in Measure for Measure." *ELH* 60 (3): 589–609 (Autumn 1993).
Draper, John W. "Honest Iago." *PMLA* 46 (3): 724–737 (September 1931).
Fagan, Patricia. *Plato and Tradition: The Poetic and Cultural Context of Philosophy.* Evanston, IL: Northwestern University Press, 2013.
Ferrari, G.R.F. "Glaucon's Reward, Philosophy's Debt: The Myth of Er." In *Plato's Myths.* Edited by Catalin Partenie, 116–133. Cambridge: Cambridge University Press, 2009.
Foakes, R.A. *Coleridge's Criticism of Shakespeare: A Selection.* Edited by R.A. Foakes. Detroit, MI: Wayne State University Press, 1989.
Flower, Annette. "Disguise and Identity in Pericles, Prince of Tyre." *Shakespeare Quarterly* 26 (1): 30–41 (Winter 1975).
Freydberg, Bernard. "Retracing Homer and Aristophanes in the Platonic Text." In *Retracing the Platonic Text.* Edited by John Russon and John Sallis, 99–112. Evanston, IL: Northwestern University Press, 2000.
Frye, Northrup. "The Argument of Comedy." In *Shakespeare: An Anthology of Criticism and Theory 1945-2000.* Edited by Russ McDonald, 93–99. Massachusetts: Blackwell Publishing, 2004.
Gallop, David. "Plato's 'Cyclical Argument' Recycled." In *Essays on Plato's Psychology.* Edited by Ellen Wagner, 263–280. Oxford: Lexington Books, 2001.
Garber, Marjorie. *Shakespeare After All.* New York: Anchor Books, 2004.
Gonzalez, Francisco J. "Of Beasts and Heroes: The Promiscuity of Humans and Animals in the Myth of Er." In *Plato's Animals: Gadflies, Horses, Swans, and Other Philosophical Beasts.* Edited by Jeremy Bell and Michael Nass, 225–245. Bloomington, IN: Indiana University Press, 2015.
Gordon, Jill. *Turning Toward Philosophy: Literary Device and Dramatic Structure in Plato's Dialogues.* University Park, PA: The Pennsylvania State University Press, 1999.
Gossett, Suzanne. "Introduction." In *Pericles.* Edited by Suzanne Gossett. London: Arden Shakespeare, Third Series, Thomson Learning, 2004.
Halliwell, Stephen. "The Life-and-Death Journey of the Soul: Myth of Er." In *The Cambridge Companion to Plato's Republic*, 445–473. Cambridge: Cambridge University Press, 2007.
Harding, Davis P. "Elizabethan Betrothals and 'Measure for Measure'." *The Journal of English and Germanic Philology* 49 (2): 139–158 (1950).
Henze, Richard. "*The Comedy of Errors*: A Freely Binding Chain." *Shakespeare Quarterly* 22 (1): 35–41 (Winter 1971), Folger Shakespeare Library.
Holmes, Brooke. *The Symptom and the Subject: The Emergence of the Physical Body in Ancient Greece.* Princeton, NJ: Princeton University Press, 2010.
Homer, *Odyssey.* Translated by Robert Fagles. New York: Penguin Group, 1996.
Homer. *Iliad.* Translated by Stanley Lombardo. Indianapolis, IN: Hackett Publishing Company, 1997.
Hunt, Maurice. "Slavery, English Servitude, and *The Comedy of Errors.*" *English Literary Renaissance* 27 (1): 31–56 (December 1997).

Hyland, Drew A. *Questioning Platonism: Continental Interpretations of Plato*. New York: State University of New York Press. 2004.

Hyland, Drew A. "The Animals That Therefore We Were: Aristophanes's Double-Creatures and the Questions of Origins." In *Plato's Animals: Gadflies, Horses, Swans, and Other Philosophical Beasts*. Edited by Jeremy Bell and Michael Nass, 193–205. Bloomington, IN: Indiana University Press, 2015.

Jackson, Ken. "'One Wish' or the Possibility of the Impossible: Derrida, the Gift, and God in 'Timon of Athens'." *Shakespeare Quarterly* 52 (1): 34–66 (Spring 2001).

Kahn, Charles H. "Plato's Theory of Desire." *The Review of Metaphysics*, 41 (1): 77–103 (September 1987).

Kahneman, Daniel, Andrew Rosenfield, Linnea Gandhi and Tom Blaser. "Noise: How to Overcome the High, Hidden Cost of Inconsistent Decision Making." *Harvard Business Review* (October 2016). https://hbr.org/2016/10/noise, Accessed 12 January 2017.

Kamtekar, Rachana, "Speaking with the Same Voice as Reason." In *Plato and the Divided Self*. Edited by Rachel Barney, Tad Brennan and Charles Brittain, 77–101. Cambridge: Cambridge University Press, 2012.

Kant, Immanuel. *Grounding for the Metaphysics of Morals*, Third Edition. Translated by James W. Ellington. Indianapolis, IN: Hackett Publishing Company, 1993.

Kirk, Gregory. "Initiation, Extraction, and Transformation: What It Takes to Answer Socrates's Question." *Idealistic Studies* 45 (1): 103–123 (2015).

Kirk, Gregory. "Self-Knowledge and Ignorance in Plato's *Charmides*." *Ancient Philosophy* 36: 303–320 (2016).

Lawrence, William W. "*Measure for Measure* and Lucio." *Shakespeare Quarterly* 9 (4): 443–453 (Autumn 1958).

Lear, Jonathan. "Inside and Outside the 'Republic'." *Phronesis* 37 (2): 184–215 (1992).

Lyotard, Jean-Francois. *Libidinal Economy*. Translated by Iain Hamilton Grant. Bloomington, IN: Indiana University Press, 1993.

McCoy, Marina. "The City of Sows and Sexual Differentiation in the *Republic*." In *Plato's Animals: Gadflies, Horses, Swans, and Other Philosophical Beasts*. Edited by Jeremy Bell and Michael Nass, 193–205. Bloomington, IN: Indiana University Press, 2015.

Minsky, Hyman. *Stabilizing an Unstable Economy*. New York: McGrawHill, 2008.

Moore, Jeanie Grant. "Riddled Romance: Kingship and Kinship in 'Pericles'." *Rocky Mountain Review of Language and Literature* 57 (1): 33–48 (2003).

Nightingale, Andrea Wilson. *Genres in Dialogue: Plato and the Construct of Philosophy*. Cambridge: Cambridge University Press, 1995.

Nightingale, Andrea Wilson. *Spectacles of Truth in Classical Greek Philosophy: Theoria in Its Cultural Context*. Cambridge: Cambridge University Press, 2004.

O'Byrne, Anne. *Natality and Finitude*. Bloomington, IN: Indiana University Press. 2010.

O'Connor, David K. "Rewriting the Poets in Plato's Characters." In *The Cambridge Companion to Plato's Republic*. Edited by G.R.F. Ferrari, 55–89. Cambridge: Cambridge University Press, 2007.

Ophir, Adi. *Plato's Invisible Cities: Discourse and Power in the Republic*. Savage, MD: Barnes & Noble, 1991.

Perry, Curtis. "Commerce, Community and Nostalgia in *The Comedy of Errors*." In *Money in the Age of Shakespeare*. Edited by Linda Woodbridge. New York: Palgrave Macmillan, 2003.

Petronella, Vincent. "Structure and Theme through Separation and Union in Shakespeare's *The Comedy of Errors*." *MLA Review* 69 (3): 481–488 (July 1974).

Planinc, Zdravko. *Plato Through Homer: Poetry and Philosophy in the Cosmological Dialogues*. Columbia, MO: University of Missouri Press, 2003.

Plato. *Symposium*. Translated by Alexander Nehamas and Paul Woodruff. Indianapolis, IN: Hackett Publishing Company, 1989.

Plato. "Apology." In *Five Dialogues*, Second Edition. Translated by G.M.A. Grube and revised by John M. Cooper. Indianapolis, IN: Hackett Press, 2002.

Plato. "Euthyphro." In *Five Dialogues*, Second Edition. Translated by G.M.A. Grube and revised by John M. Cooper. Indianapolis, IN: Hackett Press, 2002.

Plato. *Republic*. Translated by R.E. Allen. New Haven, CT: Yale University Press, 2006.

Raman, Shankar. "Marking Time: Memory and Market in *The Comedy of Errors*." *Shakespeare Quarterly* 56 (2): 176–205 (Summer 2005).

Rand, Frank Prentice. "The Overgarrulous Iago." *Shakespeare Quarterly* 1 (3): 154–161 (July 1950).

Rogers, Stephen. "*Othello*: Comedy in Reverse." *Shakespeare Quarterly* 24 (2): 210–220 (Spring 1973).

Rothleder, Dianne. "The Evil Deceiver and the Evil Truth-Teller: Descartes, Iago, and Scepticism." In *The Routledge Companion to Shakespeare and Philosophy*. Edited by Craig Bourne and Emily Caddick Bourne. New York: Routledge, 2019.

Rosen, Stanley. *Plato's Republic: A Study*. New Haven, CT: Yale University Press, 2005.

Rozett, Martha Tuck. "The Comic Structures of Tragic Endings: The Suicide Scenes in Romeo and Juliet and Antony and Cleopatra." *Shakespeare Quarterly* 36 (2): 152–164 (Summer 1985).

Russon, John. "Just Reading: The Nature of the Platonic Text." In *Retracing the Platonic Text*. Edited by John Russon and John Sallis, ix–xix. Evanston, IL: Northwestern University Press, 2000.

Sallis, John. *Being and Logos: Reading the Platonic Dialogues*, Third Edition. Bloomington, IN: Indiana University Press, 1996.

Satkunanandan, Shalini. *Extraordinary Responsibility: Politics Beyond the Moral Calculus*. New York: Cambridge University Press, 2015.

Schmid, Walter T. "Socratic Moderation and Self-Knowledge." *Journal of the History of Philosophy* 21 (3): 339–348 (July 1983), Johns Hopkins University Press.

Schulman, Alex. *Rethinking Shakespeare's Political Philosophy: From Lear to Leviathan*. Edinburgh: Edinburgh University Press, 2014.

Sextus Empiricus. *Selections from the Major Writings on Scepticism, Man, & God*. Edited by Philip P. Hallie. Translated by Sanford G. Etheridge. Indianapolis, IN: Hackett Press, 1985.

Shakespeare, William. *The Comedy of Errors*. Edited by R.A. Foakes. London: Arden Shakespeare, Methuen, A&C Black, Publishers, Ltd., 1962.

Shakespeare, William. *Measure for Measure*. Edited by J.W. Lever. London: Arden Shakespeare, Methuen, Thomson Learning, 1965.

Shakespeare, William. *Macbeth*. Edited by Barbara A. Mowat and Paul Werstine. New York: Pocket Books, Simon and Schuster Inc., 1992.

Shakespeare, William. *Othello*. Edited by E.A.J. Honigmann. London: Arden Shakespeare, Third Edition, Thomson Learning, 1997.

Shakespeare, William. *Pericles*. Edited by Suzanne Gossett. London: Arden Shakespeare, Third Series, Thomson Learning, 2004.

Shakespeare, William. *Merchant of Venice*. Edited by John Drakakis. London: The Arden Shakespeare, Third Series, Bloomsbury Academic, Methuen, 2010.

Shakespeare, William and Thomas Middleton. *Timon of Athens*. Edited by Anthony B. Dawson and Gretchen E. Minton. London: Arden Shakespeare, Third Series, Cengage Learning, 2008.

Skura, Meredith. "New Interpretations for Interpretation in Measure for Measure." *boundary 2* 7 (2): 39–60 (Winter 1979).

Smith, Thomas. "Love of the Good as the Cure for Spiritedness in Plato's Republic." *The Review of Metaphysics* 70: 33–58 (September 2016).

Sohmer, Steve. "The 'Double Time' Crux in *Othello* Solved." *English Literary Renaissance* 32 (2): 214–238. (Spring 2002).

Spence, Michael. "Can We Regulate Systemic Risk?" *Project Syndicate*, 13 August 2010. http://www.project-syndicate.org/commentary/can-we-regulate-systemic-risk-, Accessed 12 January 2017.

Thayer, H.S. "The Myth of Er." *History of Philosophy Quarterly* 5 (4): 369–384. (October 1988).

Thorne, W.B. "Pericles and the 'Incest-Fertility' Opposition." *Shakespeare Quarterly* 22 (1): 43–56 (Winter 1971).

Thucydides. *The History of the Peloponnesian War*. Translated by Rex Warner. New York: Penguin Classics, 1972.

Vlastos, Gregory. "Justice and Psychic Harmony in the Republic." *The Journal of Philosophy* 66 (16): 505–521. (August 1969).

Wasson, John. "Measure for Measure: A Play of Incontinence." *ELH* 27 (4): 262–275 (December 1960).

Weiss, Roslyn. "Wise Guys and Smart Alecks in *Republic* 1 and 2." In *The Cambridge Companion to Plato's Republic*. Edited by G.R.F. Ferrari, 90–115. Cambridge: Cambridge University Press, 2007.

Wilberding, James. "Curbing One's Appetites in Plato's Republic." In *Plato and the Divided Self*. Edited by Rachel Barney, Tad Brennan and Charles Brittain, 128–149. Cambridge: Cambridge University Press, 2012.

Yunis, Harvey. "The Protreptic Rhetoric of the *Republic*." In *The Cambridge Companion to Plato's Republic*. Edited by G.R.F. Ferrari, 1–26. Cambridge: Cambridge University Press, 2007.

Index

Achilles, xviii, xxiv, 32
Adeimantus, 22–27, 35n33, 37n37, 100
Adelman, Janet, 125n6
Adriana (from *The Comedy of Errors*), 69, 71, 73, 75–80
Agathon (from the *Symposium*), xiii, xiv
Alcibiades (from the *Symposium*), xiii, xiv, 181, 185, 188, 190, 191, 197–212
Angelo (from *Measure for Measure*), 25, 198, 214–30
Angelo (from *The Comedy of Errors*), 71–72
Annas, Julia, 91–92
Antiochus (from *Pericles*), 25, 127–42, 144, 147, 155, 191
the Antipholi (from *The Comedy of Errors*), 67–71, 78, 81
Antonio (from *The Merchant of Venice*), xvi, xx, 89, 109–24
Apemantus (from *Timon of Athens*), 183, 185, 188–91, 194, 211
Apollodoros (from the *Symposium*), xiii
Apology, xiii, xiv, 31n13, 33n20, 95, 150, 179n11
Aristodemus (from the *Symposium*), xiii
Aristophanes, xiii, xiv, xv, xxiiinn1–2, 38n39, 62

Aristotle, 3–8, 11–13, 29, 40, 213, 221, 228–29, 230nn4–6
Arragon (from *The Merchant of Venice*), 117

Baracchi, Claudia, 17, 28, 31n10, 32n17
Barnardine (from *Measure for Measure*), 225–26, 229
Bassanio (from *The Merchant of Venice*), 109–24
Bates, Jennifer Ann, 57n2
bedtrick, 214, 216, 224, 226, 229, 230n1
Bellario (from *The Merchant of Venice*), 120–24
Benardete, Seth, 23, 29, 32n19, 37, 38nn39–42, 94
Berger, Harry Jr., 57n1, 58nn5–6, 58n10, 59n11, 106–7, 107n7
Berman, Ronald, 230n1
birth, xv, xvi, xx, xxi, xxii, 7, 10, 32, 65–70, 104, 139–43, 154, 160–64, 173, 174, 176, 181, 182, 184, 198, 214
Blondell, Ruby, 35n33
Bobonich, Christopher, 107n16
Bolt (from *Pericles*), 148–50
Book X (of the *Republic*), xv, xvi, xvii, xviii, xxi, xxiii, xxiv, 9, 11, 15–28, 36–37n35, 40, 50, 57, 92, 99, 130,

243

244 Index

132, 149, 152, 159, 169, 174, 197, 206, 222, 229
Boose, Lynda E., 130–31
Brabantio (from *Othello*), xix, 39–46, 49, 52–56
Brennan, Tad, 106n5
Brill, Sarah, 37n35
Burger, Ronna, 38n39

cannibalism, xx, 18, 105, 127, 133–34, 137, 139, 185, 188, 212
Cartesian, xviii, 4, 13, 14, 18, 29, 30, 57, 61, 77, 81
Cavarero, Adriana, 178n8
cave (from the *Republic*), xxi, 18, 37n36, 150, 160–61, 164, 171–75, 177n3, 178n5, 178n6–8, 179n13, 204–6
Cavell, Stanley, 59n12
Cephalus, xvii, xxi, 14–30, 31n10, 33n20, 34nn22–27, 64, 66, 86, 88–98, 103, 105n3, 159, 169, 222–23, 227
Claudio (from *Measure for Measure*), xvi, 214–28
Cleon (from *Pericles*), 133–34, 139–55, 165
the *Clouds* (Aristophanes), xiii, xiv
Coates, John, 111–12
Coleridge, Samuel Taylor, 58n9, 230n1
comedy, xiii, xiv, xv, xviii, xix, xxii, xxiii, xxiiin2, 4–13, 21, 26–29, 39–42, 45, 47, 50, 51, 56, 58n8, 61–68, 78, 81, 86, 159, 160, 164, 173, 214, 233–34
The Comedy of Errors, xv, xix, 5, 6, 61–73, 88–89, 127, 139, 159

Daniel, Drew, 112–13
Davidson, Clifford, 185, 186
Dawson, Anthony B., 188
death, xiv, xvii, xix, xxi, xxii, xxiv, 5–12, 16, 28, 39–45, 48, 50, 53–56, 62–66, 69, 78, 88, 103, 109, 112, 119–22, 128–29, 135–36, 138–40,

143–45, 151–52, 155, 160, 170, 174–76, 181–82, 185–87, 197–98, 200, 204, 208–9, 211, 214, 216, 217, 220–25, 233
debt, xv, xvii, xx, xxi, xxii, 10, 15, 28, 35n31, 72, 92–95, 101–2, 105n3, 115, 120–21, 124, 136, 139–49, 155, 160–76, 181–230
Derrida, Jacques, xvii, xviii, xxi, 3, 12–14, 30, 33n20, 34n27, 45, 61, 177n3, 179n13, 187, 234
Descartes, 14
Desdemona (from *Othello*), xix, 39–59
Dickinson, John, 215
Digangi, Mario, 228
Dionyza (from *Pericles*), 104, 133, 139–40, 143–51, 155–56, 163–65, 169–70, 175, 199
Diotima (from the *Symposium*), xiii, xiv
discovery, 6–8, 11–14, 56, 81, 124, 197
dopamine, 111–12, 120–24, 131
Draper, John W., 58n8
the Dromios (from *The Comedy of Errors*), 66–74, 80, 81, 104, 159
the Duke (Vincentio, from *Measure for Measure*), xxi, 25, 213–30

economy, xix, xx, 10, 24, 25, 31n16, 37n35, 38n41, 71, 85–156, 159–60, 164, 170–72, 181, 183, 186, 192, 195–96, 199, 203–34
Egeon (from *The Comedy of Errors*), 62–63, 65, 66, 68–77
Elbow (from Measure for Measure), 228
Emilia (from *Othello*), 46–57, 58n9, 143, 163–65, 169–70, 178n5
enemy, 94, 96–97, 105n3
error, xvi, xix, 4, 18, 20, 29, 44, 61–81, 91, 98, 109, 130, 144, 181, 186, 197, 205, 207, 216, 221, 226, 229–30, 233–34
Escalus (from *Measure for Measure*), 217, 221, 224, 228, 230
the *Euthyphro*, 10

Fagan, Patricia, 33n19, 177n5, 178nn5–6
fated to eat his children, (from the *Republic*), 19
Ferrari, G.R.F., xxivn6, 35n31
first soul to choose, (from the *Republic*), xvi, xxi, 12, 32n19, 42, 100
Flavius (from *Timon of Athens*), 190–96, 203–8, 211
flow (and stock of capital), 69, 86, 90, 115–16, 190, 195–96
Flower, Annette, 144
Form of the Good, 23, 173, 228
Freydberg, Bernard, xxiiin2, 33n19
friendship, xviii, 3, 4, 12–14, 30, 41–42, 49, 57, 61, 81, 98, 182–83, 185–89, 193–94, 200, 203–4, 211, 218
Frye, Northrop, 62–63

Gallop, David, xxvn13
Garber, Marjorie, 154
gift, xvii, xxi, xxii, 37n36, 114, 134, 151–52, 160, 176, 179n13, 181–212, 226, 229
Glaucon (from the *Republic*), 9, 22–23, 27, 32n19, 35n33, 37n37, 96, 99–101, 107n17, 161–62, 166, 168, 177n2, 179n12, 227
Gonzalez, Francisco J., 31n16
the Good (from the *Republic*), 23, 25, 28, 36n35, 100, 102, 166–69, 173–74, 227–28
Gordon, Jill, 35n33
Gossett, Suzanne, 130, 134, 137, 139
Gower (from *Pericles*), 127, 138, 144–45, 154
Gratiano (from *The Merchant of Venice*), 122
The Groundwork (Kant), 181
Gyges (from the *Republic*), 22, 25, 99

Halliwell, Stephen, 30n9
Henze, Richard, 72
Holmes, Brooke, 35n30

The Hour Between Dog and Wolf, 111
Hunt, Maurice, 67–68
Hyland, Drew, xxiiin1, xxivn9
hysteresis, xvii, xviii, xxii, xxvn11, 8, 9, 11, 32n18, 50, 63, 69, 124, 197, 208

Iago (from *Othello*), xix, 39–57, 57n1, 58nn5–12, 159, 163, 165, 170, 178n5
the *Iliad*, xviii, xxivn6, 32n19, 37n36, 107n14
incest, 129–31, 138, 150
incontinence, xxii, 107n16, 160, 176, 213–14, 228–29
incredulity, xv, xvi, xxi, 3, 5, 7–11, 14, 17–19, 24, 26, 28–29, 36n35, 56, 63, 78, 81, 86, 89, 96–100, 109, 113, 121–22, 124, 128, 130–32, 138–39, 146, 149–59, 168, 176, 182, 192, 194, 197, 199, 200, 203–5, 211, 214, 223, 226, 228–29, 234
infinite debt, xxi, 10, 172, 176
intelligible, 170–74, 179n11
internal colony, (from the *Republic*), 163–64
investment, xxii, 4, 13, 24, 91, 93–94, 96, 110–13, 131, 184, 194
Isabella (from *Measure for Measure*), xxi, 176, 213–31

Jackson, Ken, 187
Jessica (from *Othello*), 109, 119, 121, 136
Julietta (from *Measure for Measure*), 216, 220–22, 225, 228
justice, xvi, xvii, xix, xxii, 9, 13–30, 31nn12–13, 34n22, 35n31, 36n34, 37nn35–39, 38n39, 49, 64–66, 68, 88, 90, 93–105, 119–24, 141, 143, 150, 154, 159, 160, 175, 182, 197, 200, 202, 206, 210–12, 216–29

Kahn, Charles, 36n35
Kahneman, Daniel, 32n18
Kamtekar, Rachana, 235n2

Kirk, Gregory, 34n23, 35n34
kleos, xxivn6, 32n19, 37n36

Lady Macbeth (from *Macbeth*), 51
Lear, Jonathan, xxivn7
Leonine (from *Pericles*), 140, 143, 144, 155
Leontius (from the *Republic*), 37n39, 38n39
libidinal economy, 24, 25, 38n41, 87, 89, 105, 113, 129
the line (divided line analogy from the *Republic*), 23, 164, 169–71, 173, 178n6
Luciana (from *The Comedy of Errors*), 75, 79, 80
Lucilius (from *Timon of Athens*), 184, 191
Lucio (from *Measure for Measure*), 218–20, 222, 225–27
Lucius (from *Timon of Athens*), 189
Lucullus (from *Timon of Athens*), 189
Lychorida (from *Pericles*), 139, 144
Lyotard, Jean-Francois, 38n41
Lysimachus (from *Pericles*), 146–51, 153–55, 176

Macbeth, 51
Madoff, Bernard, 19
Mariana (from *Measure for Measure*), 214–18, 224–26, 228–29
Marina (from *Pericles*), 104, 130, 135, 139–56, 164, 166, 169–70, 174, 176, 183, 186, 193, 203, 205
masochism, 112–13
McCoy, Marina, 107n17
Measure for Measure, xv, xxi, xxii, 25, 160, 176, 224, 213–31
melancholy, 20, 62, 69, 105, 109–25, 135, 139, 142, 146, 150, 151, 153, 159, 182, 211
the *Meno*, xv
The Merchant of Venice, xv, xix, xx, 87, 89, 91, 105, 109–25, 159
mercy, xxii, 62, 66, 73, 160, 181, 197–200, 208–12, 216, 217, 219–22, 225, 226, 229, 230

Michael Cassio (from *Othello*), 45–46, 48, 50, 52–55
Minsky, Hyman, 87–88, 105n2
Minton, Gretchen, 188
misanthropy, 160, 183, 189
Mistress Elbow (from *Measure for Measure*), 228
money, xx, 16, 31n13, 43, 44, 51, 64, 67–73, 86–96, 101, 103–5, 109–24, 127, 134, 141–43, 150, 159–60, 164, 168, 179n13, 181–85, 189–203, 208, 211, 220
Moore, Jeanie Grant, 131, 136, 139, 141, 147
moral hazard, 198–99, 229
Morocco (from *The Merchant of Venice*), 117
Myth of Er (from the *Republic*), xv, xvi, xxivn6, 9, 21, 25, 29, 30n9, 31n12, 93, 94, 96, 99, 117, 155, 179n17
Myth of the Metals (from the *Republic*), 162

Nerissa (from *The Merchant of Venice*), 122
New Comedy, 62
Nicomachean Ethics, 29, 230n4
Nightingale, Andrea Wilson xxiiin3, 31n11
noon at two o'clock, 234

O'Byrne, Ann, 177n1
O'Connor, David K., 37n37
Odyssean, 61, 81, 135
Old Athenian Gentleman (from *Timon of Athens*), 184–85, 191
Old Comedy, 62
Ophir, Adi, xxvn10
Othello, xvi, 39–59, 61, 64, 159

Pander (from *Pericles*), 141–42, 145, 148, 150
Pentapolis, 135, 136, 138–39, 154
Pericles, xv, xx, 25, 87, 89, 105, 127–56, 160, 162, 174, 176, 212n9

peripety, 6–8, 11, 13, 14, 50, 54, 56, 63, 70, 81, 124, 197
Perry, Curtis, 69, 73
Petronella, Vincent, 67–68
the *Phaedo*, xiv, 33
pharmakon, 33n20, 178n9
philanthropy, 160
philosophy, xiii, xvi, xvii, xviii, xxii, xxiii, 7, 11, 13–21, 30, 32nn18–19, 36n35, 38n39, 57, 90, 93–94, 103, 106, 107n7, 178nn5–9, 179n13, 234
Piraeus, xxi, 15, 18, 31n10, 98
pirates, 141–42, 149, 152, 205, 216, 229
Planinc, Zdravko, 32n19
pleonexia, xxiii, 18–19, 21, 36–7n35, 91, 106n7
the *Poetics*, 5
poetry, 30n9, 32–33n19, 93–95, 178n5, 233–34
Polemarchus (from the *Republic*), 9, 14–17, 20, 22–23, 26–27, 30, 33n20, 34n27, 36n34, 64, 66, 86, 92–95, 105n3, 227
politeia, 86
The Politics of Friendship, xviii, 3, 30, 34n27
polity, xix, xx, 85–92, 95, 98, 100, 105, 106n5, 109–10, 112, 114, 116, 118, 120–24, 127, 134, 137–38, 140–41, 159–60, 164, 234
Pompey (from *Measure for Measure*), 217, 229
Portia (from *Merchant of Venice*), 25, 109, 114, 116–29, 136
private, xx, 16, 23, 38n39, 79, 93, 101–5, 159, 161, 173–74, 214, 226
Provost (from *Measure for Measure*), 213, 215–17, 220, 222, 226–28

Ragozine (from *Measure for Measure*), 216
Raman, Shankar, 72, 73
Rand, Frank Prentice, 58n9
repetition compulsion, 89, 105, 124, 127, 160

Republic, xv, xvi, xviii, xviii, xx, xxi, xxii, xxiii, xxivnn6–9, xxvn10, 3–38, 40, 42, 43, 50, 57, 66, 85–107, 109, 130, 132, 141, 149–50, 152, 155, 159–79, 181–82, 197, 206, 214–16, 228–29, 233–34
rewards, xxivn6, 9–11, 13–14, 16, 19, 24–25, 27, 29, 35n31, 91, 94–100, 105, 107n9, 111–12, 116, 139, 151, 156, 159, 162, 164, 172, 194, 197, 199, 209
riddles, 127–29, 132, 135–37, 155
Ring of Gyges (from the *Republic*), 25, 99
risk, xvi, xvii, xviii, xix, xx, xxi, xxii, 25, 27, 48, 53, 68, 85–93, 96, 98–100, 103–4, 106n5, 109–25, 127–42, 145, 147, 149–56, 159–60, 163–64, 173–74, 179n13, 198, 200, 203, 229, 233–34
Roderigo (from *Othello*), 39–44, 50–52, 55–56
Rogers, Stephen, 39–40
Rosen, Stanley, 93–95
Rozett, Martha Tuck, 63
Russon, John, xvi, 34n22

Salanio (from *The Merchant of Venice*), 110
Salarino (from *The Merchant of Venice*), 110–11
Sallis John, xxivn9, 17, 28, 31n10, 34n26, 35n32, 105n3, 107n15, 177n2
Satkunanandan, Shalini, xxvn11, 35n31
Schmid, Walter T., 34n25, 178n9
Schulman, Alex, 125n25
Shylock (from *The Merchant of Venice*), xx, 89, 104, 109, 113–59
Simonides, (from the *Republic*), 17, 94
Simonides (from *Pericles*), 135–37
Skilling, Jeffrey, 19
Skilling John Taylor, 19
Skura, Meredith, 213, 230n1
Smith, Thomas, 36n35
Socrates, 1–235
Sohmer, Steven, 59n11

Solinus (from *The Comedy of Errors*), 63–66, 73, 77, 80
Spence, Michael, 87–88
Spindle of Necessity (from the *Republic*), 233
suitors, 54, 114, 116–18, 120–21, 128–29, 132, 135–37, 142, 148
the Sun (in the *Republic*), xxi, 164, 167, 168, 171–73, 178n6
the *Symposium*, xiii, xiv, 38n39, 94, 107n17, 223

Tarsus, 133–34, 136, 139–40, 148, 152–53, 155, 165
Tha sa (from *Pericles*), 137–39, 141–42, 153–55
Thaliard (from *Pericles*), 131–32
Thayer, H.S., 31n12
Thorne, W.B., 131
Thrasymachus (from the *Republic*), 17–18, 20–22, 25, 30, 34nn25–27, 35nn33–34, 36nn34–35, 49, 66, 88, 90, 95–98, 100, 104–5, 106nn3–7, 107n14, 192, 222, 227
Thucydides, xiii, 106n7
Timon (from *Timon of Athens*), xv, xxi, xxii, 176, 181–212, 212n9

Timon of Athens, xv, xxi, 134, 160, 176, 181–212
torch (in the *Republic*), 26–27, 38n42, 86, 98
tragedy, xiii, xiv, xv, xviii, xix, xxii, xxiii, xxiiin2, 4–13, 18–22, 26–29, 39–40, 43, 45, 47, 51, 55–57, 57n2, 58n8, 59n12, 61–63, 65–66, 68–69, 74, 78, 81, 86, 127, 159–61, 164, 179n11, 233–34
tragic incredulity, 9, 18, 19, 159
transaction, 28, 71, 73, 86–87, 93–105, 122, 182, 187, 222–23
Tubal (from *The Merchant of Venice*), 115
Tyre, 133, 137–39, 144, 154

Ventidius (from *Timon of Athens*), 183–87, 191, 194–95
Vlastos, Gregory, 37

Wasson, John, 213, 228–29
Weiss, Roslyn, 35n33
Wilberding, James, 36n35

Yunis, Harvey, 234n1

www.ingramcontent.com/pod-product-compliance
Lightning Source LLC
Chambersburg PA
CBHW022010300426
44117CB00005B/121